ON EDGE

A Journey Through Anxiety

ANDREA PETERSEN

"Petersen writes in vivid, memorable deta
acute anxiety.... Offers insight a

D0042171

Praise for

ON EDGE

"Petersen writes in vivid, memorable detail about what it's like to experience acute anxiety. . . . Books like [hers] offer insight and hope."

—NPR

"This brave, hopeful, sensitive account, grounded in the latest neuroscience, will be both enlightening and comforting to the millions who struggle with anxiety."

—Susan Cain, author of *Quiet*

"Revelatory . . . Petersen's account is enlightening and informative."

—*Booklist*

"Petersen's thoughtful and encouraging treatise on living and thriving despite these disorders will be helpful reading for many, and her honesty opens a much-needed doorway onto a significant health problem that is often underreported but on the rise."

—*Kirkus Reviews*

"Deft and affecting, heartbreaking and fascinating, *On Edge* completely captures what it feels like to live with anxiety."

—*Bustle*

"Petersen, a veteran *Wall Street Journal* writer covering health and psychology, deftly intercuts her own narrative with wide-angle reporting, tracing a checkered history of treatments ('pelvic massage' helped pave the way for early vibrators) as well as leading-edge research on genetics and neurofeedback."

—*Vogue*

"Required reading for anyone working with those who have [an anxiety] disorder."

—*Library Journal*

"A compelling read; it's personally relatable to those who have had similar experiences, highly informative on an emotional and factual level to those who have not."

—*Jezebel*

"*On Edge* is both moving and informative, and recommended for those who suffer for similar reasons, as well as those who are simply curious about the workings of the mind."

—Joseph Ledoux, university professor and professor of neural science, New York University, and author of *Anxious*

"Andrea Petersen has crafted an engaging blend of memoir and science that will open your eyes—and heart—to a condition that is usually invisible but deserves a broader spotlight."

—Maria Konnikova, author of *Mastermind* and *The Confidence Game*

"*On Edge* is a remarkable achievement—poignant, funny, illuminating, and unflinchingly honest."

—Jordan Smoller, professor of psychiatry, Harvard Medical School, and author of *The Other Side of Normal*

"In this fascinating book, science reporter Andrea Petersen deftly combines an honest, wry account of her own challenges with anxiety with a thorough examination of contemporary research."

—Gretchen Rubin, author of *The Happiness Project* and *Better Than Before*

"Everyone dealing with anxiety—the common cold of mental disorders—will benefit from the important information in this entertaining and erudite reflection on coping with the burden of anxiety."

—David H. Barlow, professor of psychology and psychiatry emeritus, Boston University, and founder and director emeritus, Center for Anxiety and Related Disorders

"Andrea's story is a beacon in the darkness for those living with anxiety disorders in silence. Stories like hers, shared openly, can change lives by reducing the stigma and discrimination that still surrounds mental illness."

—Former First Lady Rosalynn Carter, cofounder, The Carter Center

"Andrea Petersen raises the bar for anyone attempting to explain the complex science of the anxious brain. I was fascinated by the candid, painful, often humorous account of her own struggle and her quest for the best information about anxiety."

—Karen Cassiday, president, Anxiety and Depression Association of America

"For those with a family member, friend, or employee who is battling with this invisible demon, *On Edge* can shed light down the dark cavern and help them support their loved ones when 'uncertainty far too easily morphs into inescapable catastrophe.'"

—*Shelf Awareness*

ON EDGE

A JOURNEY THROUGH ANXIETY

ANDREA PETERSEN

BIDIWIY
BROADWAY BOOKS
NEW YORK

Copyright © 2017 by Andrea Petersen

All rights reserved.

Published in the United States by Broadway Books, an imprint of the
Crown Publishing Group, a division of Penguin Random House LLC, New York.
crownpublishing.com

Broadway Books and its logo, B \ D \ W \ Y, are trademarks of
Penguin Random House LLC.

Originally published in hardcover in the United States by Crown, an imprint of the
Crown Publishing Group, a division of Penguin Random House LLC, New York,
in 2017.

Library of Congress Cataloging-in-Publication Data
Names: Petersen, Andrea.
Title: On edge : a journey through anxiety / Andrea Petersen.
Description: First edition. | New York : Crown, [2017] | Includes bibliographical
    references and index.
Identifiers: LCCN 2016050111 (print) | LCCN 2016059341 (ebook) |
    ISBN 9780553418576 (hardcover) | ISBN 9780553418590 (pbk.) |
    ISBN 9780553418583 (ebook)
Subjects: LCSH: Petersen, Andrea—Mental health. | Anxiety disorders—
    Treatment. | Anxiety—Patients—Biography.
Classification: LCC RC531 .P4227 2017 (print) | LCC RC531 (ebook) |
    DDC 616.85/22—dc23
LC record available at https://lccn.loc.gov/2016050111

ISBN 978-0-553-41859-0
Ebook ISBN 978-0-553-41858-3

Printed in the United States of America

Cover design by Na Kim

10 9 8 7 6 5 4 3 2 1

First Paperback Edition

For my parents

CONTENTS

PROLOGUE 1

1. THE ANTICIPATION OF PAIN
DEFINING ANXIETY 5

2. SCARY CLOWNS AND THE END OF DAYS
ANXIETY IN CHILDHOOD 36

3. MY GRANDMOTHER'S MADNESS
THE GENETICS OF ANXIETY 58

4. FROM CBT TO KARAOKE
NONDRUG THERAPIES FOR ANXIETY 93

5. MAY CAUSE DIZZINESS
MEDICATIONS FOR ANXIETY 126

6. COLD CALLS, AIRPLANES, AND INDECISION
ANXIETY AT WORK AND ON THE ROAD 159

7. THE ISOLATION CHAMBER
ANXIETY IN LOVE AND FRIENDSHIP 188

8. WORRIES ABOUT MY DAUGHTER
THE EDUCATION OF AN ANXIOUS PARENT 217

9. STAYING GROUNDED
LEARNING TO LIVE WITH ANXIETY 244

NOTES 261

ACKNOWLEDGMENTS 291

INDEX 295

This is a work of nonfiction. Although Kate, Scott, Brad, Alice, and Michael are pseudonyms, all others who appear in the book are identified by their real names, and none are composites. I have made every effort to be accurate, but memory is fallible and some of the events I and others recall here happened decades ago. Whenever possible, I have corroborated events through medical records and interviews with people who were there.

Fear ambushes me.

It is early on the morning of December 5, 1989. At least early for a college student, which is what I am. A sophomore at the University of Michigan in Ann Arbor, a bucolic campus of creaky A-frame houses, earnest politics, fraternity sweatshirts, and dollar pitchers of beer.

I am in the basement of a 1940s academic building staring at a wall covered in long sheets of dot-matrix printer paper detailing which classes have slots for the upcoming semester: Economics 101, Introduction to Buddhism, a Jane Austen seminar. Other sleepy students, jeans-clad and tousle-headed, are scribbling in notebooks nearby.

I feel fine. Groggy from a late night of studying, yes. Touched by a bit of that midwestern late-fall dread, anticipating another long winter of fierce winds and sleeping-bag-shaped coats. But I'm fine.

And then, a second later, I'm not.

A knot of fear erupts at the base of my spine and travels upward. My stomach flips, and I break out in a thin film of sweat. My heart rate shoots up—I feel the erratic *thump thump* banging against my ears, my stomach, my eyes. My breathing turns shallow and fast. Fuzzy gray blotches appear before my eyes. The letters before me warp, words dip and buckle.

There is no warning, no prodrome. The onset is as sudden as a car crash. Something in my body or brain has gone dramatically and irrevocably wrong. My noisy internal monologue—usually flitting from school to boys to a laundry list of insecurities—coalesces around one certain refrain: *I'm dying. I'm dying. I'm dying.*

I flee the building and somehow make it home, crawling into my bottom bunk in the room I share with two other girls. I hug my knees into my chest and huddle against the cinder-block wall—my breathing still shallow, my heart still racing, the hot terror still there. Remarkably, it seems, I am alive. Any relief that gives me, however, is short-lived: *If I'm not dying, I must be going crazy.*

Crazy like my grandmother.

Like the woman who clutched knives and thought Catholics were trying to kill her. Like the woman who spent three years in a mental institution, had electroshock therapy, and tried to burn the house down with my nine-year-old father and his brother and sister in it. Like the woman who died in my grandfather's arms when I was two years old. She had suffered a heart attack but was too terrified to go with paramedics to the hospital.

Crazy like that.

I lie still. Perhaps if I cease all movement, even the tiniest shudder, become frozen, waxlike, I can quiet the torment. My insides feel noisy, in flux. Everything is revved up—as if the blood in my veins were running faster and the synapses in my brain were firing, or misfiring, at warp speed. I can feel the loud, frantic presence of every organ—liver, intestines, spleen. The cells in my body are vibrating, it seems, knocking awkwardly against one another. If

I move at all, I will shatter, scattering bits of blood and bone all across the salmon-hued sorority house. I am sure of that.

Later that afternoon my boyfriend drives me to my parents' house, all windows and suburban beige, about ninety minutes away. Over the next five weeks, I barely move from the living room sofa. I spend the days with my fingers pressed against my neck, feeling my pulse, counting the beats, reassuring myself at any given second that I'm alive. I keep still, trying to will my frenzied molecules to quiet. At night I have vivid, violent dreams. I develop weird new symptoms: tingling in my face and feet, chest pain, constant vertigo. The world is flat and out of focus, as if I'm wearing someone else's glasses. My thoughts careen toward heart attacks, stroke, insanity.

I see a doctor. He listens to my story of how I've been transformed from a slightly silly sorority girl to a terrorized shut-in in just a few weeks' time. He examines me, takes blood, does an EKG, and orders an echocardiogram, which details the chambers of my heart. His diagnosis: mitral valve prolapse, an anomaly of the heart that can cause palpitations but is generally benign. He prescribes a beta blocker, which he says will stop my heart from racing.

Except that it doesn't.

This doctor is only the first of more than a dozen I will see over the next year. During that time, I will have several more EKGs, countless blood tests, another echocardiogram, a CAT scan and an MRI of my brain, and an EEG to check my brain's electrical activity. I will take multiple trips to the emergency room, each time leaving without a diagnosis. This medical odyssey will cost my parents thousands of dollars. Doctors will suspect multiple sclerosis, a brain tumor, Epstein-Barr virus, and chronic fatigue syndrome. I will be told that I am fine. One doctor will fire me. I will drop most of my classes and barely leave my room. I will peer over the banister of a rooftop parking garage and think of jumping. I will go to a psychiatric emergency room and be sent home. I will have six sessions of psychotherapy, in which I'm asked whether I'm angry with my father. I'll largely stop eating.

And still no one will know what is wrong with me.

Fast-forward to the beginning of the next school year. I am sitting in a psychiatrist's office at the campus health center, telling the doctor that I won't—I can't—leave until she does something. She says she can prescribe Prozac, an antidepressant, or she can refer me to the anxiety disorders program at the University of Michigan hospital.

Anxiety disorder. It is the first time anyone has spoken the words.

1

THE ANTICIPATION OF PAIN
DEFINING ANXIETY

Eleven different anxiety disorders are listed in the fifth edition of the *Diagnostic and Statistical Manual of Mental Disorders*, commonly referred to as the diagnostic bible. I had symptoms of four. I was having panic attacks—sudden, intense periods of blinding terror, rapid breathing, and chest pain—several times a day (diagnosis: panic disorder). The rest of the time I worried, living with the nervous expectation of imminent disaster (diagnosis: generalized anxiety disorder, or GAD). I had developed a long list of particular fears, too: dentists, flying, driving on highways, taking medication, touching dirt, using a new tube of toothpaste, and licking envelopes. I did my best to avoid them all (diagnosis: specific phobia). My world was becoming smaller and smaller as more places became no-go zones: movie theaters, stadiums, lines. The potential for panic attacks—and the difficulty of escape—was too great (diagnosis: agoraphobia).

I had symptoms of a couple of cousin disorders, too. A twisted perfectionism turned the smallest decision into a colossal obstacle; I felt a sense of sinister foreboding if I didn't choose the "right" dress to wear, the "right" water glass (diagnosis: obsessive-compulsive disorder). I agonized over every odd sensation or twinge of physical pain. A headache was clearly an aneurysm; a bruise, leukemia (diagnosis: illness anxiety disorder, previously called hypochondriasis).

The estimated number of people who will have at least one anxiety disorder during the course of their lives is staggering: one in three Americans ages thirteen or older. If we look only at women, the number is even higher—about 40 percent. In any given year, about 40 million American adults have an anxiety disorder. And those numbers do not include the millions of garden-variety worriers and insomniacs whose anxiety, though not debilitating, leaches joy and steals peace of mind.

A certain amount of anxiety is good. It motivates us to study for tests, prepare for presentations, and save for retirement. It spurs us to get a physical or check the gas gauge. Too much anxiety, however, can be incapacitating and costly. In a 1999 study, the most recent estimate available, anxiety disorders cost the United States about $63 billion a year, more than half of it attributed to doctor and hospital visits. Other costs included psychiatric treatment, prescription drugs, and the value of lost productivity at work. There's also mounting evidence that out-of-control anxiety wreaks havoc on the body, increasing the risk of heart disease and weakening the immune system. Ironically, being a hypochondriac may actually make you sick.

It is tempting to think of our era—with its wars, terrorist attacks, rising sea levels, and economic insecurity—as, to borrow the poet W. H. Auden's phrase, "the age of anxiety." But cultural commentators throughout history have viewed their own times as equally fraught. In the 1880s, the telegraph, the steam engine, and even women's intellectual pursuits were blamed for the nation's unease. In the 1950s, it was the atomic bomb. Our world, it seems, always provides ample fodder for fear.

What is disconcerting is that rates of anxiety disorders—and depression—seem to be increasing among young people, particularly college students. According to a spring 2016 survey by the American College Health Association, 17 percent of students were diagnosed with or treated for anxiety problems during the previous year, and nearly 14 percent were diagnosed with or treated for depression. That is up from about 10 percent each for anxiety and depression in the fall 2008 survey. Parents and professionals are perplexed. While some of the rise may be because of increased prevalence, it could also be that more people are comfortable asking for help and admitting their troubles to researchers.

Depression may get most of the headlines and the research dollars, but anxiety is more prevalent. In people with a history of both an anxiety and a mood disorder, anxiety usually makes an appearance first. Anxiety disorders strike young, too: They have a median age of onset of fifteen, compared with twenty-six for mood disorders. And while anxiety disorders are pretty miserable in and of themselves, they are increasingly being thought of as gateway illnesses that can lead to a host of other problems, such as depression, substance use, and even suicide.

In fact, anxiety can be deadly. Depression is the mental illness most strongly associated with suicidal thoughts, but it doesn't often lead to suicidal acts. Recent research has found that it is anxiety disorders and other illnesses, like problems with impulse control and addiction, that are more likely to lead to suicide attempts.

In most cases, the consequences aren't fatal. Still, anxiety disorders can derail lives. Someone who develops an anxiety disorder at a young age is less likely to attend college. Anxious people who work have lower incomes. They are less likely to marry and, if they do, more likely to divorce. Anxious women face a greater risk of getting into unhealthy relationships and being the victim of domestic abuse.

That, thankfully, is not my story. If you met me now, you probably wouldn't even notice my anxiety. (When I began telling acquaintances the topic of this book, they almost uniformly said, "I would never have guessed you're anxious.") I have a career I love, as a reporter writing stories for the *Wall Street Journal*. I'm happily married, with an adorable seven-year-old daughter. I have friends, laugh a lot, go to parties, and bake pies. My affliction is often invisible.

I have had many advantages. I grew up in a loving home, lived in safe neighborhoods, and went to good schools. I have almost always had health insurance and the ability to pay for therapy and medication. While these privileges didn't prevent me from falling apart, I know they were critical in putting me back together.

But it has been a struggle. In tough years, I take medication and cycle through new therapies. In easy years, I still have to be diligent: Sleep eight hours. Do yoga. Take it easy on the wine. Pare down my responsibilities. And still I grapple with worry-induced insomnia. I tend to procrastinate, terrified of making the wrong choices. I have odd, unexplained physical symptoms—a tingling arm, chest pain. I can't drive on highways. Anxiety affects how I work, how I love, and how I parent.

So what is anxiety?

The *DSM* calls it "anticipation of future threat." Søren Kierkegaard, the nineteenth-century Danish philosopher, called it "the dizziness of freedom." But the most cogent definition I've heard comes from Christian Grillon, a neuroscientist at the National Institute of Mental Health (NIMH). "Anxiety is the anticipation of pain," he told me. "It could be physical pain or emotional pain."

Anxiety is related to fear but is distinct. Whereas fear is concrete and imminent, anxiety is, as Grillon says, "sustained uncertainty." It's a chronic sense of uneasiness about a vague future, a gnawing worry about what may or may not happen.

Anxiety is universal, but the language we use to talk about it varies by culture, and so do its symptoms. The word *anxiety* comes from the Latin *angere*, which means "to choke or throttle." In Cambodia, *khyâl* ("wind") attacks involve neck pain, dizziness, and ringing in the ears. In Vietnam, *trúng gió* ("wind-related") attacks are characterized by headaches. In Latin America, *ataques de nervios* ("attacks of nerves") can include uncontrollable screaming and crying.

Differing cultural perceptions of anxiety make it difficult to accurately compare rates of anxiety disorders in countries around the world. Yes, studies show that, in Japan, only about 4 percent of the population has an anxiety disorder in a given year, and that the French have a rate (13.7 percent) more than double that of the Spanish (6.6 percent). But these statistics are influenced by everything from how researchers define the word *worry* to who responds to surveys. (You could argue that the most anxious people are the least likely to answer a stranger's probing questions.)

Anxiety also exists on a continuum. There is no sharp boundary between mental health and mental illness, and no doubt other cultures draw the boundary differently than we do. When I asked Ron Kessler of Harvard Medical School, the country's leading mental health epidemiologist, why so many people have anxiety problems, he said it was because "we have decided it is a disorder." Still, even if we have become alert to the idea that everyday anxieties can be symptoms of a disorder, a formal psychiatric diagnosis requires that the person suffer from "clinically significant distress or impairment" in functioning. No matter the symptoms or the name you give it, anxiety is a problem if it keeps you from living— and enjoying—your life the way you want to.

. . .

I've tangled with severe anxiety for more than twenty-five years. Looking back, my troubles didn't actually begin that December day in college, though it wasn't until then that it spiraled out of control. I had been having strange "spells" for months. They started when I was living at home the summer after my freshman year. During the day, I was working as a receptionist at a company that made steel forgings, the kind of place where the women were called by their first names while the men were all Mister So-and-so. At night, I waitressed at an Irish bar in East Lansing, where I checked fake IDs, dodged the advances of horny Michigan State guys, and learned to perfect the head on a pint of Miller Light. Between jobs, I took step aerobics classes.

One night I was at the apartment of my boyfriend, Scott, a Michigan State student and Christopher Reeve doppelgänger I had begun dating in high school. The evening's goal was, to paraphrase him, to get me high. I had tried smoking pot once or twice before but very tentatively. (I, seriously, tried not to inhale.) Frankly, I was afraid of it. I had been around enough of the stuff when I was a kid at my parents' and my friends' parents' parties, the blue sheen of bongs glinting off Pledge-buffed coffee tables. Pot always seemed to make people silly and stupid. But Scott, an enthusiastic stoner, had been touting its effects for month. I was in.

We started smoking a joint and waited.

Nothing.

"Take another hit," Scott said.

I did. And when Scott took one, he grabbed me and kissed me, blowing smoke into my mouth.

Several more minutes went by.

Then it hit me.

My heart beat faster. My mouth went dry. I felt breathless. My equilibrium and vision contorted; it was as if I were on a roller coaster the moment before the big plummet. I lay down on Scott's bed, trying to take deep breaths and calm down. My legs felt like they were stretching, *Alice in Wonderland* style. I looked down and could have sworn I saw my feet on the other side of the room.

Desperate for distraction and wanting to feel grounded in some way, I reached for Scott and we started having sex. But I could barely feel him. My body was numb, deadened. I panicked.

"I can't breathe," I cried, sitting bolt upright.

"Sure you can," Scott said, taking my hand. "Just relax."

"I can't. And my heart is beating so fast, too fast," I said. "Something must have been in that pot. It must have been laced with something."

I darted around the room, pacing and gulping air. "Or maybe I'm having an allergic reaction. Something is really wrong. I think I need to go to a hospital." I threw on sandals, a T-shirt, and a pair of Scott's boxer shorts. He scrambled to get dressed, too. I was already turning the doorknob to leave. Scott grabbed his car keys and followed.

At the ER, the bright lights, shiny linoleum, and bureaucratic questions sobered me up fairly quickly. I was not the only college student whose visit was spurred by chemical overindulgence. One drunken kid threw up on the waiting room floor. Another sobbed incoherently. In the exam room, a technician hooked me up to a heart monitor. A few hours later I was told I could go. A doctor scribbled my discharge instructions: "Avoid THC," he wrote of the active chemical in marijuana.

I did that easily. That one episode was more effective than an entire adolescence of antidrug After School Specials. But the spells of breathlessness, racing heart, and, increasingly, fear, recurred every month or so. They seemed to come from nowhere. I had one while eating fried cheese sticks at Bennigan's. I had another in the middle of a women's studies class. I feigned a bathroom emergency and spent the rest of the class crouched in a ladies' room stall. The attacks subsided after twenty or thirty minutes but left me jelly-legged and shaky for hours.

I don't remember thinking much about the episodes during the intervals between them. I brushed them off, telling no one but Scott and hoping they'd vanish as abruptly as they'd begun.

According to the *DSM*, a panic attack is "an abrupt surge of intense fear or intense discomfort that reaches a peak within minutes." After that, it usually subsides. But when I landed on my parents' sofa that December, it felt as though I were having a monthlong panic attack. Sure, my fear had peaks and valleys, but it was always there. Soon I was nearly immobile, a pajama-clad heap with greasy hair, one hand checking my galloping pulse, the other on the TV remote control, switching from MTV videos to *Love Boat* reruns and back again. I couldn't read. I wasn't actually watching the TV either. The noise was just a soundtrack for my fear.

My parents were bewildered and scared. My fourteen-year-old sister, Dana, would sometimes sit next to me, but mostly she tried to stay out of the way. "Nobody really told me what was going on," she said recently. "I just knew that you were sick and needed some time off from school to get better. Everybody was tiptoeing around. I felt like I should not be trouble because Mom and Dad were clearly worried about you."

It was only a few weeks before final exams, but I didn't make it back to school. I took incompletes in my classes and planned to take my tests after winter break, when, I hoped, I'd feel better.

My dad was alarmed to see me transform overnight from an energetic young adult into a listless lump. "It scared the shit out of us," he recently recalled. "The next thing you know you're rolled up in a fricking ball in bed."

My parents took me to a doctor. I was terrified that something was wrong with my heart. "You thought it was going to explode," my dad says. I started having strange neurological symptoms, too. Once, when I'd gathered the courage to venture to the mall with my mother, my peripheral vision vanished next to an Orange Julius. I had vertigo, too. The floor would rise up and the walls would tilt at odd angles. But the only diagnosis I was given was a fluttery heart valve, the mitral valve prolapse.

Nights were increasingly difficult. I was exhausted but had a tough time falling asleep. When I did, I had terrifying nightmares that became increasingly gory. Sometimes I was being chased by an unknown assailant. I dreamed I was shot in the head. Other times my face was being torn apart by an electric drill. The violence had a Tarantino vividness, but without the humor and gloss. I'd wake up shaking, with tears running down my face.

Rules crumbled. My boyfriend started spending the night with me in my high school bed, an almost life-size poster of Morrissey and his pompadour looking over us. Nothing sexual happened. Scott was more of a nocturnal life raft. I'd clutch his arm, hoping the warmth of his healthy twenty-year-old body would somehow heal me.

After a couple of weeks of infirmity, and with no real answers from the doctor, my parents began losing patience. It was right before Christmas, and we had plans to drive to the small southern Illinois town where my grandparents, aunts and uncles, and a mess of cousins lived, but I couldn't imagine moving from my sofa. I begged them to let me stay home. They refused. I said I wouldn't leave. They could go without me.

I didn't win that fight. Instead, I ended up in the backseat of our blue Ford Thunderbird for the seven-hour drive to Salem, Illinois, a town of dried-up industry and oil wells, chain fast-food joints, and vast starlit skies. I don't recall much from that trip. Did I eat my grandmother's famous divinity—white sugary blobs topped with a single half walnut? Did I make small talk with cousins? Could anyone tell how scared and screwed up I was? Terror has a way of blacking out the details.

I do know that I took my pulse a lot, trying to will it back down to double-digit-per-minute territory. The vertigo and a growing exhaustion made it difficult for me to stay upright. I leaned against walls and car doors. And I soon found a spot on another sofa, this one in my grandparents' house, and spent most of the time quaking under the orange and brown afghan my grandmother had crocheted. I spoke little and smiled wanly at the parade of relatives.

Back at home in Michigan, winter break was coming to an end. The new semester would be starting soon. The arguing with my parents intensified. I didn't see how I could go back to school. I was too fragile. I still didn't know what was wrong with me. I wanted to stay on that ridiculous beige-striped sofa (who knew there were so many shades of beige?) until I was better.

"You have to go back," my parents said, unified in their decision.

"This is tough love," said my father.

I was furious with them. I felt tossed out. Abandoned.

"We were concerned that if you stayed in your bedroom much longer, you would never go back to school," my mom recalled recently.

"We wanted to get you off the couch. We wanted you to be normal," my dad said. "Maybe it was a sink-or-swim move on our part."

It took me years to forgive them. Now, after all my research, I know that they did the right thing. If I had stayed on that sofa, I would probably never have risen from it. Avoiding experiences that make you anxious just reinforces your anxiety.

. . .

I had to move rooms when I returned to school. I had been living with two other women, but now I would be living with three in a single room, a so-called quad. There were two sets of bunk beds, four dressers, four desks, a hodgepodge of sweatshirt-filled milk crates, and all the drama that four nineteen-year-old women can conjure.

It is awfully difficult to fall apart with no privacy, and I was almost never alone. The four of us lived in a stately, white-columned sorority house with close to a hundred other young women. We ate meals together, cooked by a surly, spice-averse man. We had weekly meetings where we'd debate which fraternities to party with and honor women who'd been "lavaliered," given necklaces graced with the Greek letters of their boyfriends' fraternities, a "going steady" move that was only one step away from engagement. It was hard for me to feign the required gushing.

I wasn't alone even in the shower. The house had communal bathrooms, and the shower was a three-person affair, a white-ceramic-tile-covered stall with three metal showerheads. Fear had stolen my appetite, and I had lost fifteen pounds over the previous month. I had started to become afraid of food itself, worrying about unknown allergies or food poisoning. In that shower, I felt so fragile and ashamed as I compared my skeletal nakedness to the spirited curves of my sorority sisters. I did my best to shower at off-peak times—in the very early morning or during happy hour.

Trying to hide my terror and appear "normal" was exhausting, so I came up with a cover story. I told my roommates and others I was recovering from mono, the quintessential college "kissing" disease. That was meant to explain why I skipped parties, stayed in bed a lot, and escaped to my parents' house on weekends. And to a certain extent, I faked it.

In pictures from that semester, I don't look haunted or timorous. In fact, apart from the awkwardly layered bangs, I look surprisingly okay. The extra-large men's sweatshirts that were in fashion then hide my skinniness. I pose perched on bunk beds and smile widely with my arms flung around other girls. Flipping through the photos, I'm reminded of something Ned Kalin, a psychiatrist at the University of Wisconsin, told me, that patients with anxiety fascinated him because they often seemed so together, even when they were plagued by intense worry and fear.

I had seemingly normal conversations with friends about boys they liked, about the fall of the Berlin Wall. I attended classes and did some schoolwork. (But only a minimal amount. I completed only two courses that semester.) Yet these efforts were undertaken, it seemed, by no more than a tiny sliver of my brain. The rest was stuffed with a litany of fears: my heart, my breathing, never being well again.

I had always been a quick, voracious reader, but ever since my spell on the couch, I found that I read pages, then had no recollection of their contents. My eyes skipped around, missing entire paragraphs. I'd finish a passage feeling inadequate and confused.

I still had to make up my final exams from the previous semester. I met with the dean in his office, and he explained the process of taking the exams, when and where they would happen. I nodded my head. After we had wrapped up, almost as an afterthought, he asked, "So what do you have?"

"Mitral valve prolapse," I said. It was the only diagnosis I had been given, and I didn't want to trot out my mono lie to an authority figure.

"Really? My wife has that," he said, clearly unimpressed.

"It makes my heart race," I mumbled weakly as I left, cheeks burning with shame.

Getting through each day was becoming harder and harder. My heart raced, my fear spiked, and I had difficulty breathing (these were clearly panic attacks, though I still didn't know it at the time) when I stood in a line or went to a movie theater. So I stopped standing in line. Stopped going to see movies. Even more nonsensical things started to scare me, too. I became terrified of contamination, of dirt, of being infected by some ferocious bacterium. Using something new—a bottle of shampoo, a toothbrush—took major effort. (Perhaps it had been tampered with, my paranoia whispered.) I'd panic for a good hour or so afterward, waiting for some dire physical reaction. Choosing a plate or glass at dinner turned into a ten-minute struggle. I'd check carefully for dried food, lipstick marks, chips. Even if I found a pristine cup, it still might not "feel right." Sometimes the easiest thing was not to drink or eat at all.

New fears cropped up everywhere. I licked an envelope, then recalled reading that LSD was sometimes delivered via paper. *Was there LSD on that envelope?* I thought. I knew the thought was ridiculous, yet I couldn't shake it. (I haven't licked an envelope since. I heartily thank the inventor of self-sticking ones.) I didn't know it, but I had turned a corner in my anxiety disorder. No longer was anxiety merely rattling around my brain and body; I was now exhibiting multiple "avoidance behaviors." I could no longer do the things I wanted to do when I wanted to do them.

Avoidance behaviors are associated with more serious, harder-to-treat illnesses. Avoidance fuels anxiety in a vicious cycle. By steering clear of the things I was afraid of, I never got a chance to learn that what I feared most—dying, going crazy—wouldn't actually happen. The not knowing made me even more anxious.

I saw many more doctors in the ensuing months in search of a real diagnosis, my mother often making the hour-long drive to Ann Arbor to accompany me to assorted specialists. I also ended up at the ER several times—driven by my ever-patient college friend Susie—when my symptoms became particularly intense. I was convinced I was having a heart attack. My heart beat like an avant-garde jazz number, cacophonous and herky-jerky. It would speed up, slow down, skip. In the waiting room, Susie would try to make me laugh. She had asthma and knew what it was like to feel fragile and breathless. But after each visit, I was sent home without any answers. I think a doctor or nurse or two might have said something about avoiding stress.

I continued to have neurological issues, too: tunnel vision, vertigo, freaky depth perception. My hands and feet were often numb and tingly. A neurologist suspected multiple sclerosis, and I had an MRI of my brain. In the middle of it, I began having trouble breathing, and my heart beat so rapidly and loudly, it seemed to strain my ribs. Spots danced in front of my eyes, and I thought I would pass out. Crying, I had to be pulled out of the clanking, vibrating tube.

They did a CAT scan instead. The machine was less tomblike so I gave it a go. My mother held my hand, her body shrouded in a lead apron to protect her from the radiation bathing my brain. That scan was "inconclusive," with some vague shadow possibly suggesting a brain tumor. After a completely sleepless night picturing my slow and awful death from brain cancer, back into the MRI machine I went, this time with several milligrams of Valium in my bloodstream. The MRI was fine. My brain, I was told, was normal.

My dad now says that the scariest thing about that time was that nobody had a clue as to what was wrong with me. With no definitive diagnosis, the expanse of possibilities and prognoses was terrifying.

I was tired all the time, a bone-deep torpor. For a few weeks, I was actually excited to think that I might have chronic fatigue syndrome, a disorder that had suddenly emerged in the zeitgeist. Sure, it didn't sound like fun, there weren't really any effective treatments, and some doctors didn't believe it existed. But at least it had a name.

I like to think that none of this would happen now. Today there's a much better chance that a doctor would properly diagnose me, that the school would refer me to the counseling center, or that I would look up my symptoms online and figure it out on my own. But all this happened in an era before large-scale mental health awareness campaigns, when there was greater stigma around psychiatric disorders. In the 1980s, organizations like the National Alliance on Mental Illness and the Anxiety Disorders Association of America (now the Anxiety and Depression Association of America) mailed out their newsletters in plain envelopes. Active Minds, a robust advocacy and support organization with chapters at more than four hundred college campuses, wasn't founded until 2003. I didn't know anyone who had been to a therapist or was taking psychotropic medication.

Anxiety disorders didn't even exist as a category in the *DSM* until 1980, and it wasn't until 1987 that Prozac was released in the United States. Then in 1989 the World Wide Web was born. The internet and Prozac would dramatically change the diagnosis and treatment of mental illness. Prozac, a new selective serotonin reuptake inhibitor, had far fewer and less onerous side effects than earlier medications. And the internet made a torrent of health information available to anyone with a keyboard and made it possible to anonymously join online support groups. In 1990, the Americans with Disabilities Act spurred colleges to open disability offices that now field requests for academic accommodations like quiet rooms for test taking and extra time for assignments for students with all types of disabilities, including psychiatric ones.

Without these new supports, I had to tough it out. I did my best to play the role of the free-spirited college student, even heading to Cancún for spring break with my roommates. Although I was barely hanging on to my student status, my parents were happy to fund the trip. Maybe doing something fun and frivolous would bring me back to health.

It was a disaster.

The days were all right. We spent them sunbathing and swimming. But at night my friends headed out to bars, and despite having been an enthusiastic binge drinker my freshman year, I hadn't had a drink since I got sick. My body and brain already felt so haywire, I couldn't imagine doing anything to make it more so. (My reaction was not typical. Many people with anxiety disorders drink to relax, a way of self-medicating.) But I wasn't open about my abstinence. So there I was at Señor Frogs, a bar crammed with sunburned spring breakers, with a tequila shot in one hand, desperately trying to figure out how to surreptitiously ditch it. I lowered my hand and poured it down the leg of my chair, figuring it would blend in with the sticky sludge already on the floor.

I managed to dance a little that night, but later on, back at our hotel, I felt a pain in my neck, and my hands and feet went numb. What if I somehow had broken my neck? It was an absurd thought. I hadn't fallen. I could walk. I knew my fear was ridiculous, but I couldn't get logic to prevail. On some primitive, emotional level, I was convinced I must have fractured a vertebra.

I called the front desk and asked for a doctor. They sent someone up. The doctor examined me and said I needed an X-ray. So I got into a taxi with him and rode through the chaotic Cancún streets to an all-night medical clinic. (Why this didn't freak me out more than a completely hypothetical injury, I have no idea.)

Several X-rays revealed—surprise—that I was fine. For a second I was relieved. Then I started worrying about the thyroid cancer I would most likely get because of the radiation from the X-rays.

The next day I stayed at the hotel while my friends went to the beach. I furtively called my mother, begging her to buy me a plane ticket so I could come home early. As in, that day. She did. Then I left my friends a weird, rambling note, packed my bags, and left. I was back in my parents' house by late evening.

As the weeks wore on, I became lonelier and increasingly hope-less. Upon waking, I'd have a moment of sunny optimism—*this* would be the day I'd feel normal again. But then I'd prop myself up on an elbow, and the heart palpitations and vertigo would re-turn, and the fears would gnaw at me again.

I began to think it would be easier to not wake up at all. I didn't want to die. I'd spent months terrified of dying. But I couldn't see any other way to escape how I felt. The doctors couldn't help me. Nor could my parents or friends. And I increasingly didn't feel strong enough to continue to slog through the days and nights.

Finally, when these dark, desperate thoughts scared the hell out of me enough to share them, I called my father and asked him to come to Ann Arbor and take me to the hospital. This time he didn't tell me to buck up or that things would be better if I got some sleep. He came and got me right away.

We parked the car in a high-rise parking garage. As we walked to the stairwell, I glanced over the railing to the ground far below and had a sudden, strong impulse to jump. To erase everything. But self-preservation and a slim hope won out. I grabbed my fa-ther's hand.

At the hospital, we bypassed the regular ER and instead went to the psychiatric emergency room. It was a small, quiet waiting room, and I was the only patient in it. I remember giving someone, a psychiatrist or psychologist, a short synopsis of the last three months and my new despondency. The doctors considered admitting me but decided that I wasn't at acute risk of harming myself. (I had no actual suicide plan.) What I needed, they said, was outpatient counseling. The therapist handed me a small card with the words PSYCHIATRIC EMERGENCY SERVICES in all caps and my appointment time written in black pen. A twenty-four-hour emergency phone number was on the back.

I had several therapy sessions, but the treatment seemed irrelevant. The therapist asked me about my childhood and how I felt about my parents, but I wanted to know why my heart raced and why I was always terrified. Scratch that. I had stopped caring why. I only wanted it to stop.

For centuries, excessive anxiety was considered more of a moral failing than a medical problem. The stories of the ancient Greeks and Romans are filled with negative depictions of people who don't cope well with fear. "The skin of the coward changes color all the time, he can't get a grip on himself, he can't sit still," writes Homer in the *Iliad*, about an anxious man preparing for battle. "He squats and rocks, shifting his weight from foot to foot, his heart racing, pounding inside the fellow's ribs, his teeth chattering—he dreads some grisly death."

Specific phobias pop up in ancient writings, too. In the third century B.C., Andreas of Charystos described aerophobia, a fear of open spaces. He also defined the apex of all phobias: pantophobia, the fear of everything. In the Classical period, anxiety was considered a component of melancholia, a mental state marked by fear and despondency. The Hippocratic physicians of ancient Greece thought all illness was caused by an imbalance among the four "humors," or bodily liquids: phlegm, blood, yellow bile, and black bile. Melancholy was thought to arise from a surfeit of black bile. Practitioners treated melancholy with everything from special diets and exercise to enemas and bloodletting. The belief in humors persisted for centuries.

Religion tackled anxiety, too. Faith in God was the cure. "It was as if a light of relief from all anxiety flooded into my heart. All the shadows of doubt were dispelled," wrote Saint Augustine in the fourth century A.D. of his experience reading the teachings of Jesus Christ.

By the seventeenth century, the belief in humors as the cause of melancholia and its attendant anxiety was supplanted by the emerging concept of nervous disorders. Dysfunction in the brain and nerves was now thought to be the cause of a host of mental and physical symptoms. The nervous disorders were generally treated by neurologists and general physicians. In 1869, George Miller Beard, a neurologist from New York, coined the word *neurasthenia*, literally "tired nerves," to describe a constellation of physical and emotional symptoms, including headaches, rashes, fatigue, insomnia, and phobias. This weakness of the nervous system was caused, Beard thought, by the fast-paced lifestyle of nineteenth-century America. In particular, he blamed the stress of technological advances like the telegraph and steam power, as well as the "mental activity of women."

Anxious women who weren't diagnosed with neurasthenia were likely to be slapped with the label of hysteria. The Greek physician Hippocrates named the disease in the fifth century B.C.; he believed it was caused by the uterus wandering around the body. In Victorian-era women, hysteria was characterized by nervousness, insomnia, "excessive" sexual desire (or the complete lack of it), and a panoply of psychosomatic symptoms from headaches to fainting. It was commonly treated with "pelvic massage," with orgasm as the goal. (The development of the vibrator was heralded as a major treatment advance.)

Just two years after Beard introduced the idea of neurasthenia, Jacob Da Costa wrote about a peculiar syndrome he had seen while working as an army doctor during the Civil War. He relayed the story of WWH, a young Union soldier who had survived the bloody battle of Fredericksburg. After the battle, WWH "was seized with lancinating pains in the cardiac region, so intense that he was obliged to throw himself down upon the ground, and with palpitation. The symptoms frequently returned while on the march, were attended with dimness of vision and giddiness, and obliged him to fall out of his company and ride in the ambulance."

Da Costa saw similar symptoms in hundreds of other soldiers, too. The young men complained of chest pain and heart palpitation, difficulty sleeping, dizziness, shortness of breath, and upset stomachs. Finding the soldiers otherwise healthy, Da Costa chalked up their symptoms to an overactive heart. He called the illness "irritable heart syndrome." Today we might call it panic disorder or post-traumatic stress disorder (PTSD). Da Costa treated irritable heart with various drugs, including opium, digitalis (derived from the foxglove plant and not dissimilar to medicines used to treat heart failure today), and lead acetate.

It's impossible to talk about the history of anxiety without mentioning Sigmund Freud. In 1894, he wrote a groundbreaking paper with a cumbersome name, "The Justification for Detaching from Neurasthenia a Particular Syndrome: The Anxiety-Neurosis." Out of the broad bucket of neurasthenia, Freud adroitly defined what we now know as the anxiety disorders. His descriptions of panic attacks (which he called anxiety attacks), generalized anxiety, phobias, and even obsessive-compulsive disorder are vivid and sound incredibly modern. Freud, then working as a neurologist in

Vienna, grouped all these symptoms under the diagnosis of "anxiety neurosis," a disorder that existed in the *DSM* until 1980.

Here's Freud's pitch-perfect characterization of generalized anxiety, or what he calls "anxious expectation": "A woman who suffers from anxious expectation will imagine every time her husband coughs, when he has a cold, that he is going to have influenzal pneumonia, and will at once see his funeral in her mind's eye. If when she is coming towards the house she sees two people standing by her front door, she cannot avoid the thought that one of her children has fallen out of the window; if the bell rings, then someone is bringing news of a death, and so on; whereas on all these occasions there is no particular ground for exaggerating a mere possibility."

Freud goes off the rails, however, when he describes the cause of anxiety neurosis. It arises, he asserts, from an accumulation of sexual energy that is inadequately released. Abstinence, premature ejaculation, and coitus interruptus are primarily to blame for anxiety neurosis in both men and women, Freud says. In later works, he abandoned this theory. Eventually, he came to believe that anxiety arose from unconscious threats and conflicts. This view would hold sway for decades.

We've come a long way from bloodletting and opium. Advances in brain imaging and genetics are yielding new insights into the origins of anxiety disorders and what can go awry in the brain. Groundbreaking treatments are on the horizon. Pioneering scientists are experimenting with programs intended to prevent anxiety disorders in children as young as three.

We now know that the foundation of anxiety is the defense system that nearly every organism has to detect and react to threats.

That's what trips off the racing heart, the shallow breathing, and the urge to escape—a response that makes clear sense if you're being chased by a bear. The fight-or-flight response is critical to survival.

When that response is initiated, the adrenal glands release the hormone epinephrine. Blood pressure rises and senses become sharper. The hypothalamus, a part of the brain that acts as the control center for the autonomic nervous system, releases corticotropin-releasing hormone (CRH), which in turn tells the pituitary gland and the adrenal glands to release the stress hormones adrenocorticotropic hormone (ACTH) and cortisol. This activation of the so-called HPA axis works together with the sympathetic nervous system to keep the body on high alert for danger. (Some studies have found a range of HPA axis abnormalities in people with anxiety disorders.)

At the root of this threat detection system is the amygdala, an almond-shaped structure in the brain that has been called its fear center. Probably no one knows more about the amygdala than Joseph LeDoux, a sixty-six-year-old neuroscientist at New York University and a genuine rock star in the world of anxiety disorders. (He fronts a band called the Amygdaloids.) In the 1980s, he successfully mapped the neurocircuitry of the defensive mechanism in rats.

People had speculated before that the amygdala was involved with fear. In the 1930s, Heinrich Klüver, a German-American psychologist, and Paul Bucy, an American neurosurgeon, conducted a series of experiments on monkeys. They found that removing both temporal lobes (which include the amygdala) caused monkeys to exhibit bizarre behaviors, including eating anomalies, hypersexuality, and fearlessness. Later scientists noticed similar behavior in people who had sustained damage to the amygdala and nearby brain structures due to strokes, infections, or other ailments. This came to be known as Klüver-Bucy syndrome.

Building on this work, LeDoux used a common experimental model called fear conditioning to teach his rats to react to an audible tone. When rats are threatened, say by a predator or by an electrical shock to the feet, they freeze, their hair stands on end, and their blood pressure and heart rate shoot up. In his experiments, LeDoux played a tone to the rats and followed it with a shock. After several rounds of this, the animals began to freeze as soon as they heard the tone. They had been conditioned to perceive the sound itself as a threat.

LeDoux's goal was to trace the path in the rats' brains from tone to rodent freak-out. To do this, he damaged different regions of the brain and then fear-conditioned the animals, noting what effect the various lesions had on the rats' behavior. He started with the auditory cortex, which directly receives sensory information, and worked downward to more primitive brain structures. Lesions to the auditory cortex didn't do much; the rats still froze to the tone. Lesions to the caudate-putamen, which is involved in movement and learning, also didn't affect freezing behavior. But when LeDoux made lesions in the amygdala, the rats stopped freezing. No amygdala, no threat response. The locus of fear, it seemed, had been found.

The tone takes one of two routes to the amygdala, LeDoux found. The more direct route, which he dubs the "low road," sends the stimulus right from the sensory thalamus, which relays sensory and motor information, to the amygdala, a journey that takes 10 to 12 milliseconds. The "high road," by contrast, where the stimulus travels from the sensory thalamus to the sensory cortex and then to the amygdala, takes about twice as long. The low road is a "quick and dirty processing system," LeDoux says. It unleashes the defense system almost instantly, even before a threat is consciously registered. He gives an example of a prairie dog spotting a bobcat. "The sight or sound of the bobcat goes straight to your amygdala and out comes the freezing response. If you had to make a deliberate decision about what to do . . . you could get so bogged down in decision making that you might be eaten before you made a choice."

The amygdala itself has different regions that serve different functions. The lateral nucleus, for example, is the part that receives the information. The central nucleus sends that information to the parts of the brain that control the physical responses associated with fear—freezing, respiration, heart rate, and the release of stress hormones. The hippocampus is the region that processes the context of the threat experience. This cage is where you got the shock, it tells the rat.

LeDoux then tackled the question of how animals can shake fear. Rats that have been fear-conditioned by the pairing of a tone with a shock can override that learning when the tone is repeatedly presented without the shock. Eventually they cease to freeze. This process is called extinction. In experiments in the 1990s, LeDoux found that another part of the brain, the medial prefrontal cortex, is critical to extinction. It acts, he says, by dampening the amygdala's action. "The medial prefrontal cortex is clamping down the amygdala, sort of like the brakes. The amygdala is the accelerator." Stress, however, can undo extinction. "The brake comes off," he says.

LeDoux says that in people, anxiety happens when thoughts interact with this threat-defense mechanism. While our body is going into fight-or-flight mode, our mind conjures catastrophe and dredges up memories of prior peril. The result, LeDoux says, is the conscious experience of anxiety.

On an October afternoon, I visited LeDoux at his office on the eleventh floor of the Center for Neural Science at NYU, a block from Washington Square Park in Greenwich Village. His office has a view of the Empire State Building. His desk is cluttered with books, unopened mail, and a baseball cap adorned with the image of a brain. LeDoux is the hippest-looking neuroscientist I've met, sporting dark jeans, a checked shirt, and a gray-blond soul patch. He speaks slowly, with a bit of a Louisiana drawl; he grew up in Eunice, the son of a butcher. (The part of the cow that most intrigued him? "The slimy, wiggly, wrinkled brain," of course.) He played in rock bands throughout high school and college, including one presciently named Cerebellum and the Medullas.

LeDoux takes me on a tour of his lab. We stop in a room lined with shelves, each piled with stacks of slim white boxes. "Here we have thirty years of rat brains," he says, gesturing with an arm. He takes a box down, opening it to reveal dozens of slides, each with a thin slice of brain stained a brilliant cerulean blue.

In another room, we see an apparatus designed for rodent neurosurgery, a silver bracelike contraption with various arms, knobs, and grooves indicating measurements. Brain lesions, he tells me, are usually made with an electric current. The rats themselves (two hundred or so) are out of sight, in a room that is off-limits to visitors. (After several more interviews with scientists who work with animals, I discover that it's standard policy not to let visitors see their subjects. Scientists are afraid of becoming the targets of animal rights activists.)

At one point, LeDoux confesses that he has a phobia of snakes. He traces the fear back to a traumatic childhood experience. "I remember as a kid being taken craw fishing on the bank of a bayou," he recalls. "It seemed like there were thousands of slithering black snakes everywhere. It was so disgusting." After that, he did everything he could to avoid them—a challenge given that he was an avid water-skier. "I would never get in the water ever. I'd be able to jump off the pier as the rope tightened and ski and then ski back up onto the landing."

After I visited LeDoux, I watched a video of one of his band's songs, "Fearing," based on a poem by Emily Dickinson. The Amygdaloids, which LeDoux formed with other NYU scientists, write and perform songs about emotions and the mind. In the video, LeDoux appears in the dark, ominous attic of a ruined house, wearing opaque black sunglasses and singing these words:

> *But recollecting is not forgetting*
> *It's vivid rehearsal of pain*
> *It reminds me of that day*
> *It keeps fear in my brain*

Studies have found that the amygdala and prefrontal cortex are involved in fear conditioning and extinction in people, too. Our fear response can be measured in a variety of ways, including skin conductance (a method of measuring sweating using electrodes) and fear-potentiated startle, an eyeblink reflex. Tiny sensors are placed under the eye to record the magnitude and intensity of the eyeblink. Researchers have found that people with anxiety disorders have a larger startle response than healthy people to conditioned stimuli—the colored light or tone that precedes an unconditioned stimulus, like an electric shock. And during extinction, the startle response tends to remain elevated. Simply put, anxious people catch fear easily and have a hard time letting go of it, even when there's mounting evidence they're safe. The amygdalae of anxious subjects also tend to be hyperactive even when they are not facing a potential threat. It is as if the anxious brain were always scanning the horizon for danger.

Anxious people aren't just constantly on guard; they actually see more peril in the world. If a situation is ambiguous, they are more likely to perceive it as negative or threatening. That's why when I have a headache, I think of brain tumors. And if my husband, Sean, is being quiet, I don't consider that he might be tired—I think he's mad at me. (Okay. Sometimes he is.) Scientists call this "attention bias to threat," and they think that, like lightning-quick fear conditioning, the bias is linked to a hyperactive amygdala and dampened prefrontal cortex activity.

Scientists often use the dot probe task to measure attention bias. It generally works like this: Subjects are shown photos of two human faces side by side, one angry or fearful, the other neutral. The faces disappear, and a small dot or cross (the probe) is shown in place of one of the faces. Subjects need to respond as quickly as possible (often by pushing a button) to the probe. A subject is considered to have an attention bias toward threat if they respond more quickly to the probes that replace the threatening faces versus the neutral ones. In many studies, those with anxiety disorders are shown to have this bias. This is true even when the faces are flashed so quickly that they can't be processed consciously. Nonanxious people, however, don't show this bias.

Besides being constantly ready for crisis, anxious people have a hard time with uncertainty. *What if? What if? What if?* is the endless refrain of the anxious mind. Uncertainty far too easily morphs into inescapable catastrophe. Scientists call this "intolerance of uncertainty," and it actually makes parts of the brain light up on a functional magnetic resonance imaging (fMRI) scan. Researchers at the University of California, San Diego, found that intolerance of uncertainty was linked to activity in the insula, part of the cerebral cortex that plays a role in emotion processing and body awareness. In a small experiment published in 2008, the scientists gave fourteen young adults a task called the Wall of Faces. The study subjects saw a series of pictures of thirty-two faces against a black background. Some faces had ambiguous expressions. Others were clearly happy or sad. The subjects who scored higher on a measure of intolerance of uncertainty had greater activity in the insula when they saw more faces with ambiguous expressions. Other studies have found that people with PTSD, social phobia, and GAD have increased activity in the insula when they anticipate seeing negative pictures.

Interestingly, scientists are finding that fear and anxiety may originate in different parts of the brain. The amygdala, it seems, is more closely tied to fear. It generates the raw, immediate response to an imminent threat. Anxiety, however—longer-lasting, amorphous uneasiness—may be rooted in an adjacent structure with an ungainly name: the bed nucleus of the stria terminalis, or BNST.

Michael Davis, a neuroscientist who recently retired from Emory University, has been exploring the BNST for decades. During the 1980s, he and LeDoux were in something of a race to map the neurocircuitry of fear conditioning in rats. At that time, he noticed that the BNST was connected to the same structures as the amygdala: the parts of the brain stem that control blood pressure, heart rate, and freezing. Why, he wondered, would there be a second area of the brain that appeared to serve the same function as the amygdala? Nature didn't usually duplicate itself like that.

While LeDoux was measuring fear conditioning by looking at freezing behavior, Davis began studying the startle reflex—specifically, fear-potentiated startle. Rats have a whole-body response when startled: Electrical activity can be detected in the rodent's neck muscles 5 milliseconds after a loud sound. In Davis's lab, first at Yale and then at Emory, rats were fear-conditioned by being exposed to a light followed by a shock. Then researchers elicited the startle response with a series of loud noises. Sometimes sounds followed the light that predicted the shock; other times there was no light, only sound. Not surprisingly, the startle response to the loud noise was bigger when the rats were also exposed to the light. This amplified response is known as fear-potentiated startle.

It was during these experiments that Davis stumbled on a potential role of the BNST. Over the years, he and his colleagues tested a host of compounds to see how they worked on fear-potentiated startle and, by extension, anxiety disorders. But there is a problem with fear conditioning. It involves learning: The rats have to learn that the light precedes the shock. So if a substance reduces fear-potentiated startle, you don't know whether it is because the substance is actually reducing the fear response or whether it is simply causing amnesia. It's possible, in other words, that the substance caused the rats to forget the link between the light and the shock.

With that in mind, the lab searched for a way to elicit an amplified startle without learning. Davis's colleague David Walker discovered that exposing rats to bright light for twenty minutes also enhanced startle. No learning was required. (Rats naturally avoid bright light and open spaces, which to a rodent signal danger.) "When the bright light is on for a long time, you don't know when something bad is going to happen," Davis says. Davis and Walker assumed that the amygdala was key for this extended fear conditioning, but it turned out that inactivating the amygdala didn't block the increase in startle after the twenty minutes of light. Deactivating the BNST, however, did.

The amygdala, it seemed, controlled the lightning-quick response. The BNST was switched on by longer-lasting apprehension—the expectation of pain without any certainty as to when it would occur. Scientists aren't certain when the shift from amygdala to BNST activity occurs in the face of danger, but it seems to be somewhere between four seconds and a minute.

In the 1990s, Christian Grillon, who was collaborating with

Davis at Yale, began doing similar experiments in people. Humans have a whole-body startle reflex, too, but the eyeblink part of it is the most consistent and easiest to measure. Sustained uncertainty, Grillon found, makes people jumpy for a sustained period of time. In one critical experiment, Grillon and Davis recruited fifty-eight Yale students. Most of the subjects underwent repeated rounds where they saw a blue light and received a shock to the left wrist. The students were divided into three groups. In the first group, the shock was predictably delivered a few seconds after the light. In the second, shocks were delivered randomly, with no relation to when the light was shown. (A third group saw the blue light but didn't receive any shocks.) Startle was elicited with a loud sound. Four days later the students underwent the same experiment. After being fear-conditioned, the first group startled more after hearing the sound—despite the four-day break. That wasn't surprising. But the second group had a bigger so-called baseline startle, the startle scientists elicited even before the subjects began this round of the experiment. The unpredictability of the shocks had made them on guard and ready to jump as soon as they were back in the same environment.

"In a way, anxiety is the opposite of fear. Fear is about something that is in front of you that is predictable and imminent. Anxiety is the opposite. It is worrying about something that is in the future that may or may not happen," Grillon says.

Based on the animal data, Grillon is pretty sure that the BNST is behind uncertainty-driven apprehension. One challenge for researchers is that the structure is small and hard to see on an fMRI scan. Grillon is excited about a powerful new scanner that his lab, now at NIMH, has procured. Using the new equipment, Grillon and colleagues have recently mapped the human BNST and its connections to other brain structures. It is a step toward understanding the area and its role in human anxiety. "Where is the anxious thought of a shock?" he says. "It may not be at the same place as the anxious thought of my kid not going to college or losing my job or fear of God." Perhaps the BNST will prove to be a fruitful target for new drugs or psychotherapies.

Neuroscientists caution that this kind of imaging work is still in its infancy. Other brain regions are being explored, too, and it's unlikely that there's any single route to an anxiety disorder. Also, developing anxiety is likely a dynamic process, with anxious thoughts and behaviors reinforcing the underlying neurobiology. As researchers Dan Grupe and Jack Nitschke write, "A patient with an anxiety disorder probably builds up neural pathways of anxiety just as a concert pianist strengthens neural pathways of musicianship—through hours of daily practice."

I wonder when things started to go awry in my brain. When did my amygdala go into overdrive? When did my prefrontal cortex cease to keep my body's fight-or-flight response in check? Neuroscientists are starting to see anxiety disorders as disorders of brain development that begin in childhood. And as with other neurological diseases—such as Alzheimer's disease with its telltale plaques and tangles—the brain likely shows signs of the illness long before the first panic attack or paralyzing bout of worry. The trick will be to locate those signs.

2

SCARY CLOWNS AND THE END OF DAYS
ANXIETY IN CHILDHOOD

I am seven years old, sitting at my desk at school. I have a blank piece of notebook paper in front of me and a number-two pencil at the ready. My teacher, a stony-faced young woman wearing orange kneesocks and brown loafers, is standing in front of the class.

"What's five times four?" she says.

Barely a second passes before she opens her mouth again.

"Nine times six."

"Three times four."

"Eight times two."

She's barking out math problems in an unrelenting monotone. Everyone around me is scribbling down answers. Except me. I'm frozen. My mind is blank. My mouth is dry. My hands are sweaty, tightly gripping the pencil. A hot blush rushes up my cheeks. My heart feels like it is doing penny drops, the flips I love to do on the monkey bars during recess.

I look down at my paper and see a few halfhearted numbers, a stray pencil mark, and lots of blanks.

But here's the thing. I know all the answers.

I've choked. This happens during every one of these oral math quizzes. I fail them all. So I wasn't that surprised when my first

second-grade report card came home with a big U for "unsatisfac-
tory achievement" in mathematics. In fact, I even traced over the
U in black pen, as if to highlight my shame. My parents, however,
were stunned. My math homework and written tests had come
home nearly errorless, and I hadn't told them about those awful
oral quizzes.

My father called the teacher, who told him to get me flash
cards. (In my parents' telling, the teacher was snippy and unsym-
pathetic. My dad got angry, and the teacher hung up on him.) So
he got flash cards. Every evening after dinner, my father would
sit in his chair while I sat on the floor in front of him. "What's
eight times nine? What's three times eleven?" he'd quiz. I swear
he mimicked that teacher's impatient bark and pinched, irritated
expression, too.

Although I dreaded those flash card sessions, the constant rep-
etition boosted my confidence. We didn't know it at the time,
but those sessions were very similar to exposure therapy, one of
the most effective treatments for anxiety disorders. Little by little
I began to dread the school tests less, and my terror subsided. I
started passing the quizzes. Then I started acing them.

On my next report card, I received an S for "satisfactory
achievement" in math. I got an S on the one after that. And by the
last report card of second grade, I was fully vindicated, with an O
for "outstanding achievement."

Many childhood events and experiences—from illness to
trauma to certain styles of parenting—can contribute to the development of anxiety. Although I'm not sure those mini panic
attacks—what scientists call "fearful spells"—were the beginning
of my anxiety, they were certainly a red flag. Having a panic attack
or even several isn't a disorder in and of itself. About one-quarter of
the U.S. population will have a panic attack during their lifetime.
But scientists are finding that panic attacks are often a harbinger

of future mental health problems. In a study that followed more than three thousand young people ages fourteen to twenty-four, German researchers discovered that those who reported having had panic attacks before joining the study were much more likely to develop a wide range of disorders, including specific phobias and social phobia, during the four years that followed. They also had more than double the risk of an alcohol-use disorder and more than ten times the risk of GAD.

Full-blown panic attacks are less common in kids. An adult with a panic attack has to manifest at least four out of thirteen possible symptoms, which include feelings of choking, chest pain, nausea, and fear of dying. Children, however, often experience less severe or more circumscribed attacks, like my fearful spells. A fearful spell is "a sudden experience of fear and anxiety but it does not have to be associated with all these panic symptoms like heart racing, sweating, feeling that you're losing control," says Katja Beesdo-Baum, a coauthor of the German panic attack study and a professor of behavioral epidemiology at the Technische Universität Dresden. Children who experience fearful spells have a higher risk of developing major depression and are more than three times more likely to develop panic disorder, agoraphobia, and GAD within the ten years following the spells. "Fearful spells might be an early indicator and you can assess it quite easily," Beesdo-Baum says.

But maybe my anxiety took root even earlier.

At age four, I developed an intense fear of clowns. (Yes, I realize this isn't a particularly original phobia. Clowns are creepy.) At first I was as fascinated as I was afraid—I actually dressed up as a clown for Halloween. My mother sewed the outfit herself, a turquoise suit with fluffy white pom-poms and a conical hat. I also had a deep affection for Ronald McDonald, and when I heard that he was visiting a local McDonald's, I begged my parents to take me. They did, grudgingly, even though my mother was a health nut who tried to pass carob off as chocolate and put wheat germ on just about everything. But when we arrived on that much-anticipated day, I was too scared to get out of the car. My parents cajoled, bribed, and threatened to try to get me to go meet the smiley, yellow-suited guy. I wouldn't budge. Finally, my father turned the car toward home, grumbling.

Clown-induced terror was waiting for me at home, too. From the ages of about three to five, I was hooked on *Sesame Street*, often watching it twice a day. In the 1970s, one recurring segment featured a clown with a curly red wig and painted white face with an oversize red mouth and black triangles above and below his eyes.

"I don't always look like a clown, you know," he would say, sounding sad and stoned. "I have an everyday face, too."

He'd yank off his nose and wig. Then, accompanied by a frenetic soundtrack of horns, whistles, and a panicked piano, they'd run the tape of him putting on his clown face in reverse. The triangles below his eyes and the red around his mouth were sucked back into their respective makeup pencils. The white of his face disappeared back into a small tube. At the end he was revealed to be a pasty, dour, thin-faced man.

"This is my everyday face. Which do you like best?" he would ask in a slow, dispirited voice. The screen split, barefaced man on left, clown on right. The man looked to his clown face and dejectedly said, with a small shrug, "Me, too."

The frenzied music, the aggressive unmasking, the clown's obvious depression, all of it terrified me. I'd watch *Sesame Street* in a state of nervous anticipation, one foot literally out the door as each new segment began. As soon as I saw a glimpse of that painted white face or heard the first honk of his red nose, I'd run out of the living room, yelling. I wouldn't go back in until my mother had assured me that the segment was over.

I found the clip of that *Sesame Street* segment on YouTube recently. Watching it, I wanted to give the guy a hug and hand him some Prozac.

Various fears, of course, are normal in childhood and adolescence. Separation anxiety in one-year-olds and fear of thunderstorms and the dark in toddlers. Fear of monsters and ghosts in five-year-olds and fear of social rejection in teenagers. These are all typical. According to the *DSM*, in order for a fear to be classified as a phobia, it should last at least six months and impair a person's life. For example, if you can't go to school because you're terrified of the bus getting into an accident, that's an impairment.

Specific phobia is one of the earliest of all the anxiety disorders to appear, with an age of onset generally between seven and fourteen years old. It is also the most common of the anxiety disorders, affecting 15.6 percent of Americans ages thirteen and older during their lifetime. People can develop phobias to almost anything. (I came across a case report of a nine-year-old boy who had a phobia of buttons.) The most common involve animals (dogs, spiders, bears), the natural world (heights, water, storms, earthquakes), blood, or situations like flying or being in enclosed places (claustrophobia). There are some gender differences in phobias. For example, phobias of bugs and snakes are more common among women. Both men and women are equally afraid of heights and closed spaces.

The most common phobias make a lot of evolutionary sense because they can involve real peril. The psychiatrist Randolph M. Nesse argues that these fears developed over millennia with the purpose of keeping people safe. Even modern phobias, like those of flying or driving, are primed by the age-old dangers posed by heights, speed, and being stuck in small spaces. "Our emotions are adaptations shaped by natural selection," Nesse writes.

Anyone with a phobia knows that it can be crippling. (My

driving-on-highways phobia would be a serious problem if I lived in Los Angeles, for example.) They also can foreshadow even more serious mental health problems. A 2010 study of about fifteen hundred young German women, for example, found that those with specific phobia were twice as likely to develop GAD, depression, or a somatoform disorder (mental illnesses that cause unexplained physical symptoms, including pain and distress) during the next seventeen months compared with those who didn't have a phobia.

My clown phobia was quickly surpassed by something much more overwhelming and unavoidable: a colossal fear of death. I was terrified of it—the pain, the fear, the blank blackness. I could not handle any depiction, or even mention, of death in books or movies. *Charlotte's Web* was a horror. If any creature seemed in peril, I would ask my mother, "Does he die? Does she die?" I soon became more demanding: "Promise me she doesn't die." The no death edict eliminated many children's classics: No *Bambi*. No *Wizard of Oz*. No *Snow White*.

I became increasingly alarmed by the breathless descriptions of hell—the eternal fires, the screams of the damned—delivered many Sundays by the pastor at our Baptist church. My mother had grown up Southern Baptist, which meant that my sister and I did, too. (For years, my father, who drank beer, cursed, and smoked, didn't accompany us to church, declaring that he wasn't "good enough" for it.)

According to our church, the only way you could avoid hell was to be "born again" or "saved" and to accept Jesus Christ as your Lord and Savior. At the end of every church service, while the congregation sang the hymn "Just As I Am," the pastor would invite people to come up to pray and be saved. This became my favorite part of the service. Who would escape hell's clutches this week? The pastor, in a dark suit with his hands clasped behind him, would wait expectantly in front of the wooden pulpit, his eyes scanning the congregation. Sometimes one verse, then two, would go by, and no one would stir. The singing would take on more urgency. There were days when someone would scurry up just before the choir started singing the last "Oh Lamb of God, I Come, I Come."

My favorite Bible verse became John 3:16: "For God so loved the world, that he gave his only begotten Son, that whosoever believeth in him should not perish, but have everlasting life." Not perish. Woo-hoo!

I became fixated on being born again, not because of true religious fervor but because of its get-out-of-eternal-damnation-free card. But there seemed to be some unspoken rule that you had to wait until a certain age. Nine seemed to be the magic number. That's how old I was when I finally strode down the church aisle. A few weeks later I was baptized in the hidden pool behind the pulpit. It was actually more like a big bathtub. I wore a brand-new baby-blue sundress. The pastor wore black rubber waders under his suit jacket and put a white handkerchief over my mouth and nose as he dunked me under three times: one for the Father, one for the Son, and one for the Holy Ghost.

I was elated. Salvation, however, didn't seem to let you escape this whole death thing. Sure, your spirit would live on. But your body would still conk out. Then I found a loophole: the Rapture. From church services, I gleaned that Jesus was supposed to return to Earth and that those who were alive at his second coming would be taken directly up to heaven, bypassing death altogether. What a neat trick!

Every night before I went to sleep, a stuffed animal menagerie surrounding me, I'd pray for the second coming of Jesus so I wouldn't have to die. "Please come soon. Please don't let me die, get hurt, get killed, or get scared," I'd say, making sure to leave no wiggle room in my request.

A couple of years after that, I learned that the world was supposed to end on March 10, 1982, when I would be eleven. At least that was the prediction set forth by John Gribbin and Stephen Plagemann, two Cambridge-educated astrophysicists, in their 1974 book, *The Jupiter Effect*. On that date, major planets would align on the same side of the sun. The gravitational pull of those planets, especially Jupiter, would supposedly cause all sorts of mayhem, from altering Earth's rotation to generating earthquakes, one of which would level Los Angeles.

I never read *The Jupiter Effect*. I was too busy warping my mind—and my future view of romance—with my mother's Danielle Steel novels and with V. C. Andrews's books (arsenic poisoning! incest!), surreptitiously purchased with my allowance money. But I was aware of the apocalyptic date. The prediction and the response to it were being covered by the local news. I recall seeing TV segments and newspaper articles about people—even teachers and their classes—throwing weirdly ebullient "End of the World" parties, complete with balloons and Carvel ice cream cakes.

As the date edged closer, I became more and more nervous. What would it feel like to die in an earthquake? Would I be knocked out immediately by a falling ceiling? Or would my demise be slow and agonizing? Would I be trapped under debris, calling weakly for help until I finally starved? I spent hours mulling over various outcomes, all tragic. There were no world-saving superheroes in my anxious imaginings.

March 10 was a Wednesday, so I must have gone to school that day. But what I remember is sitting immobilized in my dad's tan corduroy La-Z-Boy chair with the pop-out footrest that evening, pretending to watch *The Facts of Life* while monitoring the passing minutes on the clock, trying to will the hour hand past midnight. Then it would be March 11, and I—and the world—would be safe.

. . .

Trauma during childhood is a strong predictor of psychiatric disorders, including depression, drug and alcohol abuse, ADHD, and anxiety disorders. Researchers at Harvard Medical School and the University of Michigan analyzed data from 5,692 adults, examining the association between a host of childhood adversities—from physical abuse, sexual abuse, and neglect to divorce, poverty, and the death of a parent—and the onset of a psychiatric disorder. They found that these experiences are remarkably common: More than half of respondents had experienced at least one, with divorce, violence in the family, and the mental illness of a parent among the most typical. The most serious traumas, what researchers dubbed maladaptive family functioning (including mental illness of or substance abuse by a parent, criminal behavior, violence within the family, physical and sexual abuse, and neglect), most strongly predicted psychiatric disorders.

Scientists are trying to figure out exactly how childhood trauma can lead to mental health problems. Some studies show that early maltreatment can alter the HPA axis and cause long-term dysfunction in the body's stress response. Childhood stress affects the brain. When researchers at the University of Wisconsin gave sixty-four adolescents MRI scans, they found that a history of abuse and neglect during childhood was associated with altered connections between the hippocampus and the subgenual anterior cingulate cortex. And the adolescents who had these altered connections had more symptoms of anxiety and depression.

Interestingly, the traumas specifically linked to anxiety disorders are childhood physical illness and economic adversity. A study that surveyed nearly seven hundred high school students and their parents found that a serious illness or infection during the first year of life strongly predicted anxiety disorders by the teenage years. The risk of anxiety disorders was also higher among teens whose mothers had a history of pregnancy problems, particularly miscarriages and stillbirths.

My mother says that when I got a cold, it almost always turned into a nasty bout of bronchitis. Once when I was not quite one year old, I was coughing and then suddenly stopped breathing. My mother tells me that she was holding me and patting me on the back and that I just went limp. For a minute she thought I was dead. My father grabbed my ankles, hung me upside down, and started whacking me on the back. I finally started crying. Later the doctor said that I had nearly drowned on phlegm.

A similar thing happened when I was four, while I was recovering from another spell of bronchitis. I was playing with my Barbie dolls in my room when I started feeling funny, compelled to take deep breaths and hold them. I sat on my pink comforter, hands on knees, arms rigid, focused on pushing the air in and out of a space that soon felt no bigger than a coffee stirrer. I tried to distract myself from the sensation of breathlessness by bundling Barbie and Skipper into their RV camper. (I was never a big fan of Ken, with his suspect intentions and immovable hair.) It didn't help; I felt increasingly desperate, each breath a struggle. Panicked, I ran into the kitchen, where my parents were sitting at the table, and was able to croak out "I can't breathe" before passing out on the linoleum floor.

I woke in a car hurtling toward the nearest hospital emergency room, curled on my mother's lap in the front seat. Suddenly I looked up and said, "Where are we going?" "You popped right out of it," my father recalls.

In high school, I was diagnosed with exercise-induced asthma. In college, when I began having panic attacks, the feeling was instantly familiar. Even though I didn't have bronchitis and there was no lung-clogging phlegm, the terror and struggle to breathe were no less real. Anxiety is a fantastic mimic.

Research today is showing a link between respiratory illnesses and anxiety. A study of nearly one thousand young people by researchers from UCLA and New Zealand revealed that a history of asthma increases the risk of panic disorder in young women. Other studies have found that adults with asthma, emphysema, and bronchitis have higher rates of both anxiety disorders and depression. There's also evidence that lung problems in kids are associated with a greater risk of anxiety disorders by young adulthood. A 2008 study showed that those who had pneumonia, asthma, croup, or bronchiolitis—or a history of it—at age one were nearly three times more likely to be treated for an anxiety disorder by age thirty-four. Those who had respiratory diseases at both age one and age seven were nearly twenty times more likely to have received treatment for an anxiety disorder by thirty-four. The risk was evident even in infants. Babies with a higher breathing rate at just four months old had more than double the odds of being treated for anxiety by thirty-four.

Still, these studies show only an association; they don't prove that breathing disorders *cause* anxiety. Some scientists speculate that breathing problems and mental disorders could both be at least partly caused by immune system issues. Another hypothesis is that they share an underlying genetic or environmental source. There's evidence that people with anxiety disorders, particularly panic disorder, have an overly sensitive "suffocation alarm system," a mechanism that evolved to help people survive. Recently, scientists have located a gene that creates a protein that acts as a sensor for carbon dioxide (rising CO_2 levels can indicate impending suffocation). The gene has been linked to a risk for panic disorder.

It is not only being ill as a child that can lead to anxiety disorders. Witnessing the serious illness of a parent also increases the risk. In the UCLA and New Zealand study mentioned earlier, young women whose parents had had a stroke, heart attack, or high blood pressure during the women's childhood or early teenage years had an increased risk of panic disorder. It could be that being sick as a child or growing up in close proximity to illness elicited fears about bodily sensations. Perhaps these children were more likely to misinterpret mild shortness of breath or a fluttery heartbeat as impending catastrophe. It's also possible that the parents' ill health and fragility spurred them to become overprotective.

Of course, parents do not have to be in ill health to be overly controlling of their children. Overprotective and controlling parenting—telling kids what to think and feel and micromanaging their activities—sends the message that children aren't capable, a belief that can fuel anxiety. But scientists haven't been able to tease out which comes first—the kids' anxiety or the controlling, overprotecting parenting. It could be that moms and dads are molding their parenting style to their already anxious kids rather than shaping their kids' temperaments.

If a child is anxious from an early age, parental hovering is understandable. Kids who are genetically vulnerable to anxiety disorders may be skittish and sensitive. Parents, in turn, tend to respond to these kids by being overinvolved and overprotecting in an attempt to ease their children's distress. The trouble is, this sends the message that the world is a dangerous place and that kids can't cope on their own. Also, when parents allow their children to avoid scary or distressing situations, the kids have fewer opportunities to learn to master their fear. Thus the fear-overprotection-fear cycle goes on and on. There's also some evidence that parents who are colder, more critical, and less responsive—what researchers call rejecting—are more likely to have anxious kids.

Researchers in Australia wanted to see if and how this played out in real time. They watched 95 children ages seven to fifteen and their mothers in two five-minute experiments: 43 kids had anxiety disorders, 20 had oppositional defiant disorder (characterized by behavioral problems and anger, defiance, and vindictiveness), and 32 had no psychiatric diagnosis. Children were asked to complete two difficult tasks: a tangram puzzle, where geometric shapes need to be arranged to form particular larger shapes, and a Scrabble-type game where kids were given letters and told to form as many words as possible. The mothers were given the answers to the first task and extra letters—which would make the game easier—for the Scrabble task. Moms were told they could help their kids when they felt the children needed assistance.

A researcher rated the mothers' interactions with their children to assess the level of controlling and rejecting parental behavior. Measures included things like "degree of unsolicited help," "touching of the tangram/Scrabble pieces," "mother's tension," and "mother's degree of verbal and non-verbal encouragement/criticism." Mothers of anxious children were significantly more controlling than mothers of children without a psychiatric diagnosis. They were also more negative. Mothers of oppositional children were about equally as controlling and negative as the mothers of anxious kids. The researchers speculated that this style of parenting might be a reaction to not just anxiety but psychiatric problems in kids in general.

On the whole, though, the effect of parenting on the development of anxiety is thought to be relatively modest. In a big 2007 review of the scientific literature looking at the link between parenting and anxiety in kids, researchers found that parenting explained only about 4 percent of the variation in anxiety issues among children. Controlling parenting behaviors fueled anxiety slightly more than rejection did. The one parenting behavior that did appear to have a strong impact on a child's anxiety was "granting autonomy," which explained 18 percent of the variance in childhood anxiety. "When parents fail to provide children with the opportunity to experience control in age-appropriate contexts, it is possible that children may not develop a strong sense of self-efficacy, thereby increasing their sense of vulnerability to threat and heightening anxiety," the scientists wrote.

I'm apt to buy that parenting doesn't contribute much to anxiety because my parents weren't controlling or overprotective at all.

My mother was twenty, my father twenty-one when I was born. They had gone to high school together in Salem, Illinois, but didn't get to know each other until 1969, as students at Kaskaskia College. My mother was pretty, studious, and very shy. My father was a cutup, boisterous and popular. He had long hair and lamb-chop sideburns, and he carried a beat-up leather briefcase to classes. (This was exotic. Hippie style had yet to hit Salem.) He strode up to my mother's table in the library while she was studying, sat across from her, stared at her, and declared, "If you don't talk to me, I'm going to play with your leg." She talked to him. They fell in love. She got pregnant. And then they eloped. My mother didn't tell her parents about the pregnancy or the marriage until months later.

During the first few months of my life, I lived with my mother, her parents, and five of her six siblings in her childhood home, an old converted schoolhouse where chalkboards still lined the walls. My father lived a few hours away at the University of Illinois, in a fraternity for engineering students—then a hotbed of loud music, marijuana, and geekdom. On weekends, my mom and I took a bus there. During one visit, my parents ran out of diapers. The fraternity's housemother wrapped me in an old dishcloth.

My parents eventually landed a two-bedroom apartment in a married-student housing complex. Still, they were young and broke. One night while my father was watching me and my mother was working her job at a pharmacy, he and a friend were high on hash. My dad turned around to find me, about a year old, with a mouth full of the stuff. He force-fed me mayonnaise to make me vomit. More than once we had no food in the apartment except for baby formula and a jar of peanut butter. For my first birthday, my mother broke a piggy bank and took five hundred pennies to the bank, swapping it for a crisp bill. She had just enough to buy a cake mix and party hats.

After my dad graduated from Illinois, we bounced around the country as my father built a career as an industrial engineer: to Neenah, Wisconsin; Scranton, Pennsylvania; Appleton, Wisconsin; and Danbury, Connecticut, all by the time I was ten.

My childhood was warm and loving. I have fond memories of family sing-alongs and camping trips. But Mom and Dad's parenting style was decidedly laissez-faire. In Pennsylvania, at age seven or so, I spent weekends riding bikes and playing Red Rover with a pack of other kids. We'd stop home for dinner, then dash back outside to play Flashlight Tag until long after dark. As a teenager in Connecticut, I'd break curfew to drive around with friends in my silver Chevy Sprint, go skinny-dipping in Candlewood Lake, or head to Images, a teen dance club where kids slam-danced to Big Audio Dynamite and the Jesus and Mary Chain and gave each other Mohawks in the parking lot. I don't remember ever getting grounded.

My dad was transferred to Michigan the summer before my senior year of high school. My parents let me move in with my best

friend, Kate, her mother, and their cat for the rest of the school
year so I could graduate with my class. Kate and I were both obsessed with books and music. As preteens, we had spent hours
making up dances to the songs we loved like Joan Jett's "I Love
Rock and Roll" and Queen's "Another One Bites the Dust."

But the new living arrangement was difficult from the start.
Kate's mother was dating a ringer for Moses who blared organ
music through the T-top of his red Camaro Z-28. The couple
practiced jujitsu in the living room and left violent, pornographic
comic books on the coffee tables. Kate's mom read my mail, listened in on my phone conversations, and called my boyfriend's
mother when he cut baseball practice to hang out with me. My
best friend and I fought. I was allergic to the cat. At Thanksgiving,
my boyfriend and I drove my Chevy to Okemos, Michigan, where
my parents had moved. A week later I sent him back to Connecticut on a Greyhound bus. I stayed.

After the chaos and intrusiveness of my friend's home, I was
thrilled to be back with my family, even though it meant starting over in a new school and making new friends a third of the
way through senior year. The truth was that I craved a bit more
parental guidance and a few more rules. I felt like I was winging
it too often. And I felt unmoored by typical teen feelings of anger
and sadness.

I didn't have much of a model for dealing with negative emotions. My family didn't talk about them, or even acknowledge
that such feelings existed. My father was usually jovial and a goof,
my mother sunny and optimistic. They almost never fought. The
only time I saw my father yell at my mother was after she drove
our Oldsmobile through the garage door. The maddest I saw my
mother was once when my sister and I were arguing; she jumped
up and down and yelled, "Stupid, stupid kids," and slammed
a cabinet door, which broke off the hinges and clattered to the

ground. (The three of us laughed for a long time afterward.) Her most serious curse was "gosh darn it." When I was mopey or sad, she would tell me to "just be happy."

So I learned to bury bad feelings. And I didn't divulge teen friend and boyfriend dramas, like the time a friend was kicked out of her house and we stuffed her belongings in my hatchback. Or the times when one early high school boyfriend became psychologically manipulative ("You would if you loved me," he actually said) and even physically scary, pushing me and blocking doors when we fought.

I don't have the scientific studies to back this up, but now—after years of therapy—I think my college breakdown was, in part, my body's way of saying, *Enough already! You have to pay attention to how you feel. And that means the tough stuff, too.*

Some of the most promising research is looking into what goes on in the brains of anxious kids. About half of kids with anxiety disorders won't go on to have anxiety problems as adults. But half will. So scientists are trying to identify markers in the brain that might reveal which kids will remain anxious.

Daniel Pine, chief of the section on development and affective neuroscience in the Intramural Research Program at the National Institute of Mental Health, believes that the key to tackling anxiety is to start early in the lifespan. "If we think of mental disorders as disorders of brain development, most of the keys are going to be found by working with kids," Pine says.

Studying kids will also help scientists overcome a problem inherent in looking at the brains of anxious adults: untangling whether the dysfunctions that have been identified in mature brains are evidence of the disease or simply the brain's way of compensating for the disorders.

"Anxiety is a normal part of childhood," Pine observes. "But among that large mass of normal anxiety, hidden in there somewhere, are the seeds of most chronic emotional problems in adults. Most adult emotional problems—anxiety disorders definitely, but also depression and even bipolar disorder—will start as elevated levels of anxiety." But because anxiety is a normal part of being human, the line between illness and health is fuzzy. "The thing that keeps me up at night," he says, "is how do you sort out what's normal and what's not normal?"

Pine is perhaps the most influential person in the world when it comes to pediatric anxiety disorders and their development. His lab has scanned the brains of hundreds of anxious children and launched the careers of many anxiety experts. His arm of the NIMH has partnered with scientific institutions all over the world and funded hundreds of studies.

I visit Pine on a balmy June day. The NIMH building looks like a strange, small afterthought on the sprawling NIH campus in Bethesda, Maryland. It is tucked away on a tree-covered hill, a cream-colored house with a brown roof and accents, looking vaguely like a Swiss chalet. A flimsy, curling piece of copy paper with NIMH printed on it is taped to the door—the only indication I see of what's inside.

Danny (everyone calls him Danny) Pine's office is on the first floor, a spacious corner spot filled with beige-striped furniture that looks like castoffs from a conference room at a Sheraton. Chicago Cubs and Bruce Springsteen memorabilia dot the room; a framed *Darkness on the Edge of Town* album, a poster from *Magic*. Pine is wearing khakis, a blue polo shirt, and gold wire-rimmed glasses. He is a fifty-three-year-old father of three and has a full reddish beard. He's enthusiastic and informal, with the demeanor of a beloved professor. "That's a great question," he says, often.

Pine and his colleagues are finding that many areas of brain dysfunction are similar in anxious adults and kids. As in an anxious adult, in an anxious kid something is often amiss in the connection between the amygdala and the prefrontal cortex. The amygdala of an anxious child tends to be overactive, the prefrontal cortex underactive. One of Pine's major areas of research is on the relationship between anxiety and attention. He uses the dot probe task with kids to measure attention bias. "Attention is very tightly related to anxiety," Pine says. But the relationship is fuzzy. "In some situations, anxious people pay more attention to threat. In other situations, they pay less attention."

While we talk, Pine walks me over to the NIH's clinical building, where his research studies are conducted. Two young NIMH research fellows take me to a room where they conduct a fear-conditioning task using the "screaming lady" paradigm. It is a way to fear-condition kids without using electric shocks (used with adults but not kids, for ethical reasons). Children are presented with two different female faces—one blonde, the other brunette—via a black-and-white video screen and are told that one of the faces will be accompanied by a loud sound. "The scream happens 80 percent of the time," says Liz Ivie, one of the fellows. "The uncertainty makes the arousal higher." Various physiological measures are taken, including heart rate, skin conductance, eyeblinks, and startle response.

Ivie and Laurie Russell, another fellow, demonstrate the experiment.

As they set things up, we debate which woman is creepier. Honestly, neither one looks very pleasant even with their faces resting, but we settle on the brunette. Russell says she "looks like she's plotting someone's demise." As I await the scream, I can feel myself getting anxious; my heart rate jumps, and my stomach feels buzzy. "Just get it over with. The anticipation is horrifying," says Russell, who, like me, will be hearing the scream for the first time. When it finally accompanies the blonde, I jump. It sounds slightly strangled, and the face contorts into a twisted shriek. (NIMH has had a problem with the screaming lady being too terrifying, so much so that they lost about a third of the studies' participants. They are now working on a new paradigm that uses bells.)

In some studies, participants are also shown merged images of the two faces. After the kids are conditioned, they undergo extinction, which entails being shown the faces without the scream.

In a small study using this paradigm published in 2008, adolescents with anxiety disorders developed more fear of both women's faces, whether they were coupled with the scream or not. This speaks to the tendency of anxious people to generalize threat; fear of a situation that is genuinely scary can spill over to one that is safe, too.

Another larger study published in 2013 used fMRI scans to see what happened to two parts of the prefrontal cortex, the subgenual anterior cingulate and the ventromedial prefrontal cortex (vmPFC), three weeks after anxious adults and adolescents underwent fear conditioning and extinction with the screaming women. These parts of the brain are critical for extinction and dampen the activity of the amygdala. Both anxious adolescents and adults had less activity in the subgenual anterior cingulate than healthy people when they were asked whether or not they were afraid while viewing the women's faces during the three-week follow-up, so this pattern may be a common feature of both adolescent and adult anxiety disorders. But anxious adolescents and adults differed in the activity of the vmPFC. The researchers conjecture that certain patterns of activity in this brain region might help identify those young people most at risk of remaining anxious in adulthood.

Children tend to classify more things as dangerous, but "when kids mature they get better at recognizing the nuanced boundaries between things that are safe and things that are dangerous," says Pine. It is the prefrontal cortex that helps us do that. Pine thinks that the development of anxiety has something to do with prefrontal maturation. He explains that one of the things that separates healthy from unhealthy development is learning how to appropriately classify things that are ambiguous.

After I've been spooked by the screaming blonde, Russell takes me to a room with a fake MRI machine designed to acclimate kids to being in an actual scanner. There she shows me one of the newest research paradigms, dubbed "Virtual School." Virtual School "enrolls" subjects aged eight to seventeen and tries to replicate the treacherous social waters they have to navigate, which are particularly terrifying for children with social anxiety disorder.

Social anxiety disorder (SAD) or social phobia is one of the most common anxiety disorders, affecting more than 10 percent of the U.S. population during their lifetime. Children and adults with SAD fear meeting new people, being at parties, and other situations where they are expected to interact with strangers. Terrified of embarrassment, they often avoid such situations entirely. Some evidence shows that the brain dysfunction in social anxiety disorder may be different than in other anxiety disorders.

In Virtual School, kids are told that they will be chatting online with six other kids in a virtual school. In preparation for that, they make an avatar and answer questions about their favorite subject, color, actor, and type of music, among others. Once the experiment starts, they "attend" the virtual school while in an fMRI scanner, as their brain is being scanned. They are told that two of the other kids are mean, two are nice, and two are sometimes mean and sometimes nice. (In reality, there are no other children in the experiment. A computer generates the responses.)

Kids see an electronic rendering of a schoolroom, with various avatars sitting at desks. Bubbles appear above the avatars' heads when they are about to chat. Some of the other kids taunt them, and the information they provided about their personal likes and dislikes is used to make the teasing more pointed. A mean kid might say something like, "You like Miley Cyrus? Wow, you're such a loser."

The researchers are particularly interested in what happens in anxious kids' brains as they anticipate comments from the kids who are sometimes mean and sometimes nice, which is known as ambiguous social feedback. Other studies have shown that kids with SAD tend to interpret ambiguous social feedback as negative.

Afterward kids are debriefed and told that they weren't chatting with real kids after all. "The anxious kids are usually pretty sad," says Russell. "They usually say, 'I can't believe I didn't figure it out.' That they weren't smart enough to know that we were tricking them.

"Some of the kids come out of the scanner really upset because they got bullied." Other kids are relieved when they find out they weren't actually talking to real kids. "It actually makes a lot of them feel better," says Russell. "Some say, 'I'm glad kids aren't that mean in real life.'"

The goal of these NIMH experiments is to figure out the "neural signature" of nascent anxiety disorders. Identifying the signature could allow doctors to identify at-risk children and develop treatments to prevent the anxiety from becoming entrenched.

3

MY GRANDMOTHER'S MADNESS
THE GENETICS OF ANXIETY

It was in the middle of the night sometime in the fall of 1958 when my grandmother Gladys Schneidervin Petersen, a thirty-nine-year-old Wisconsin housewife, tried to kill her family.

She began by crumpling some papers and putting them under the beds of her two sleeping sons, nine-year-old Gary, my father, and eleven-year-old Bill. Next, she crumpled more papers, placed them between the stove and the refrigerator, and arranged a tower of garbage in a back storage room. Then she collected her thirteen-year-old daughter Susan's schoolbooks and stacked them at the bottom of the sleeping girl's bed. Finally, she moved through the house and set each spot aflame.

"I woke up and the bottom of my bed was on fire," my aunt Susan recalls. She ran to wake up her father and then her brothers; my grandfather screamed for them to leave the house. "Mom just kept saying she needed to protect us and if we were dead nobody could hurt us. That made sense to her."

"That's when Dad took her to the hospital, and she didn't come back for a long, long time," my father said recently. Gladys would spend the next three years at Mendota State Hospital, a mental institution in Madison that opened in 1860 as the Wisconsin State Hospital for the Insane.

Throughout my childhood, my grandmother was a specter. She died when I was two, and I have no memory of her. But I heard bits of stories—of the fire, of the mental hospital, of how my mother was afraid of the knives Gladys carried. While my parents were dating, my father told my mother that the only thing she could do to make him leave her would be to "go crazy."

When I got sick in college, I was terrified that I was following in my grandmother's footsteps—beginning my own descent into psychosis. My father was worried, too. "It got stuck in my head that somehow you ended up with a little bit of the wrong Petersen DNA," he said.

Mental illness is at least partly genetic. Studies of twins have found that genes are responsible for 30 to 40 percent of the variation in the individual risk for anxiety disorders. For schizophrenia, Gladys's diagnosis, the genetic toll is much higher: Genes contribute close to 80 percent of the variation in risk. Having a first-degree relative—a parent, sibling, or child—with an anxiety disorder bumps a person's risk of developing one up to five times that of the general population.

New research is showing that some of the same genes underlie different mental disorders. In a 2013 study, genetic overlap was found between five different illnesses: schizophrenia, bipolar disorder, depression, autism, and ADHD. The overlap was highest (about 15 percent) between schizophrenia and bipolar disorder and lowest (about 3 percent) between schizophrenia and autism. Researchers suspect that the genes implicated in anxiety disorders also overlap.

Scientists believe that a set of genes crucial to brain development can go wrong in many different ways, says Francis McMahon, chief of the Genetics Basis of Mood and Anxiety Disorders Section of the Human Genetics Branch at the NIMH Intramural Research Program. "The more severe mutations are more likely to be seen in cases of autism, the less severe in cases of schizophrenia, and perhaps the more subtle defects we'll see in the mood disorders and the anxiety disorders." So some of the same genes may be behind both Gladys's breakdown and my own struggles.

Genetic research into anxiety disorders has been hampered by small sample sizes, says McMahon. Some scientists believe this is because of inadequate funding. Also, anxiety disorders often coexist with other mental illnesses, such as depression, which muddies the waters. A further complication is that patients with the same diagnosis can show great variation in symptoms and severity, which means that scientists risk comparing apples to oranges. And since anxiety is a normal human emotion, it can be difficult to ascertain where disorder begins.

McMahon believes that the number of genes involved in anxiety disorders is "probably going to be in the many hundreds." Each one likely contributes a tiny amount to the overall risk.

Gladys had been deteriorating for years before the fire. Indeed, her children can't remember a time when she was healthy. However, old friends of my grandmother told my aunt Susan that, in her youth and when she first married, Gladys was "a wonderful woman. She cared about people, taught Sunday school, was active in church, and was there to help anybody that needed it." In my favorite photo of my grandparents, from the early 1940s, my grandfather Pete Petersen is dashing in his army uniform. (He was a fighter pilot in the Pacific during World War II.) My grandmother, wearing a chic white suit and dark blouse, her brown hair lustrous and curled, leans tenderly into him. They look joyous and hopeful.

In 1950, when the children were five, three, and one, my grandfather had a tragic accident. He had become a carpenter after the war and was making repairs on a church roof when he fell thirty feet and punctured a lung. Then, while recuperating in the hospital, he caught polio. He spent several months in an iron lung, a cylindrical respirator that did the work of his paralyzed chest muscles, and was not expected to survive. Although he ultimately recovered, he used crutches because of his weakened legs until his death in 1979.

Even before the accident, the family's lifestyle was hardly luxurious. The family lived in a one-bedroom home (the boys slept in a screened-in porch and Susan slept in the living room) on the banks of Eagle Spring Lake in Eagleville, Wisconsin. There was no indoor plumbing, and my grandmother hauled water down from the lake so that she could wash clothes and the family could bathe. "Mom would do the laundry, then she'd do us," my dad recalls. As the youngest, he went last and "got the grimiest stuff" at bath time. There was an outhouse and a jerry-rigged contraption to fall back on during the cold Wisconsin winters—a wicker chair with a hole and a bucket under it. But on idyllic summer days they swam in the lake and picked wild black raspberries, asparagus, and rhubarb.

Because of Pete's polio, the whole family was under quarantine for weeks. "There was a big colored piece of paper on our front door that boldly said QUARANTINED and warned people not to approach us or the property," my aunt Susan relays in a life history she wrote for her daughter. My aunt was barred from attending first grade for several weeks. Food was dropped off outside the fence surrounding the yard, including a piece of birthday cake left over from a party she had to miss. Money dried up. "Our relatives called us the 'poor Petersen kids,'" my dad says.

Pete's illness seems to have been the catalyst for Gladys's decline. "It kind of ripped her to shreds. She was never the same again," my dad recalls.

Gladys spent two months at Waukesha County Hospital near her home, where she underwent insulin coma therapy (ICT), a widely used psychiatric treatment from the 1930s to the 1950s. Patients were injected with large doses of insulin that sent blood sugar levels plummeting, inducing temporary comas. The comas—characterized by profuse sweating, muscle twitching, and sometimes seizures—were ended with infusions of glucose. Higher doses of insulin were used for schizophrenia, lower doses for "nervousness." ICT would not be discredited until the 1960s, when it was supplanted by new antipsychotic drugs and electroconvulsive shock therapy.

The records are sketchy, but it's likely that doctors saw little improvement, because she was transferred to Mendota on July 12, 1955, and stayed there for more than a month. In her medical records from that stay, under "present illness," it says: "Symptoms she recalls are loss of memory, of articles just read and program [sic] just seen on T.V. and crying herself to sleep at night after working continuously day after day. . . . She also remembered being alarmed about reading an article in a newspaper in which the names, Sharon [sic], Gary and Bill, appeared being killed by a truck backing over them, the names being those of her children." The notes give two potential diagnoses: "schizophrenic reaction, paranoid type" and "SIMPLE SCHIZOPHRENIC or REACTIVE DEPRESSION." On August 3, doctors wrote that she "went into remission." She was released on August 17.

Reading the records from her first Mendota admission, I feel like I'm trespassing. There are weirdly intimate details: when she learned about sex and how many sanitary pads she used during her period. At times I sense a tone of disapproval, as in the first line of the case summary: "The patient [is] a dependent individual with little self-confidence."

It is eerie how similar my grandmother's early symptoms were to some of mine: fuzzy memory, strange superstitions, and a fixation on catastrophe. My own doctors have hypothesized that, if she were treated today, Gladys might have initially been diagnosed with severe obsessive-compulsive disorder and GAD.

In the 1950s, schizophrenia was a bit of a catchall diagnosis. In Mendota's 1955 annual report to the State Board of Public Welfare, patients are given only a handful of diagnoses, such as schizophrenia, syphilis, alcoholism, "senility," and "psychoneuroses." Until 1960, Mendota patients were divided into "quiet" and "disturbed" groups.

After my grandmother's first hospitalization, she declined further. She was so afraid of something terrible befalling her children that she had trouble letting them out of her sight. She forbade Susan to see friends and followed her to the school bus stop. Then the fear curdled into psychosis. She became terrified of Catholics and "bad spirits." (My grandparents were Lutheran. My aunt says my grandfather told her that Gladys had been raped by a boyfriend who was Catholic.) She was afraid of being poisoned. She tucked a screwdriver into her purse for self-defense. She also carried a pocket mirror and would tilt it to catch the sunlight, a habit she thought would protect her family. Once she tried to force Susan to take the pills she had been prescribed at Mendota.

"I was afraid to go to sleep," Susan says. "I would lie on my stomach with my face to the wall and the covers over my head so I couldn't see her. I knew she was going to come and kill me."

Then Gladys set the fires.

"She was trying to save us from all the terrible things that were going through her mind. She was going to send us to heaven. She thought that's what needed to be done to protect us," my dad says.

My grandfather put out the fires, and it seems that no authorities were notified. Pete took Gladys back to Waukesha County Hospital, and she was transferred to Mendota on November 28, 1958. In the admissions report from her second stay, under "mental status," it says: "Heard rumblings under floor, threatening voices, both male and female. Became doubled over in the middle—'they were putting the screws on me' and believed her 'insides were empty.' . . . Has expressed fears about being placed in a pinball machine." This time the diagnosis is more definitive: "SCHIZO-PHRENIC REACTION, CHRONIC UNDIFFERENTIATED IN TYPE."

In 1958, my grandmother was one of 936 patients at Mendota. The most common diagnoses that year were "schizophrenic reactions" and alcoholism. About 28 percent of patients had been at Mendota for less than three months; 8 percent had been there for a decade or more. Space was tight, and resources were taxed. The original main building had become a drafty firetrap, and there were plans to abandon it. Goodland Hall, a new building for "chronic disturbed patients," opened that year.

The year of her admission marked the beginning of a movement to provide more freedom for Mendota patients. Six locked wards were now unlocked during the day, and the administration gave some say to an advisory board made up of patients. There was swimming, archery, and field trips to sporting events at the University of Wisconsin. The hospital received a new 35-millimeter projector for watching movies. Attendance at the Sunday worship service reached nearly two hundred, and communion was given every twelve weeks. A volunteer group, the Gray Ladies, came each week to visit patients and write letters for them.

During her time in the hospital, Gladys was treated with psychotherapy. In her records are several notations about her level of "insight" into her problems, a reflection of the supremacy of Freudian psychoanalysis at the time. My grandmother was also prescribed a few of the new antipsychotic medications just coming to market. At various times, she was on Thorazine, first synthesized in 1950, and Mellaril, a medication that largely disappeared from the market in 2005 over concerns about cardiac arrhythmias. During at least one period, the medication seemed to be helping her. The records say her thinking was better "organized" after the dose of one drug was raised.

Antipsychotic drugs were instant hits at mental hospitals like Mendota. In February 1955, 147 patients were being treated with the new "tranquilizing" medications. Less than a year later, by May 1956, four hundred patients were on the drugs. By 1960, staff members were complaining that some patients whom the hospital relied on to work in the facility—particularly in food service and the laundry—were "so heavily sedated that their work output is limited."

Gladys herself worked in Mendota's kitchen. But at some point, she developed paranoid fears about the job and refused to continue. Later hospital staff encouraged her to do a shift in the laundry, but she refused to go, saying she was worried about her heart. At least one staffer was downright grumpy about her noncompliance, noting in her records that "she always uses her health as an excuse for not doing something."

In May 1961, doctors noted that my grandmother had begun to experience a disturbing new hallucination and decided that shock therapy, also referred to as ECT or EST, was imperative. "Her hallucinations stem from the fact that she feels that her son is someplace in the hospital. She takes walks around the grounds hoping to find him. It is recommended that the patient have EST. If we do not obtain permission for shock therapy it is recommended that the patient be transferred to the county hospital."

The message was clear: Undergo shock therapy or be kicked out of the hospital. Gladys was terrified of ECT, but she did ultimately have the treatments.

Electroconvulsive therapy was first employed in Rome in 1938. Ugo Cerletti, a psychiatry professor, had been tinkering with electricity in his research on epilepsy, using it to induce seizures in dogs. (About half the dogs died; their hearts stopped.) Cerletti became intrigued by the use of insulin and other compounds to induce convulsions in psychiatric patients and wanted to see whether electricity could be safely applied to people to similar therapeutic effect. His assistant, Lucio Bini, built the first ECT machine for humans, which delivered 80 to 100 volts of electricity via electrodes placed on the temples. The first patient was a thirty-nine-year-old engineer with hallucinations. Not only did the patient survive the treatment, he seemed to get better. ECT spread rapidly to mental hospitals around the world, used primarily to treat patients diagnosed with schizophrenia and depression.

In its early years, ECT caused violent convulsions, and it was not uncommon for patients to fracture their spines as they thrashed about. Soon doctors began using muscle relaxants and short-acting anesthesia to keep patients still and prevent broken bones. By the time my grandmother underwent ECT, the treatment was considerably safer, although some patients were troubled by aftereffects such as headaches and short-term memory loss. (Today ECT has been largely redeemed: It is one of the most effective therapies for treatment-resistant depression and suicidal ideation.)

According to my grandmother's doctors, the treatment was effective. A note from September 26, 1961, says: "The patient has also completed a series of 18 EST Treatments" and states that she is hallucinating less and seems less suspicious and paranoid.

During Gladys's time at Mendota, my grandfather made the hour-and-a-half trip every weekend to visit her. Often he would take their children. "All I remember is people screaming," Susan says. "That just frightened the heck out of me. Mom didn't [scare me]. But in the background you could hear the screaming." On the way home, as a reward, my grandfather would stop and buy the kids Neapolitan ice cream.

It's a chilly October night, and Aunt Susan and I are going through hundreds of family photos in her office at home in Waukesha. We stop at a haunting picture of my grandmother shot during a week-long visit home from Mendota in the fall of 1960. Gladys is staring at the camera, grim-faced and weirdly vacant, her dark hair tightly curled. She's wearing a checked dress and a black cardigan and holding a white stuffed dog she made at the hospital. "What a sad face," my aunt says.

My grandmother was released from Mendota on January 3, 1962. During the 1960s, a movement arose to shift treatment away from inpatient psychiatric facilities to outpatient programs, and Mendota, like many other mental hospitals, was aggressively looking to discharge patients. The final note in her medical records reads, "The patient shows some improvement over her status previously, but she is not well by any means." She was transferred to the county hospital and then sent home. She didn't take medication or have any outpatient treatment after her release.

For the first six months or so after she was back, Gladys seemed better, but soon enough the intense fear and paranoia returned. By then Susan had graduated high school and studied keypunch, an early form of computer data entry. She moved to Racine and married. "I wanted out," she recalls. The rest of the family moved to Salem, Illinois, where my grandfather, an actuary at an insurance company, had been transferred.

My grandmother never recovered. "She talked to herself all day," my dad says. "She'd rail against the Catholics and just crazy shit." As a teenager, my father never invited friends over. Still, Gladys made rhubarb pies and sticky buns that my father still raves about, and she was able to take care of the house. She also liked to walk to downtown Salem and visit the shops. Her favorite was one that sold yarn, thread, and material.

Despite her delusions, my father was always able to make my grandmother laugh. She loved it when my father would come up behind her while she was washing dishes and give her bear hugs. He would talk in silly voices, make up nonsense words, and snap a towel on her behind. "She was usually so serious because she was so worried," my mom recalls. "But when your dad was around, she really brightened up."

When I was a baby, my grandmother doted on me. She would sit next to whoever was holding me and coo and smile. She was particularly delighted when I began walking, dragging a Raggedy Ann doll around by its tuft of red hair. But my grandfather never allowed Gladys to hold me. She had started carrying knives again. No matter where she was in the house, no matter what she was doing, she kept a large kitchen knife nearby.

Gladys died in 1972, when she was fifty-two years old. She had long had heart problems, perhaps caused by the rheumatic fever she'd had as a child. On the night she died, she had chest pains, and my grandfather called an ambulance. When it arrived, however, she wouldn't let EMS take her to the hospital. My grandfather pleaded with her, and so did the emergency responders. No. She wouldn't go. She was terrified of doctors and of being confined to a hospital again. Terrified of more shock treatments.

My grandfather stayed with her to the end. "He loved what she was and she loved him, too," my father says. "But she was living in a whole different world."

· · ·

I visit what is now called Mendota Mental Health Institute for the first time on a sunny fall afternoon. Because of my panic around driving on highways, I take the back roads from my sister Dana's house in nearby Janesville. I drive past dairy farms and drying cornfields, ignoring the incessant "recalculating" pleas from the GPS trying to nudge me back on the highway. I had originally planned on asking Dana to be my driver, but she had scheduling issues. And, it turns out, in the last few years she's started to panic on expressways, too. Genes indeed.

The street leading up to Mendota's entrance is lined with modest vinyl-sided homes that look to be from the 1940s and 1950s—many probably built during the time period when my grandmother was inside. Mendota isn't what I expected. I'm not sure what I thought it would be like, exactly—something more foreboding, perhaps, that portended the human misery inside. But the original building was razed in the 1960s, and nothing of it remains but a stately line of trees. Now Mendota looks like a graceful college campus. I can see Wisconsin's capitol building across Lake Mendota, which abuts the four-hundred-acre campus. Sunlight glints off the water and dapples the gold and orange leaves overhead. Burial mounds from the Ho-Chunk Indians dot the grounds, graceful green hills in the shape of a deer, panther, and eagle. Banners proclaiming HEAL, RESPECT, HELP, and HOPE line the roads.

Mendota now has 315 inpatients and 825 staff members. Almost all are so-called forensic patients, part of the criminal justice system. People are taken here so that clinicians can assess whether they are competent to stand trial. If they are found not to be, Mendota treats them until they are deemed competent. About 150 residents are long-term patients who have been acquitted of their crimes—almost all violent—by reason of insanity. (The vast majority of people with mental illnesses are not violent. In fact, those with psychiatric disorders are far more likely to be the *victims* of violence than the perpetrators.) There's also a small geriatric ward for patients with dementia and an innovative juvenile treatment program housing twenty-nine teenagers. Most patients in the facility are men; female forensic patients are sent to a different state hospital.

I'm here to meet with Gregory Van Rybroek, Mendota's director. Van Rybroek is fifty-nine years old with close-cropped gray-blond hair and small, rimless rectangular glasses. He's dressed in a gray polo shirt featuring the word MENDOTA and an image of an eagle. His baseball cap also sports an eagle and the word MENDOTA, along with 1860, the year the hospital was founded. The employee badge around his neck says HOW CAN I HELP YOU? He looks like a college athletic director and is both self-deprecating ("I'm not that smart," he jokes periodically and very unconvincingly) and profane. He has a Ph.D. in psychology and a law degree and started working at Mendota as a student in 1980.

We get into Van Rybroek's decade-old silver Acura, and he gives me a tour of the grounds. Mendota divides its facilities into maximum security, medium security, minimum security, and "minimum plus." Patients are assigned to a facility based not on the severity of their crimes but on how well they are recovering. (You're just as likely to find a killer in minimum plus, where residents have jobs mowing the lawn, are allowed to make excursions into town, and can attend college, as you are in maximum security.) Most patients come in with psychotic symptoms and are diagnosed with disorders such as schizophrenia, bipolar disorder, and major depression.

Van Rybroek points out a new greenhouse where some patients

work and that provides flowers to the governor's mansion. He tells me about plans to build a new "skilled learning center" that will include a house where patients can practice the skills they'll need to live independently. "You should be able to make a bed and fry an egg," he says.

We drive by Goodland Hall, a beige brick building that houses maximum and medium security wings. There are bars on its windows. In a grassy courtyard hemmed in by a barbed-wire fence, a young bearded guy in jeans and a tie-dyed shirt runs around a track. Other men sit at picnic tables near an unused volleyball net. One man in a blue short-sleeved shirt leans back to catch the sun on his upturned face.

We move on to Stovall Hall, which houses minimum-security and geriatric psychiatric patients. In its courtyard, there's an incongruous white gazebo and red flowers. Men play basketball and sit in lounge chairs. The "minimum plus" facility is a low-slung brown and white building that looks faintly Swiss. RECOVERY THROUGH INDEPENDENCE says a plaque above its front door. The perky language and bucolic setting should not lead to any misperceptions, though, Van Rybroek says. "You try to help people who are sick. These people can be dangerous. It is not Disney here."

Contrary to the perception (which, I admit, was mine) that criminals who enter a psychiatric facility are never released, Van Rybroek says that currently four hundred former inpatients have been released "on conditions"—meaning that their housing, medication, and future treatment have been planned in detail. Those who have been acquitted of their crimes because of insanity have the right to petition the court for release every six months. Van Rybroek says the recidivism rate of those released is just .25 percent.

We stop at a building that houses an employee conference

center and a cafeteria for employees and minimum-security patients. In the hallway, Van Rybroek stops to congratulate a pleasant white-haired man who looks to be in his sixties. I take him for an employee who is moving to a new job, but after the man walks away, Van Rybroek says, "He killed his mother twenty years ago." After about a dozen years at Mendota and successful treatment, the man is about to be released. Van Rybroek was congratulating him on overcoming a hurdle to his release by finding a place to live near a sister who was willing to check in on him.

In the employee conference center, where staffers are participating in a "leadership seminar," historical photos and maps of Mendota line the walls: The grand 1860 main building with its striking cupola and white terraces. A steam yacht outing to a Norwegian Sunday school picnic in 1879, complete with boat schedule. Boats "to asylum for insane and maple buff" depart at one, three, and five, it says. Rows of nurses in starched white hats and cat-eye glasses, circa 1960.

A glass cabinet in a corner holds artifacts: A photo of the "1901 Wisconsin Hospital for the Insane Band," a group of grim-faced men with natty ties, tubas, and trombones. A prescription dated 1927. A photo of the "dayroom" in 1870 with rocking chairs, upright piano, easel, and chandelier. My eyes fix on a foot-long brown box with black knobs and gray plastic tubing: a vintage Medcraft Mark II ECT machine. So this is the device my grandmother was so afraid of. It looks no more sophisticated than my childhood Lite-Brite.

"In college I spent a lot of time holding people down" while they were getting electroshock, Van Rybroek says. He says he would hold one arm and one leg of a patient. Someone else would pin down the patient's other arm and leg, and a third person would hold the patient's head still. (The first time, Van Rybroek didn't hold tight enough and when the electric current was switched on the patient socked him on the side of the head.) Afterward, ECT patients often had short-term memory problems. "They didn't remember who I was or where they were," Van Rybroek says. Gradually, their memories returned and some patients got better, though he's not certain it was solely because of the shock treatments.

We drive past a boarded-up brown brick building constructed in 1922 for World War I vets with "shell shock," or what we now call PTSD. Van Rybroek wants to turn it into a drug and alcohol treatment facility. As we drive around more, with Van Rybroek pointing out some of the burial mounds and the view to the calm, shimmering surface of Lake Mendota, he sighs and says, "All the terrible tragedy all mixed up with the beauty."

My grandmother's records don't reveal where she lived while she was here. But Van Rybroek thinks she most likely was in Stovall Hall or Lorenz Hall. Lorenz was built in 1953 and housed adult civil patients until the 1970s. I'm not allowed into any of the occupied patient zones, but one wing is empty. It is being transformed into a forensic wing, so security must be added before patients can move in. Lorenz is yet another low-slung beige brick building, but there's a chic Mad Men–like concrete entrance and steel-rimmed walls of windows. Van Rybroek takes me inside.

We head down a series of hallways, through two sets of doors. The ceiling is low, with white perforated squares. Fluorescent lights illuminate a floor made up of yellowish-green tiles. The hallway opens into a dayroom filled with tables and modular chairs like those in an airport terminal, where patients relaxed between treatment sessions. Big windows offer views of the autumn trees. An enclosed nurses' station—shrouded in steel and tempered glass— sits in the center. There's also a smaller "secure" dayroom with a locking door for patients who couldn't handle being around so many other people. Along one wall are five "seclusion" rooms for patients who behaved violently—nine-by-twelve-feet cinder-block cells (stained with a slight green tinge) illuminated by fluorescent lights. Each has a steel door with a small window. A camera beamed video to the nurses' station.

One of the seclusion rooms has a "restraint" bed, a low silver metal platform with small circular holes punched into it that's used to prevent self-harm. The bed is bolted to the floor. Green, blue, and purple leather straps lie across it, the cheerful colors incongruous given their function.

We walk down another hallway with patient rooms, small cinder-block spaces with dressers bolted to the walls. A bulletin board offers suggestions for things patients can do when they're bored. Among them: Draw pictures. Play Yahtzee. Clean your room. Make paper airplanes.

In the days after my visit to Mendota, I often think about the march of mental illness across my family tree. Gladys's brother, Harold, spent years at a psychiatric hospital in Utah; he died there in the late 1980s, of lung cancer. Susan thinks that he, too, was diagnosed with schizophrenia. Susan herself has bipolar disorder. Her daughter, my cousin Renee, has GAD and for years self-medicated with alcohol. My father struggles with depression. About fifteen years ago he asked his doctor for Zoloft because "maybe I've just never been happy," he says.

Susan muses hopefully that as time has passed, the illnesses have become less severe—that in three generations we've gone from psychosis to anxiety. Maybe my daughter and Renee's three children will be even more lightly touched.

My mother's side isn't completely even-keeled. My mother is

a worrier with frequent insomnia and an anxiety-fueled cleaning compulsion. Growing up, Dana and I knew that if we heard the vacuum cleaner running before seven a.m., we needed to tread carefully. My mom's siblings can be tightly wound, too. Their group texts are a constant volley of concerns and comfort. Two of my cousins deal with recurrent panic attacks.

Over time anxiety has become an issue for my sister Dana, too. She's always been introverted and shy, more comfortable one on one than in big groups, and she's dealt with a bit of social anxiety, but none of these things ever impaired her life in a significant way. She always had friends and boyfriends. And I still remember her, age seven or so, decked out in a red satin and silver-sequined outfit, shaking it onstage to Prince's "Little Red Corvette" at one of our yearly dance recitals. Then, during her twenties, Dana had a handful of panic attacks while driving. Bridges and interstates were the triggers. More recently, she says that anxiety has taken up permanent residence.

"I feel like my nervous system is on overload compared to normal people," she says. "Sometimes I just don't feel calm, don't feel present or as able to interact. I feel like I just drank coffee even when I haven't." She's started to avoid highways (not an easy thing to do in Wisconsin) and driving at night. She's afraid of flying.

At the time Dana and I have this conversation, she knows that I've been dealing with a serious set of anxiety disorders for more than twenty-five years and that I've been working on this book for the last three. Yet this is the first time she's ever talked to me about her own anxiety. She hasn't told her husband about it either. And she's had a hard time even admitting it to herself. "For a long time, I didn't think about anxiety in terms of myself. You were always the one who had that, and I didn't," she says. "I think it kind of crept up on me. It's scary to talk about because that means admitting you have an issue. I was in denial."

. . .

Scientists have been searching for the genes behind anxiety disorders for at least twenty years. For the first decade or so, researchers focused on individual "candidate genes."

One of the most extensively researched is the SLC6A4 gene, which makes a protein called the serotonin transporter. The protein's job is to pick up excess serotonin from the space between neurons (the synapse) and suck it back into the neuron. It isn't particularly surprising that scientists landed on this gene: SSRI drugs like Prozac, which alleviate depression and anxiety, block the serotonin transporter so more serotonin remains in the synapses. This extra serotonin is thought to account for the drugs' therapeutic effects. So for scientists trying to home in on the genes that might confer risk for anxiety disorders, zeroing in on the serotonin transporter gene was as good a guess as any.

The SLC6A4 gene has a "promoter region" that regulates how active it is and how much serotonin transporter protein it makes. Some studies found that people who had one or two copies of the "short" version (or allele) of this region were more likely to have anxiety symptoms than those who had two copies of the "long" allele. Researchers also discovered that when people with at least one short allele were put into an fMRI scanner, their amygdalae had stronger responses to angry and fearful faces than those with two long alleles.

Unfortunately, the science isn't consistent. Other studies haven't shown an association between the variation of short and long alleles and anxiety disorders.

Many other individual genes have been implicated in anxiety disorders, too. Indeed, there's a veritable alphabet soup of genes that have been explored, some with a heftier body of evidence behind them than others. However, geneticists say that much of the research on candidate genes isn't that useful. Even in the best-case scenario, it just confirms preexisting hypotheses.

Thankfully, about a decade ago technology evolved to enable genetic research that is likely to be more fruitful. Genome-wide association (GWA) studies let scientists cast a wide net and scan across the genome. GWA studies are leading researchers to genes they never even suspected might contribute to anxiety disorders. The hitch is that very large sample sizes are needed for this research. Groups of scientists are now collaborating to build these big data sets.

Still, genetic research on anxiety disorders lags behind other psychiatric illnesses.

"There's been very little funding for anxiety genetics despite the fact that it is a massive public health problem," says Jordan Smoller, a professor of psychiatry at Harvard Medical School and a leading genetic researcher. "Anxiety disorders don't quite have the visibility" of schizophrenia, bipolar disorder, and autism. "People underrecognize the toll that [anxiety] takes on people's lives."

One of the most exciting areas of research is the interaction of genes and the environment. We already know that childhood trauma increases the risk of anxiety disorders, but it turns out that the level of that risk depends, at least in part, on your genes. Some scientists are focusing on the gene FKBP5, which makes a protein that regulates the cellular response to stress hormones like cortisol. People with a certain version of the gene—the T allele—who are exposed to trauma during childhood, may be more likely to later develop PTSD and major depression than those with a different version of the gene.

The hope is that genetics will be able to guide patients to the most appropriate treatments. One person's genetic profile might make her responsive to CBT, for example, while another person might be more responsive to an SSRI. Also, genetic research could lead to entirely new ways of understanding the biology of anxiety disorders, which could lead to better treatments.

There is no greater risk factor for anxiety disorders than being born female. Women are about twice as likely as men to develop one, and women's illnesses generally last longer, have more severe symptoms, and are more disabling. The bad news doesn't stop there. Anxious women are also more likely to develop an additional anxiety disorder, an eating disorder, or depression. In general, women worry and ruminate more than men.

What is it about being female that makes women vulnerable to anxiety? Are women born anxious, or are we raised to be that way? Scientists are looking at how gender differences in upbringing can fuel anxiety. Intriguingly, as newborns, it is boys who are more fussy and irritable. Michelle Craske, director of the Anxiety and Depression Research Center at UCLA, says that boys' cantankerous early temperaments may actually protect them from developing anxiety later on. Several studies have noted that mothers are more likely to match their sons' facial expressions and the direction of their gazes, which makes them more in sync with sons than with daughters. Craske conjectures that irritable baby boys may be better able to harness their mothers' attention than more placid baby girls. Mothers' greater harmony with sons may give boys the sense that the world is a predictable place, one over which they have some degree of control.

By the time babies are a few months old, however, the temperaments of boys and girls don't differ as much. And when girls hit age two, they start to show more "negative affect," expressing more fear and acting more inhibited than boys. Researchers note that two is also the age when kids begin to exhibit traditional gender role behaviors—stereotypically, boys gravitate to trucks and soccer balls, girls to dolls and dress-up clothes. By this age, parents have also begun encouraging their daughters—more than their sons—to exhibit empathy and help others; they urge their daughters to share toys with other children and consider others' points of view more often than they do their sons.

It could be that instilling empathy in very young girls has a downside. There's evidence as early as toddlerhood that girls "catch" fear more easily. Girls and women are better able to identify facial expressions, so scientists conjecture that they may be more vulnerable to internalizing the threats they see reflected on others' faces.

In one study, mothers presented two toys—a rubber snake and spider—one at a time to their toddlers. In one trial, the mothers were instructed to make fearful or disgusted faces and describe the toy as "horrible, scary, or yucky." In the other trial, they made positive, joyful expressions and described the toy as "fun, cute, and nice." Ten minutes after completing both rounds, mothers showed their children the spider and snake again. (This time moms were told to hold a neutral expression.) Both boys and girls were warier of the toys in the trials when mothers made frightened expressions and used negative words. And the effects of the moms' words also stuck: The kids continued to be fearful and avoided the toys even after the ten-minute delay. Girls generally had more extreme avoidant responses and seemed more afraid of the toys than the boys did.

People—particularly parents—respond to children's fears in markedly different ways, too, depending on gender. When girls are anxious, adults are more likely to be protective and allow them to avoid scary situations. Boys are told to suck it up. "There's an assumption that boys should be courageous and they should overcome their fears and face their fears. With girls, we are a little bit more accommodating, and we permit this sort of reluctance or avoidance of situations," says Carmen McLean, an assistant professor of psychology in psychiatry at the University of Pennsylvania School of Medicine who has studied gender and anxiety. But this protection, she says, has lasting consequences. "You are teaching the girl, 'If I feel a little bit nervous, that means I should not do something.' A boy learns, 'If I feel this way, I should act anyway.' He learns, 'I can do it, and my anxiety goes down.' He feels more confident and has more efficacy. A little girl doesn't learn that lesson." It is as if boys are engaged in continual exposure therapy. Perhaps this inoculates them from future anxiety disorders.

A large body of dispiriting research shows just how much boys are encouraged to be independent and brave while girls are dissuaded from the same behavior. Parents have been found to be more controlling with daughters than with sons, which puts girls at greater risk of an anxiety disorder. In a University of California, Berkeley study, researchers videotaped ten-minute interactions of mothers and fathers with their preschool-age children. The families were told to "create a world" out of a sand tray and small toys. When boys asserted themselves by, for example, telling their parents where to put a toy, parents were more likely to praise them. When girls were assertive, parents were more likely to interrupt, talk over, or disregard them. This gives girls the message that they don't have control over their environment. Feeling out of control is, of course, a core belief in the anxious mind.

I take some solace from the fact that this particular study was conducted in 1993. Surely we must be more enlightened now?

I pose that hopeful question to McLean, and she quickly shuts it down. She tells me about a conversation she recently had with the father of a newborn daughter and an older son. "He was telling me how having a girl is so different than having a little boy.

He said he felt a lot more protective, like his daughter was more fragile," she recalls.

Barbara Morrongiello, a professor of psychology at the University of Guelph, has conducted a fascinating series of studies looking at how parenting interacts with gender to affect children's risk-taking behaviors. When Morrongiello was on maternity leave in the early 1990s, after her oldest son was born, she spent a lot of time at playgrounds and noticed huge differences in what boys and girls were encouraged to do—and not to do. In the sandbox and on the jungle gym, "I saw much more encouragement [expressed] to boys and caution to girls," she says. Morrongiello had a hunch that these different messages might be contributing to high injury rates for boys: After age two, boys have two to four times more injuries than girls. Their injuries also tend to be more serious.

Although Morrongiello isn't an anxiety researcher, her findings may be critical for understanding the gender disparity in rates of anxiety disorders. Morrongiello and her colleague Theresa Dawber conducted a study that observed forty-eight sets of parents and toddlers on a playground. Parents and kids first played freely on a slide, swings, and jungle gym for ten minutes. Then the grownups were instructed to teach their children how to slide down a pole similar to what you'd see at a fire station.

Both boys and girls were just as skilled at navigating the playground equipment. Still, parents more often warned girls about safety and the risk of getting hurt, whereas they tended to encourage independence in boys. They also were more likely to physically help girls, even when girls didn't ask for assistance. For example, parents spontaneously helped girls during 67 percent of their attempts to slide down the pole. By contrast, they physically helped boys only 17 percent of the time. Incredibly, even when boys requested help, parents often initially denied their requests and urged them to try again on their own. Parents were so hands-off with their sons that several boys tumbled off the pole and onto the ground.

Indeed, by school age, girls seem to have learned to be vigilant to threat. In other research, Morrongiello and colleagues found that when six-to-ten-year-old girls and boys assessed the same potentially dangerous scenario—such as riding a bicycle without a helmet—girls tended to see it as riskier than boys.

Parents also have different emotional reactions when sons and daughters do things that could get them hurt. When girls engage in risky behaviors, mothers, in particular, respond with disappointment and surprise. When boys do it, mothers react with anger. Parents are also more likely to chalk up their sons' injuries to personality, a "boys will be boys" mentality. When girls are injured, however, parents are more likely to blame the child. They are more likely to think that if only their daughters were more careful or listened better, they wouldn't get hurt.

While these messages may protect girls from physical injury, Morrongiello conjectures that they could pave the way for feelings of vulnerability and self-blame. Boys are told that being a daredevil is just part of being a boy, whereas girls are taught that if something bad happens, it is their fault. "To the extent you're telling girls you are responsible for your own negative outcomes, you can see girls being more anxious and more self-evaluative and self-critical," she says.

By late elementary school, girls are less likely to expect that they will succeed and more anxious about the prospect of failing. When facing stressful events, boys are more likely to problem solve on their own. Girls are more likely to seek support from their friends.

There is, however, one "equal opportunity" type of anxiety: social anxiety disorder. McLean tells me that this makes sense given how boys and girls are socialized. Girls are expected to master small talk, be charming, and make friends. Parents may consider it socially acceptable for a daughter to be afraid of snakes or dogs and avoid them, but they likely communicate that it's *not* all right to refuse to say hi to a teacher or withdraw during a playdate.

Surprisingly, men's *physiological* reactions to stressful events are stronger than women's. Levels of the stress hormones epinephrine and norepinephrine tend to spike higher in men when they undergo stress-inducing laboratory experiments, like taking a difficult test. Researchers say this makes evolutionary sense since a hair-trigger fight-or-flight response would have been adaptive when hunting or fighting adversaries. Women, on the other hand, have a more muted fight-or-flight response, which scientists have dubbed "tend and befriend." According to this model, women respond to stress by producing more oxytocin, a hormone thought to promote attachment, which spurs them to tend to their young and befriend other members of their group. The disadvantage to the tend-and-befriend response is that it could fuel anxiety by reinforcing worry and a pattern of avoiding threats.

Men and women also often try to ease their anxiety in different ways. Anxious men, for example, are more likely to self-medicate with alcohol or drugs and develop a substance-use disorder. For years my friend Mike, a fellow journalist, turned to alcohol and drugs to try to ease his anxiety and depression. Mike is handsome, smart, and wickedly funny, but when his anxiety is full throttle, he constantly churns over conversations with editors and friends, worrying that he's offended someone or said something stupid. The physical symptoms of anxiety are even more debilitating: His stomach churns, his skin tingles, and he feels constantly light-headed.

For Mike, marijuana and narcotics like Vicodin were a revelation. They took away the worrying. They calmed his twitchy body. "When you find something that makes that go away, you'll do anything," he says. But after a while, the marijuana turned on Mike. It started making him more anxious. His drinking and use of narcotics slid into addiction. He went to rehab. He relapsed. He kicked the drugs and alcohol again. Now he combats anxiety with an SSRI, daily exercise, and a strong spiritual practice.

There's evidence that estrogen and other sex hormones affect how women learn fears and how they override them. Women with anxiety disorders often say their symptoms worsen before their periods. Fluctuating estrogen levels could be partly to blame. Some studies show that when estrogen is high, fear responses are lower and vice versa. In one study, thirty-four women underwent a fear-conditioning procedure in which a picture of a lamp was paired with a shock to the hand. The women later underwent extinction, where the lamp picture was followed by no shock. Level of fear was measured by skin conductance. Women with higher levels of estradiol, a form of estrogen, had stronger extinction recall (meaning that they maintained a lower level of fear) than women with lower levels of estradiol. The women with high estrogen also had greater activation in the brain network implicated in fear extinction, the vmPFC, and amygdala.

It isn't just genes, hormones, and socialization that contribute to women's greater vulnerability to anxiety disorders. The risk of sexual assault and abuse does, too. Men generally encounter more traumatic events—such as serious accidents and experiencing or witnessing violence—in their lives than women. Women, however, are more likely to be the victims of sexual abuse and assault. Because sexual trauma is so uncontrollable and unpredictable, Craske argues, it is more likely to lead to PTSD and other anxiety disorders.

. . .

Scientists can identify some people at increased risk for anxiety disorders when they are infants. Researchers do it by assessing temperament, that unique, innate fingerprint of personality.

Temperament is a "biologically-based bias, usually inherited, that affects the chemistry of the brain," Jerome Kagan, a professor emeritus of psychology at Harvard University, tells me. "It is analogous to the behavior and mood of a dog breed. You know the difference between a laid-back Labrador and a Pekingese or a pit bull?"

Kagan, who is now eighty-seven, has spent his career studying two particular temperaments—what he calls high-reactive and low-reactive—that relate to how we respond to new objects, situations, or sounds. High-reactive babies thrash their arms and legs, arch their backs, and cry when confronted with novelty. Low-reactive babies remain relatively quiet and relaxed. Kagan has found that, as toddlers, high-reactive babies tend to be shy, quiet, socially reticent, and fearful, or what he calls behaviorally inhibited. Low-reactive babies, by contrast, generally become more boisterous, outgoing, and daring. Kagan calls them uninhibited. Studies by Kagan and others have found that inhibited children are much more likely than uninhibited kids to develop anxiety disorders. About one-third to one-half of inhibited kids develop anxiety disorders—most often social anxiety disorder—by adolescence. Behavioral inhibition (BI) is largely genetic. Twin studies have found that the heritability of BI is anywhere from 40 to 75 percent.

Kagan started his temperament work in 1957 at the Fels Research Institute at Antioch College in Ohio. At the time, the institute was conducting a longitudinal study of children born between 1929 and 1939. The researchers noticed that a small group of participants who were very fearful as small children remained cautious and introverted into adulthood. Kagan, along with colleagues at Harvard, where he began teaching in 1964, hypothesized that the root of our differing reactions to novelty lay in the amygdala. Since the amygdala projects to brain regions that control motor activity and the autonomic nervous system, the theory was that babies with more excitable amygdalae would thrash and cry more and have higher heart rates and blood pressure. In 1989, Kagan and colleagues recruited five hundred four-month-old infants. The researchers conducted a series of experiments (what scientists now call the Kagan paradigm) to assess how the infants reacted to new things.

Each baby was put in an infant seat for the forty-five-minute assessment. First, the mother was told to look at her baby and smile but not talk, while researchers took the infant's resting heart rate via electrodes. The baby was then presented with a series of noises, including a taped female voice reading sentences and nonsense syllables and a balloon popping behind the child's head. Mobiles with colorful toys were dangled in front of the baby's face. A researcher placed a cotton swab dipped in alcohol in front of the baby's nose.

The researchers characterized about 20 percent of the babies as high-reactive, meaning they cried and moved their arms and legs around during at least 40 percent of the experiments. About 40 percent were low-reactive. (The rest were a mix of the two.)

Kagan and colleagues continued to assess the children every few years.

When the babies were two years old, each toddler was asked to put a finger in a glass of black liquid and to let a researcher put a drop of water on his or her tongue. The child was approached by a stranger wearing a white lab coat and gas mask, a moving toy robot, and a person dressed as a clown. Toddlers who were fearful, cried, and avoided at least four of the objects or situations were tagged as behaviorally inhibited (BI).

About 46 percent of the high-reactive infants went on to become inhibited four-year-olds. Two-thirds of the low-reactive infants became uninhibited kids. When the kids were seven, they were assessed for anxiety symptoms. About 45 percent of high-reactive babies developed anxiety problems by age seven. Only 15 percent of low-reactive babies, however, became anxious. Kagan also discovered that blond, blue-eyed, fair-skinned children were more likely to be inhibited, a finding that, he believed, may indicate that the same genes influence both eye color and temperament.

Of course, if nearly half of BI kids will go on to have problems with anxiety, it means that half won't. Nathan Fox, a developmental psychologist at the University of Maryland and a former graduate student of Kagan's, is trying to discern which kids are most at risk. Fox notes that BI kids can still be shy without developing a disorder. "They are not your cheerleaders and football captains. But they end up being professors or computer scientists."

Fox is leading two longitudinal studies of behavioral inhibition. The first began in 1991 with 156 four-month-old babies. By the time they were fifteen, he discovered that about half the BI babies had developed an anxiety disorder; 40 percent had developed social anxiety disorder. By age twenty-three, about 19 percent had a mood disorder.

One October morning, I head to College Park, Maryland, to see Fox. Meeting me in his office, he looks professorial, with a graying mustache and wire-rimmed glasses. A toy Oscar the Grouch, complete with garbage can, sits on his desk, a relic from his years as a consultant for *Sesame Street*. Idyllic photos of Lake Como, Italy, are blown up on his walls, souvenirs of a trip he took while writing a book about his work in Romania with orphan children.

Fox brings a laptop over to a table and shows me a video. A little blond boy I'll call Michael, fourteen months old, leans against the legs of his mother, who sits behind him in a chair. The boy, Fox tells me, was a high-reactive baby. Meanwhile a research assistant, off camera, plays with blocks and tries to entice the child to join her. The toddler rebuffs the advances, clutching his mother's legs and burrowing his head in her lap. While this is happening, we can hear the mother telling the researcher about the boy's first birthday party. "We had a bunch of people over. He wouldn't open his presents. He wouldn't eat his cake. He cried the whole time. That was a fiasco." He's scared, she says, of most adults but is fine around children.

Fox shows the next video, which features Michael at age four. The study paradigm is a "play quartet" with the target child and three unfamiliar children. I see three boys playing in a room strewn with action figures, cars, and dolls, but no Michael. Then I hear crying and then a loud, plaintive "Nooooo!" coming from off camera. A woman, his mother, then carries a flailing Michael into the room. He tries to run out the door, but she drags him back in. He sobs and sobs. After a few minutes, he stops crying and slumps in a corner, defeated.

"He's just going to watch the other three kids for the rest of the time. He's not going to play by himself," Fox says. At one point, a little boy comes over to Michael and says, "You don't like being here."

The third video Fox shows me is of Michael at age seven. The paradigm is again a play quartet that includes the target child and three unfamiliar peers. Three of the boys walk into the room and immediately start exploring the toys on the floor (Legos, action figures). Michael, on the other hand, simply looks around and doesn't pick up any of the toys. "He's going to go and stand in the corner of the room for the entire fifteen minutes," Fox tells me. Indeed, Michael does just that. He looks miserable, as if he's hoping the floor will swallow him up. At one point, a boy walks over to Michael and puts his arm around him, but Michael shrugs the arm off. The other boy walks away.

I ask Fox if he knows what became of Michael, who now must be about twenty-three. Michael, he says, did develop an anxiety disorder and, later, depression. Fortunately, he got treatment and was prescribed medication. He graduated college and seems to be coping reasonably well.

Fox and colleagues have found that, while parenting may not contribute much to the development of anxiety disorders for children who aren't inhibited, it matters a lot for BI kids. In one study, the researchers found that only those BI kids whose mothers were overcontrolling developed greater social anxiety symptoms by adolescence. They cited various examples of this kind of parenting behavior during playtime including mothers dominating the conversation, giving frequent and unnecessary instructions, interrupting the child, or taking away a toy. In other studies, the researchers found that BI kids who are put in day care during the first few years of life became less inhibited. Being exposed to new people and experiences at day care—and possibly getting a break from controlling parenting at home—helps kids become less fearful.

Fox and his fellow researchers are finding that particular cognitive processes of some BI kids raise the risk of anxiety disorders. They have found that behaviorally inhibited toddlers who have an attention bias to threat are more socially withdrawn at five years old and are more anxious in adolescence. BI kids who don't have an attention bias to threat don't end up socially withdrawn and anxious. "We find that BI kids way before they show any signs of anxiety are showing this attention bias to threat," Fox says. "So it is not a symptom of an anxiety disorder. It is an underlying mechanism which facilitated the emergence of anxiety."

Fox and his colleagues have found that some cognitive processes protect BI kids from developing anxiety disorders. Kids with BI who are adept at attention shifting (being able to shift one's attention in order to complete a task or to achieve a goal) are less likely to develop anxiety disorders. This skill could help kids divert their attention away from threatening stimuli.

BI kids who have higher levels of inhibitory control, however, are more likely to develop anxiety disorders. Inhibitory control is the ability to override an ingrained response that is maladaptive and respond in a more beneficial way. For kids without BI, this is thought to be adaptive, but it doesn't seem to be for BI kids. Scientists aren't quite sure why. One hypothesis is that, because BI kids already have a trigger-happy fear system (that twitchy amygdala), having a strong voluntary control system on top of it leads to overcontrol and inflexibility. In other words, researchers say, such kids "may be better able to monitor their response and reflect on past errors, leading to increased levels of rumination and increased anxiety symptoms."

In one study, Fox and colleagues assessed inhibitory control by asking behaviorally inhibited four-year-olds to say the word *day* when shown a picture of a white moon and stars with a black background and *night* when shown a picture of a yellow sun on a white background. This is known as a Stroop task, and it requires participants to override a powerful response. Kids who were more accurate in the task were considered higher in inhibitory control. Researchers assessed attention shifting by asking the children to sort a set of cards based on a given rule by color. Then they were asked to sort the cards according to a new rule, by shape. The greater a child's accuracy, the greater their ability to attention shift. The study found that BI kids who had lower levels of attention shifting and higher levels of inhibitory control had anxiety problems. But BI kids who had higher levels of attention shifting and lower levels of inhibitory control seemed to be protected from excess anxiety. The hope is that this research might lead to new interventions for BI children that could prevent anxiety disorders from developing. A therapy that increases attention shifting and decreases inhibitory control is one possibility.

I ask Fox what his personal temperament is. "I don't think I was highly inhibited, but I think I was somewhat inhibited," he says. "I think I was—more so than I needed to be—an overly sensitive kid, just in terms of friendships and entering into peer groups and all that. High school was not a pleasant time as I remember." What helped him was having a best friend. "I had one very good friend, and I think that was a very important anchor for me." Not all BI kids have this. In his studies, when the children come in for their nine-year-old assessments, researchers ask them to bring in their best friend. "We had some kids where the mom said, 'Can he bring his cousin?'"

I was not an inhibited child. I made friends easily, was independent, and could be a bit of a show-off, dancing and making up skits for any audience I could find. My mother says that once, at age two, I walked by myself from our house to the park—a distance of several blocks. My father, who was supposed to be keeping an eye on me, was washing his lemon-yellow Ford Torino in the driveway and didn't see me leave. "I just wanted to go to the park," I said calmly when my parents found me after a frantic search.

A couple of years later I got lost in a department store while shopping with my mother. "There's a little lost girl named Andrea," my mother heard over the loudspeaker, with directions on where to collect me. She found me sitting happily on top of a checkout counter, a lollipop in my mouth, being fawned over by a group of young saleswomen. We continued shopping and I quickly vanished again, this time deliberately, in search of more sweets and attention.

In doing this research, I have realized that my temperament is probably not the root of my anxiety disorders. It is doubtful that I'll ever find a single smoking gun, although genes most likely play a part. Mental illness isn't like tuberculosis, which is always caused by one particular bacterium. Anxiety disorders almost certainly have multiple causes—from genetics to childhood trauma to how your parents interact with you. And for any given person, the mix of these factors will be as singular as a fingerprint.

4

FROM CBT TO KARAOKE
NONDRUG THERAPIES FOR ANXIETY

Anxiety Disorders Program, Evaluation Summary,
November 20, 1990

Ms. Peterson [*sic*] is a 20-year-old single student who is a
junior at the University of Michigan who was referred to the
anxiety disorders clinic by Dr. Pitt. She comes with a chief
complaint of a one-year history of panic attacks. . . . The
patient presented as an attractive young women [*sic*] who
was appropriately dressed and presented as mildly anxious.
Thoughts were fluid and coherent, affect was appropriate to
the content of discussion. There was no evidence of impairment of memory or judgment. Our conclusions are as fol-
lows: Panic Disorder with Agoraphobia. OCD (mild).

It is the fall of 1990, nearly one year since that December day I
fell apart, and I'm sitting in a small, nondescript conference room
with about ten other people—all women, all anxious. We are in
a group therapy session in the Anxiety Disorders Program at the
University of Michigan Health System. At twenty, I'm decades

younger than most of the other participants. Looking around the room, I glimpse the sad progression of my own life if I let anxiety control me. Plagued by panic attacks, several of the women have been practically homebound for years, their trips to "group" one of their few (white-knuckled) outings each week.

We go around the room and talk about our "homework" for the next week. One of the homebound women has an assignment to leave the house each day and walk to the mailbox. Mine is to buy multiple travel-size tubes of toothpaste and open a new one every day. This is exposure therapy, the most effective—and most excruciating—treatment for anxiety problems. The idea is for us to actively face our fears by eliciting anxiety symptoms and gathering evidence that experiencing them won't lead to whatever catastrophe we've conjured. Gradually, week by week, the assignments become more difficult. The goal is to scale our emotional Everests.

Exposure therapy is the workhorse of what is known as cognitive behavioral therapy (CBT). Remember the fear-conditioned rats that stopped freezing when the tone was no longer followed by the shock? Learning that the tone was safe overrode the association of the tone with the shock. Some scientists think exposure therapy does the same thing in people. Each time I used a new tube of toothpaste and didn't drop dead reinforced the reality that it wasn't, in fact, dangerous.

The toothpaste was item one on the "fear hierarchy" my therapist had me create, a list of things and situations I avoided because of anxiety. As the weeks went by, I tackled each one. Standing in line at a coffee shop. (Lines made me feel trapped.) Taking a vitamin. (I was afraid it would make me sick.) Running up a flight of stairs. (I panicked when my heart rate went up.) My therapist even had me breathe rapidly to induce hyperventilating, one of the classic symptoms of my panic attacks.

My therapist also helped me tackle my catastrophic thoughts.

This was called cognitive reappraisal. Each time I had a calamitous thought, I was to challenge my negative beliefs by amassing evidence and then calculating the actual odds of disaster on a scale from 0 to 100. For example, say my heart rate kicked up suddenly. Typically, my first thought was: "Maybe I'm having a heart attack." Cognitive reappraisal went something like this: "This has happened before, and I've never had a heart attack. I'm only twenty years old, and I've had several tests to rule out heart disease. The symptoms I'm having are also the same as a panic attack. What is the actual likelihood that I'm having a heart attack? Maybe 3 percent."

I can't say I was always persuaded by these arguments. The tiny voice of rationality was often drowned out by the loud, demanding symptoms of my body. In the battle between my racing heart and logic, the heart usually won.

But as time went on, as I exposed myself to more scary situations and continued not to die, the symptoms became slightly less urgent, the rational thoughts a little sturdier. By the end of the group sessions, I certainly wasn't back to my old self, but I was more functional. My world—which had pretty much narrowed to a few classes and my room—expanded. I took on a full course load. I ventured out for pizza. I remembered more of what I read. I even made it to a fraternity party and had an energetic dance-off to Madonna with my friend Lisa.

CBT, which usually involves twelve to fifteen weekly sessions with a therapist plus daily homework, is effective: About half of anxiety disorder patients experience clinically significant improvement. In a meta-analysis of twenty-seven studies comparing CBT for adult anxiety disorders to a placebo, CBT was found to have a "medium to large" effect on the severity of anxiety symptoms. Neuroimaging studies show that successful CBT treatment changes the brain—some reveal reduced activity in the hyperactive amygdala and increased activity in the listless prefrontal cortex. In one 2016 study, CBT actually shrank the amygdala.

Nondrug treatments for anxiety have a colorful history. In the nineteenth century, people flocked to spas to ease their anxiety, a practice that had begun earlier but was now booming. Hydrotherapy was used to treat all manner of chronic illnesses, including psychological ones. Charles Darwin, for example, frequented Malvern in England for his hypochondriasis. The Italian and French Rivieras were recommended for the treatment of nervous problems. In the major cities, "hydros," private mini-spas, cropped up. Paris had dozens. Depending on the diagnosis, patients were sprayed with water, alternately hot and cold, and then dunked into arctic swimming pools. Massage and electrotherapy were on offer, too. Hydros competed with private "nervous clinics," which were overseen by a growing cadre of "nerve doctors," usually neurologists or general physicians. Psychiatrists, by contrast, who were called alienists, worked almost exclusively in asylums, grim places that housed the psychotic and the criminal. Treatment there was generally limited.

One of the most popular therapies for neurasthenia, the "tired nerve" disease of the late 1800s, was the rest cure. In 1875, Silas Weir Mitchell, a nerve doctor in Philadelphia, popularized a souped-up rest cure: a stringent regimen of bed rest, massage, and a high-fat diet rich in milk. Patients often took the cure in spa clinics, staying for as long as three months. (Needless to say, this was a therapy available only to the well-off.)

Some found the cure more harrowing than the illness. The writer Charlotte Perkins Gilman described her experience with the rest cure in the autobiographical short story *The Yellow Wallpaper*, published in 1892. In the story, the heroine is separated from her baby and mostly confined to a room in a rented summerhouse. She is forbidden to write or do housework and is admonished not to even think or imagine too much. "So I take phosphates or phosphites—whichever it is, and tonics, and journeys, and air, and exercise, and am absolutely forbidden to 'work' until I am well again," Gilman writes. "Personally I believe that congenial work, with excitement and change, would do me good. But what is one to do?" Deprived of distraction and any intellectual life, the heroine spends hours staring at the yellow wallpaper in her room, gradually descending into madness, her unraveling revealed through her hallucinatory descriptions of the wallpaper.

The rest cure was primarily prescribed to women. When Theodore Roosevelt was diagnosed with neurasthenia, his doctor sent him to a dude ranch in the Dakotas for a spell of riding and hunting.

The seeds of CBT were also planted around this time. The origins of the treatment go back to the Russian physiologist Ivan Pavlov and his concept of the conditioned reflex, an automatic form of learning. In his famous experiments with dogs in the 1890s, Pavlov found that if the sound of a buzzer was followed by food, the animals eventually learned to associate the buzzer with food and would salivate as soon as they heard the sound, even before they saw the food.

John Watson, an American psychologist, expanded upon Pavlov's ideas. In 1913, he published a paper delineating his belief that psychology must be rooted in observable behavior. In the 1920s and 1930s, pioneering psychologists like Hans Eysenck and B. F. Skinner fleshed out the approach. Skinner asserted that people act to gain a reward or avoid pain and behavior changes through either reinforcement or discouragement. Eysenck said people become neurotic through learning experiences undertaken to avoid anxiety. Healing happens when these experiences are "unlearned." The behaviorist school of psychology was born.

Meanwhile psychiatrists continued their love affair with Freud, who had trained as a neurologist and studied hysteria with Josef Breuer. Working with Breuer, Freud claimed he was able to bring relief to hysterical patients by hypnotizing them and having them zero in on the psychological origins of their symptoms, a process the duo called "catharsis." Over time, his psychoanalytic method evolved. Instead of relying on hypnosis, patients—with the help of their analysts—could supposedly uncover the unconscious conflicts that were the origin of their distress simply by talking, saying whatever came to mind. Psychiatrists throughout Europe and the United States adopted his "talking cure" to treat people with anxiety problems and other mental illnesses.

In the 1950s, while Freudian psychoanalysis reigned, therapy for anxiety disorders took a huge step forward with Joseph Wolpe, a South African psychiatrist. Wolpe began his career as a staunch follower of Freud. But when he began working with soldiers suffering from "war neurosis" (what we now know as PTSD), he was disillusioned to discover that the treatments he had been trained to provide—talk therapy and medication—didn't seem to work. He began exploring alternatives. Eventually Wolpe developed a treatment called "systematic desensitization," an early form of exposure therapy. The treatment rested on his belief that it was impossible to simultaneously feel anxious and relaxed. It entailed teaching people with phobias relaxation techniques, then gradually exposing them to the things they feared while they employed the relaxation tools they had learned. Soon Wolpe's teachings spread to psychologists around the world.

In the 1960s, Aaron T. Beck, a psychiatrist at the University of Pennsylvania, developed cognitive therapy, initially as a treatment for depression. Beck said that psychopathology was largely the result of distorted thinking. Treatment focused on identifying maladaptive thoughts, challenging them, and replacing them with more realistic ones.

Frustrated at the dismal success rates of traditional analysis and psychotherapy, a handful of renegade psychiatrists and psychologists took the behaviorist and cognitive theories and began to experiment further with new ways of treating anxiety. Like Wolpe, they largely abandoned the idea of trying to uncover the root cause of a patient's anxiety, focusing instead on relieving the symptoms. In the 1960s, they were dismissed as quacks and charlatans by the psychiatric establishment.

In 1971, psychiatrist Manuel Zane opened the country's first phobia treatment center at White Plains Hospital in New York. He treated his patients in the community, driving over bridges with those with bridge phobias, riding elevators with those with elevator phobias, and tape recording every panicky pronouncement. Soon he began sending patients out to tackle their fears with "phobia aides," trained people who had recovered from their own phobias.

Meanwhile in California, psychiatrist Arthur Hardy was taking a similar approach. He developed a behavioral treatment for agoraphobia (which he dubbed territorial apprehension) and generated a huge amount of press coverage.

These iconoclasts and others eventually banded together and formed an organization to educate other clinicians and raise money for research. In 1977, about three hundred patients, psychiatrists, and psychologists convened in an auditorium at White Plains Hospital for the first meeting of the Phobia Society. Since renamed the Anxiety and Depression Association of America, the group now publishes one of the field's key scholarly journals and holds a yearly research conference that attracts more than a thousand scientists and clinicians from around the world. Neuroimaging experts mingle with CBT trainees. Geneticists chat with mindfulness experts. All are focused on improving the lives of the chronically anxious.

It took nearly a year and numerous doctors for me to be diagnosed and treated. I'm unusual, however, in that I sought help from the medical system at all. People with panic disorder wait an average of ten years before discussing their symptoms with a doctor, psychologist, or other professional (including an acupuncturist or "spiritual advisor"). Those with social phobia delay sixteen years; those with generalized anxiety disorder, nine years. With specific phobia, the wait is twenty years. And when they do seek help, patients may not receive appropriate treatment. This is particularly true of African Americans. Though they have lower rates of anxiety disorders than whites, studies have found, their illnesses are more chronic and severe and the quality of care they receive is generally lower.

In the months after my stint in group therapy, I continued to get better. The panic attacks and overall anxiety abated. I went to class and started working part time at a funky clothing store called Splash where our manager judged employees' success not by how much we sold but by how much we flirted with customers. Scott and I broke up. During spring break in South Padre Island, Texas, I met Joel, a sweet, goofy MBA student. I stayed in Ann Arbor for most of the summer to spend time with my new boyfriend before he moved to San Francisco. Throughout the fall of my senior year, I felt pretty good. I was taking a full load of classes again,

going dancing with friends, and flying to visit Joel when time—
and cash—allowed.

Then the day after Christmas, I relapsed.

I am in my parents' car, sitting in the backseat. It is the middle
of the night. My sister is sleeping next to me, my mother nodding
off in the passenger seat. My father is driving, blasting Led Zep-
pelin on a classic rock radio station to keep himself awake. We are
in the middle of the fourteen-hour drive from San Antonio, Texas,
where my parents had moved more than a year earlier, to Salem,
Illinois, on our way to visit family.

Suddenly I feel a slight pressure on my chest. I try to ignore it,
silently singing along to the radio: "Oh oh oh oh oh oh. You don't
have to go oh oh oh oh oh." It quickly becomes a weight. The air
in my lungs seems to have turned from a gas to something more
solid. Breathing starts to feel like a struggle or at least a conscious
action. If I stop paying attention, I think, it will stop. And I will
die.

I try to use some of the techniques I learned in group therapy.
I'm okay, I tell myself. *I'm still breathing. This is just a panic attack.*
But my puny thoughts are no match for the powerful, catastrophic
sensations. For the rest of the ride, I huddle against the car door
and focus on moving the air in and out of my lungs. When we arrive at my grandparents' house, I head right for the afghan-strewn
sofa. The terror abates enough—or I am able to mask it enough—
for me to get through the trip without a visit to the ER, but when
we get back to San Antonio, I crumble.

The weight on my chest is constant. Sometimes it feels like
my ribs have shrunk a few sizes. Other times I imagine the pressure as the anvil that eternally drops on Wile E. Coyote. I am too
scared to sleep. If I sleep, I can't concentrate on breathing. In my
mixed-up mind, sleep equals death. All night I lie on the sofa in

my parents' living room, the TV turned to Nick at Nite's *My Three Sons* marathon. At times my mother stumbles half-asleep out of her bedroom, sits next to me, and silently strokes my hair. I nod off for a half hour, an hour, and wake up with a heart-racing start. The weight on my chest is always there.

I see my mother's doctor, who thinks I might be having an asthma flare-up. She puts me on an oral steroid, which makes me jittery and does nothing to lift the burden on my chest. That doctor sends me to a pulmonologist and a cardiologist. They find nothing wrong. When I tell the cardiologist that I have had perhaps ten hours of sleep over the entire week, he prescribes Xanax. I'm still afraid of taking medication, but I'm so desperate that I swallow half a tablet and zonk out for fourteen hours.

My parents call my therapist back in Ann Arbor.

ANXIETY DISORDERS PROGRAM: Progress Note

PETERSON [*sic*], Andrea

January 16, 1992

Andrea comes in after a 6-month absence from the clinic. . . . She comes complaining of difficulty breathing, shortness of breath, light-headedness, dizziness, occasionally experiences derealization, depersonalization, and describes anxiety over many catastrophic thoughts that she has about her physical well being. We reviewed her symptoms and again reviewed the behavioral and cognitive interventions that have helped her in the past.

Back in Ann Arbor for the winter term, I resumed weekly therapy. Because the fears of food and contamination had reappeared, causing me to lose ten pounds, my first homework was to eat four to six small meals and drink eight glasses of water a day. I was also to take a vitamin pill.

I also embarked on another medical odyssey, looking for some reason other than anxiety—and the mild asthma I already knew I had—for my shortness of breath and weight on my chest. Through the winter and spring, I was a regular at the Pulmonary Function Laboratory at the University of Michigan Hospital. I had multiple spirometry tests to see how much air I could quickly blow in and out of my lungs and a methacholine challenge test, where I had to breathe in a substance that makes the airways constrict in people with asthma. I had a test to measure my blood gases during exercise: I jogged on a treadmill while blood was taken from an artery in my wrist. The diagnosis? Mild asthma.

The fatigue and constant fear returned, along with weird new physical symptoms. The tingling in my feet that I had felt off and on before settled into a constant throb. It slowly crept up from the soles to the tops of my feet, to my ankles, then licked the bottoms of my shins. I had a test to assess the nerves in my feet and legs using pinpricks, electric currents, and vibrations. I visited the Chronic Fatigue Clinic and even the Infectious Disease Clinic. I was convinced that I had some rare fatal disease the doctors just couldn't identify. I started to sneak around. I'd make an appointment with a new doctor without telling the previous one. (I was mortified when my doctor at the University Health Service received a detailed letter from a doctor I had seen at the Infectious Disease Clinic.)

Why didn't the CBT techniques prevent this? Maybe it was because, after two years, the major physical symptom of my anxiety had changed from a racing heart to chest pressure. Or maybe it was simply because the effects of CBT can wear off. One study followed sixty-three panic disorder patients, most of whom had responded well to a course of CBT; nine of them relapsed during the following two years. And more than one in four participants sought additional treatment within those two years because of persistent symptoms.

Psychologists are tweaking CBT to boost its performance. Very simple adjustments, such as scheduling appointments in the morning or asking that patients nap or run after therapy, may make it more effective. A 2016 study found that exposure therapy appointments in the morning were more helpful than those later in the day. Higher levels of the stress hormone cortisol occur naturally in the morning, and researchers concluded that they were responsible for at least part of the benefit of the earlier sessions. A surge in cortisol can facilitate learning, they said.

Napping after therapy was shown to be beneficial in a 2014 study of people with spider phobias. The subjects did a session of exposure therapy using virtual reality: Using a head-mounted display, they moved through simulated rooms containing virtual spiders. After the session, some subjects were given ninety minutes to nap. Others watched a video. Then they were asked to approach a live tarantula in a cage. At that point, there were no significant differences in anxiety symptoms between the groups. However, an appointment a week later yielded different results. Compared to those who didn't sleep after exposure therapy, the people who had napped had a greater reduction in anxiety and catastrophic thoughts about spiders as they moved toward the tarantula. Scientists believe that sleep can strengthen the memories of new learning that occurs during therapy.

Psychologists are also adding other components to improve CBT. In a 2016 study of patients with severe GAD, CBT was augmented by motivational interviewing, an approach where therapists focus on expressing empathy and validating patients' feelings. Those who got the combined therapy saw a greater reduction in worry and distress over the one-year period after the treatment ended, compared to those who got only CBT. In addition, far fewer patients who had the combined therapy—about half as many— dropped out of treatment. David H. Barlow, a CBT pioneer and founder of the Center for Anxiety and Related Disorders at Boston University, has, along with colleagues, developed a treatment called the Unified Protocol that they are using to treat a range of anxiety disorders and depression. It builds on CBT and includes sessions to teach patients to fully experience their emotions. Barlow says the dropout rate is much lower than traditional CBT.

Michelle Craske and colleagues at UCLA are finding that asking patients to vividly imagine happy scenes before therapy may improve learning during exposure and make the treatment work better. Craske is also finding success in modifying exposure therapy. Modifications include varying where and how patients do the therapy and intensifying exposure to the feared object or situation. For example, a person with a dog phobia might encounter two dogs at one time.

Craske will soon launch a study to see whether exercise after exposure therapy boosts its effectiveness, since exercise increases the level of a protein that is critical for the consolidation of memories.

Anne Marie Albano, director of the Columbia University Clinic for Anxiety and Related Disorders, says that it is important to do periodic booster sessions of CBT, particularly during times of stress and big life changes, like getting married, getting divorced, having a child, or losing a parent. "Demands become different over time. The person's ability to adapt to that is challenged," she says.

Psychologists have also developed a number of other therapies for anxiety disorders. The most heavily researched is acceptance and commitment therapy (ACT). Whereas in CBT you're taught to challenge your anxious thoughts, weigh the evidence, and modify them so that they are more realistic, in ACT you're taught to accept your thoughts and feelings. "Trying to get rid of your pain only amplifies it, entangles you further in it, and transforms it into something traumatic," writes clinical psychologist Steven Hayes, one of the creators of ACT.

Acceptance doesn't mean succumbing to anxiety, though. Rather, you're taught to distance yourself from your anxious thoughts and feelings, to see them more objectively. This is known as cognitive defusion or a way, as Hayes writes, to "look *at* thought, rather than *from* thought." ACT therapists use dozens of different defusion techniques, including having clients say one word over and over for twenty to forty-five seconds until it seems stripped of its meaning. Patients do this for benign words like *milk* and then move on to emotionally charged words like *weak* or *stupid*. Other exercises include visualizing thoughts as leaves floating by on a stream or stating fears in a silly voice or as lyrics to a song.

ACT involves a variety of mindfulness techniques. Derived from ideas from Zen Buddhism and yoga, mindfulness, says Hayes, is the "nonattached, accepting, nonjudgmental, deliberate awareness of experiential events as they happen in the moment." ACT includes meditations on bodily sensations, walking meditation, and such exercises as mindfully eating a raisin or drinking a cup of tea.

Like CBT, ACT also includes exposure. But in ACT, exposure is presented as a way to achieve personal goals. Therapists have patients identify core values through exercises such as writing their own eulogies and epitaphs. Clients are encouraged to see exposure as helping them move toward what they find personally meaningful.

Hayes was already working with anxiety patients when he had his own first panic attack in 1978. He was in a contentious meeting with colleagues at the University of North Carolina at Greensboro when he moved to ask his coworkers to "stop fighting and to start cooperating." "I couldn't make sound come out of my mouth," he told me. "My heart rate was going so fast." Over the next three years, the panic attacks worsened. He tried relaxation tapes and exposure therapy, but nothing worked, and he felt himself spiraling downward.

It was only when he went back to the influences of his hippie youth, he says, that he started feeling better. He had dabbled in meditation, lived in a spiritual commune, and gotten involved in the so-called human potential movement that came out of the Esalen Institute in California. He began combining what he had learned from these experiences with the behavioral therapies he had studied and, with like-minded colleagues, launched the research that would lead to the development of ACT.

A 2012 study revealed that twelve sessions of ACT or CBT were about equally effective at reducing the symptoms of anxiety disorders. Another 2012 paper found that ACT was more effective for anxiety patients who also suffered from depression, while CBT was better for those without depression and those with "moderate levels" of anxiety sensitivity. Anxiety sensitivity is the belief that anxiety symptoms like a fast heartbeat and dizziness are dangerous.

Anxiety is a future-oriented state, so it's not surprising that learning to focus on the present would help to subdue it. Not only ACT but mindfulness practices of all kinds are increasingly being used to treat anxiety disorders. Mindfulness-based stress reduction (MBSR) focuses on meditation and yoga. Applied relaxation (AR) teaches people to identify early symptoms of anxiety and quell them using fast-acting relaxation techniques. Mindfulness-based cognitive therapy (MBCT) and emotion regulation therapy (ERT) combine meditation with practices from CBT.

These treatments are effective for many patients. In a meta-analysis of thirty-nine studies involving more than a thousand people in total, mindfulness-based therapies significantly reduced symptoms in patients with anxiety disorders.

Knowing what a magic bullet they can be for some people with anxiety disorders, I've tried meditation. *How hard can it be?* I asked myself. It's incredibly popular. Kids learn it in school. You can download meditation apps on your smartphone. There's even a book that teaches you to meditate with your dog.

It is very unfashionable to say that you suck at meditation.

I suck at meditation.

I know that one can't really be awful at meditation. It is, devotees tell me, all about the practice. Still, I can't get into it. I've tried. But my mind jumps around so much, from worries to the ache in my hip to the dust on the carpet. I usually abandon the practice after a few days.

I decided to visit Jeffrey Rossman, a clinical psychologist and the "director of life management" at Canyon Ranch, a luxury spa and health resort in Lenox, Massachusetts. Rossman treats anxiety with mindfulness and a range of other alternative therapies including biofeedback and EMDR (eye movement desensitization and reprocessing), which entails having clients recall traumatic memories while moving their eyes rapidly back and forth. The treatment is supposed to ease the intensity of the memories and reduce anxiety.

Rossman is trim and youthful with a wide, toothy smile and voluminous salt-and-pepper hair. He tells me that anxiety (and its cousin, stress) is what brings most people to Canyon Ranch. "You would think people are coming to lose weight," he says, "but we have more people coming to deal with stress in their lives than any other reason. People working seventy, eighty hours a week, commuting two hours a day, sleeping four hours a night. That's an extreme version, but I see it."

After chatting for a while, Rossman does a biofeedback session with me. With biofeedback, you're hooked up to sensors that monitor functions like heart rate, skin temperature, and muscle tension, and you're then taught strategies to modify those functions. Rossman attaches a sensor to my ear, and a digital chart of my heart rate shows up on his computer screen. He has me close my eyes and guides me through a brief meditation. "Breathe peacefulness in," he says over and over.

After a few minutes, he says "good" and tells me to open my eyes. He points to a line on my chart that is sharp and jagged with abrupt peaks and deep valleys. That is my heart rate before the meditation, when it was jumping from one hundred beats a minute down to sixty and all points in between. The good news, according to him, is that my heart rate variability means that my heart is "very dynamic. You've got a healthy young heart," he says. "My guess is you have a lot of adrenaline in your system." Then he shows me a different part of my chart, where the jagged peaks become rolling hills. If this were a ski run, it would go from black diamond to easy green. This, he says, is my heart rate during meditation. "You need some of this," he says, pointing to the smooth hills. "People need recovery time." As soon as I open my eyes and begin asking questions again, the jagged peaks have returned. Rossman points to them and says, "If somebody stays in this state for a long period of time . . ." His voice trails off. I know that whatever he left unsaid isn't good.

Rossman advises people to "punctuate the day with many moments of mindfulness" so that over time they can rewire their nervous system. "There are some people who are on medication who don't need to be," he assures me. "If they practiced mindfulness, yoga, and meditation, they could train their brains."

Yoga and massage: They help tremendously when I'm relatively healthy. They keep me on an even keel and make relapses less likely. However, when anxiety has a tight hold on me, I turn to CBT and medication. These other things don't help at all. In fact, they seem to make things worse. I've had panic attacks while having my shoulders kneaded and while in Downward Dog. I've had to clamber off massage tables while mumbling apologies to a surprised therapist, slink off to the locker room, and down some Klonopin.

I've had mixed results with other "alternative" therapies as well. I'm still traumatized from my first acupuncture treatment, with a doctor who practiced "integrated medicine," which combines Western approaches with mindfulness, herbs, and acupuncture. (There's emerging research that acupuncture can ease anxiety before surgery and reduce the symptoms of GAD.) My amygdala feels like it has been on overdrive for months. Brad, the man I'm living with, is emotionally distant and critical, and the stress of the relationship is taking a toll. I'm having trouble sleeping and experiencing near-daily episodes of a racing heart. I've lost ten pounds.

That's why I'm lying on a table in a dark room with needles in my ankles, arms, and face.

"I've had great success helping people with anxiety with acupuncture," the doctor says as he works. I barely feel a pinch as the needles pierce my skin.

"Don't put too many needles in. I've never done this before, and I'm pretty nervous," I say.

"We'll go slowly. You'll be fine," he says. "You should start to feel very relaxed." Then he leaves the room.

I close my eyes and scan my body. I notice that my heart rate has slowed; the beats feel more regular and even. The tension in my muscles eases slightly. I sink lower into the table.

My mind, however, is whirring just as swiftly. The worries mount and collide, interrupting one another like rude dinner guests.

Where is the doctor? Is he ever coming back? Am I stuck here? I'm alone. I'm alone and I'm trapped.

The mismatch between my torpid body and my frenetic mind makes me even more freaked. It is as if the telephone wire between body and mind has been severed. I feel completely out of control.

"Excuse me. Excuse me!" I call.

No answer.

"Excuse me! Excuse *me!*" I yell.

The doctor comes back into the room.

"Are you okay?" he asks.

"No. Please take the needles out. This isn't working for me," I say. As soon as they're out, I hurry off the table. Needless to say, I don't make another appointment.

It turns out that I'm not the only anxious person who loses it while trying to chill out. A phenomenon called relaxation-induced anxiety appears in the scientific literature at least as far back as the 1980s. In one admittedly tiny study of fourteen people with chronic anxiety, four felt increased tension during progressive re-laxation, a technique where people tense and then relax various muscle groups in the body. Seven became more tense during a meditation exercise. Another small study of college students who said they felt anxious at least half the time incorporated similar relaxation techniques. Again the findings were counterintuitive: A handful of subjects felt increased anxiety during the relaxation exercises, and their heart rates jumped by ten to twelve beats per minute.

Researchers have various theories about relaxation-induced panic. The physical changes caused by relaxation, such as floating sensations and muscle twitches, can be jarring for anxious people. It can feel like a loss of control. Practices like meditation and muscle relaxation encourage people to focus on their bodies and breath, which can make anxious people overly aware of their revved-up thoughts and distressing bodily sensations. And calming the body and mind can, paradoxically, open up more mental space for worrying.

There's been a flurry of research activity recently around yoga in particular. A 2016 meta-analysis of seventeen studies found that yoga had a medium effect on anxiety symptoms. Stefan Hofmann, a professor of psychology at Boston University, is in the middle of a $4 million NIH-funded study of yoga as a treatment for GAD. The study compares the effectiveness of CBT to Kundalini yoga and a stress-education program. Kundalini, sometimes called "the yoga of awareness," focuses on breathing techniques and mindfulness. Hofmann says that the results from a pilot study are encouraging. "The effects we observe with Kundalini are actually quite strong," he tells me. The deep, slow breathing that is a hallmark of Kundalini can modify the level of CO_2 in the blood and kick-start the parasympathetic nervous system, and mindfulness counteracts the excessive worrying that plagues those with GAD.

"GAD is a disorder where people are overly focused on the future, on what could go wrong. They are in this loop that is the essence of worrying—what could happen?" says Hofmann. "Mindfulness encourages individuals to stay in the here and now. The present-moment awareness at the heart of mindfulness works directly against these worrisome cognitive tendencies." Hofmann's study will measure changes in how focused the mind is on the current moment and on "respiratory sinus arrhythmia," or variation in the heart rate that occurs with breathing. Hofmann says certain heart rate patterns are linked to GAD; they are one of the few biomarkers scientists have associated with worry.

For me, attending yoga classes sounds definitely more palatable than slogging through sessions of CBT and daily exposure therapy homework. I've done yoga fairly regularly for more than fifteen years. I stumbled onto it when I was in my twenties, living in Manhattan's Chelsea neighborhood. I used to walk by the local Sivananda yoga studio and see relaxed-looking, clear-eyed patrons milling about after their classes, yoga mats tucked under their arms. I started going to beginner classes and immediately liked the low-key vibe and the emphasis on strength and stretching.

The habit took, and I soon began exploring other studios. I went to midnight yoga, where class was accompanied by live drumming and frantic flirting. I went to packed popular classes frequented by models and got used to being splashed with other people's sweat. I went to my first ashram in upstate New York, where I was awakened by a gong at five-thirty a.m. and shoveled manure as part of "karma yoga." I went to a conference filled with celebrity yogis: One teacher autographed students' mats after class. Taking a challenging yoga class grounds me in the present moment. If I don't concentrate on what I'm doing, I might literally fall over. There's a reason many teachers call yoga a "moving meditation."

There are only a handful of Kundalini studios in New York. Online reviews of one of them mentioned the dirty light-blue carpet and cultlike environment, with most participants wearing white. One reviewer even said she'd had a panic attack midclass! I passed on that one. Instead I went to Golden Bridge Yoga in Nolita one bright and balmy fall afternoon. Until then my yoga experience had been mostly secular, the only nod to the spiritual practice a few *oms* chanted at the beginning and end of class and maybe a photo of a guru stashed in the corner. From that vantage point, Kundalini seems pretty eccentric. The name *Kundalini* refers to a coiled-up energy shaped like a serpent that is housed in the base of the spine. The yoga practice is supposed to unwind this energy along the chakras, energy centers in the body.

When I peeked into the studio, I saw a woman sitting cross-legged on a platform flanked by several photos of serene-looking elderly men. She was wearing a white scarf over her long curly dark hair and had her eyes closed while chanting in Sanskrit. She opened her eyes and welcomed me, saying I might be the only student that day. Thankfully, five others soon arrived.

Many yoga classes include some kind of breath work, called *pranayama* in Sanskrit. Kundalini takes this to the extreme. We did seven minutes of "breath of fire": You suck in your belly sharply while you exhale audibly through your nose. After only a couple of minutes, my hands and the skin around my mouth began tingling, and I felt light-headed. No way was I going to make it. I stopped, then started again. It went on and on. Everyone around me seemed fine. I, however, felt as if I were going to pass out. The sound of everyone exhaling puffs of air was accompanied by a recording of a woman singing "Guru Ram Dass" over and over at high volume. Very trippy. This is what a yoga rave would be like, I thought.

We followed that with some deep breathing, then countless leg lifts and stomach crunches. Chakras were mentioned several times. During one move, the teacher said we were going to "make our auras all shiny." Next we sat on our heels, raised our arms, clasped our hands behind our head, elbows pointing outward, and chanted *HUD* (the acronym for the Department of Housing and Urban Development, I thought) over and over, thrusting our elbows back with each *HUD*. The music (still Guru Ram Dass) seemed to swell and fill the room. After a couple of minutes, my arms started aching; a few minutes more, and they were throbbing. The muscled, heavily tattooed guy on the mat in front of me lowered his arms and massaged them. I dropped mine, too. I felt a faint euphoria.

As I was leaving, thrust back into the reality of a downtown New York City afternoon (a guy was slurping soup on the front stoop next door), I realized that my mind had not wandered once during the class. Despite the ridiculously sore muscles I knew were in store, I felt genuinely peaceful.

I'm lying on a mat with a tennis ball under my butt trying to learn to relax. I'm in Lenox, just a few minutes away from Canyon Ranch, at the Kripalu Center for Yoga & Health for a weekend Yoga for the Nervous System workshop with Bo Forbes, a Boston-based clinical psychologist who has developed a yoga practice that she says can heal anxiety and depression.

"This is a release," says Forbes, as I and about ninety other anxious people roll around on our tennis balls, attempting to massage our piriformis, a muscle deep in the hip. The woman on the mat next to me and I look at each other and giggle.

Later we're all walking around the room trying to find a particular spot on the scalene muscles in our neck. "This is a direct release valve, a direct pathway to our nervous system," says Forbes, clad in snakeskin-print yoga pants and a red top adorned with a silver lotus flower. (Sunday's pants feature an image of a cow skull.) Three gold earrings dangle from each ear. Three gold necklaces encircle her neck. Her long, straight red hair is pulled back in a black scrunchie. She's wearing a headset microphone, a black foam ball a few inches from her mouth, like Lady Gaga.

I'm confused, and I must look it, because Forbes strides over to me, puts her fingers on my neck, and pushes. I gasp. It hurts!

The workshop takes place in what must have been the church

of this former Jesuit seminary, with soaring ceilings, eight modern chandeliers, and a grand piano on a dais. Instead of a cross, there is a screen to project Forbes's PowerPoint presentation and a fabric scrim in soothing pink, orange, and gold. A metal statue of Shiva, standing on one leg, four arms outstretched, stands by it. We're in the middle of an early September heat wave (upper eighties and high humidity), and the room has no air-conditioning. An industrial fan and several white boxy models have been brought in. A few participants were savvy enough to bring paper fans and are waving them wanly.

Forbes is thin and punctuates her sentences with big smiles. She tells the story of a woman who recently attended the workshop and said that her husband had sent her there with an ultimatum: She must learn to be calm, or he would divorce her. Yikes! As she talks, I start to get her quirky Bo-isms. When she wants us to explain something, she asks us to "language it." She's going to "curate" some tools to help with our anxiety. She speaks a lot of the various "boxes" she says we put ourselves in.

Forbes began her career doing traditional talk therapy. After she became a yoga teacher, she started integrating yoga poses, fascia release, and breath work into her sessions. She soon realized, she says, that it was the yoga, not the talk, that was making her patients better. Now she believes that the body, not the mind, is the key to relieving anxiety and depression. "Breath and simple restorative poses are most effective in our clinic for anxiety and depression," she says. Telling our "stories" too often, she says, can exacerbate anxiety. She's critical of current mindfulness practices, too, saying they have become too removed from the body. No clinical trials have been published to assess Forbes's specific methods, though she makes several references during the weekend to neuroscience and to others' scientific studies.

In one exercise, she has us pair off and tell our partner a difficult story from our life. A fashion designer from Manhattan tells me of the engagement she regrets breaking off several years ago. I tell her about an awful fight my husband and I had in the presence of our baby daughter—one that made her cry. Forbes has us notice how our bodies feel after telling our stories. My stomach feels tight, my heart beats faster.

Then she has us use one of our new tools. I lie in Child's Pose, head resting on a block, breathing slowly through my nose. I do feel better. She teaches us about interoception, our sense of the physiological condition of our body. "Being with the changes in our bodies moment to moment is most calming to the nervous system," she says.

At Kripalu, breakfast in the main dining room is a silent meal. (When I forget that one morning, I get a stern lecture from one of the volunteer staff members.) We wear name tags and collect our food from metal vats, piling it onto too-small, scuffed black plastic trays. It is a cross between grade school and *Orange Is the New Black*, except with delicious food and middle-aged women in lululemon yoga pants and tank tops. During dinner—when we're allowed to speak—I meet a neurologist and several therapists, all of whom struggle with anxiety. I debate the merits of Klonopin versus Xanax with a massage therapist from Nyack.

Forbes doesn't teach typical yoga here, the very physical vinyasa classes that are popular in most gyms and yoga studios, the ones that can lead to taut arms and tight abs. Her approach is subtle. In one exercise, she has us count our pulse for one minute. Mine is galloping along at ninety-six. Then she has us clasp our hands together and press them to our forehead, stimulating our vagus nerve, she says, while we breathe slowly. After a few minutes, she has us check our pulse again. Mine has slowed to a more respectable eighty-three.

After the weekend, when I feel twitchy or sleepless at one a.m.,

I find myself doing this, and it seems to have a calming effect. While the workshop didn't hand me any cures, I did learn a few useful tricks. And it felt freeing to be surrounded by so many of my fellow anxiety sufferers. Every so often, I wonder what became of the woman whose husband gave her the ultimatum. Did she learn enough to save her marriage?

CBT and ACT were developed decades before the latest advances in neuroimaging and genetics. New technologies are spawning treatments that aim to directly target the brain dysfunctions that underlie anxiety disorders. One such approach is called attention bias modification (ABM). It often uses a simple—actually quite boring—computer task to try to normalize the attention bias toward threat that many anxious people have.

One version of ABM is a variation on the dot probe task that scientists use to assess attention bias. In this version, however, subjects are trained to attend to *non*threatening stimuli. In the task, participants might see two faces side by side—one with a neutral expression, the other with an angry or scared expression. There are also two buttons, one corresponding to each face. The faces vanish, and a probe (it could be one dot or two) appears in the same position as one of the faces. Participants must then push the button that corresponds to the placement of the probe. In ABM the probe always appears in the same spot as the nonthreatening face. Sometimes, instead of faces, ABM uses threatening words (such as *explosion* or *humiliation*) and neutral ones.

Treatment varies, but participants often spend ten to fifteen minutes doing the task twice a week for a month, says Yair Bar-Haim, a professor of psychology and neuroscience at Tel Aviv

University in Israel and a leading researcher on attention bias modification in anxiety disorders.

In a small study with GAD patients, half the patients no longer met *DSM* criteria for their disorder after eight sessions of ABM. By comparison, only 13 percent of patients who had the control treatment no longer met criteria for GAD. A study with social phobia patients yielded similar results: Half the patients who got ABM treatment no longer met criteria for social phobia, compared with 14 percent of those who got the control treatment.

I spent a week playing with one ABM app called Personal Zen, a free download available at the Apple iTunes app store. On a field of green grass, two little blue heads pop up: One creature wears a cheerful expression while the other has an angry scowl. The heads appear for only a second, but a trail of waving grass lingers where the happy creature was. Players have to trace the trail of grass with a finger as quickly as possible. After using the app, I didn't feel noticeably more relaxed, but I did get quicker at the game. And I was better able to ignore the grumpy guy.

ABM doesn't seem to work as well as CBT or ACT, although some evidence shows that combining ABM and CBT has benefits. In a 2015 meta-analysis, ABM had a "medium effect" in reducing anxiety symptoms. ABM appears to be most beneficial for GAD, social anxiety disorder, and PTSD. The meta-analysis also found that the treatment didn't work well when participants used it online on their own. Instead, ABM seems to ease anxiety primarily when mental health professionals oversee the treatment.

"You don't know how the people on the internet were doing the treatment," Bar-Haim, one of the authors of the meta-analysis, told me. He speculates that they might have been "sitting on the bus and paying half of their attention to doing the task and half on 'where's the next bus stop and where do I get off?'"

Bar-Haim also notes that not all anxious people have attention bias to threat, so the treatment isn't likely to work for everyone. Researchers are also trying to figure out the appropriate "dose." Could a person overdose on ABM? And what would overdosing mean—becoming too blasé in the face of real danger? Bar-Haim reminds me that our threat-detection system is critical to survival.

There's also the issue of boredom. Bar-Haim's group is collaborating with others to try to jazz up the ABM tasks. "We have color versions, but it doesn't help with the boredom," he says. "It would be great if we could create a Candy Crush version."

Another relatively new technology is transcranial magnetic stimulation (TMS), which has been approved by the FDA as a treatment for migraines and for treatment-resistant major depression. Now researchers are exploring whether it could effectively treat anxiety disorders. TMS is noninvasive; a device that generates a magnetic field is placed above the scalp directly over the part of the brain researchers want to stimulate. While the science is preliminary, TMS has shown benefits for people with GAD, PTSD, and panic disorder. It can cause some transient side effects like headaches and light-headedness.

Probably the coolest, most sci-fi-sounding new treatment is fMRI neurofeedback. Patients can see the workings of their own brains and then—in real time—modify the dysfunctions. In neurofeedback's newest iterations, patients lie in a functional magnetic resonance imaging scanner. (Older methods use EEG, a test that records electrical activity in the brain, but EEG cannot target brain structures as precisely as fMRI.) They're told to conjure memories or look at pictures while their brains are being scanned, and a computer analyzes the activity of the relevant brain regions. Patients see real-time feedback from their brain activity, often presented in the form of a thermometer or colored bar. Depending on what their brain is doing, the subject is told to enhance or suppress that activity. Patients "need to train their brain like they train their muscles when they want to be fit," says Anna Zilverstand, a postdoctoral researcher at the Icahn School of Medicine at Mount Sinai in New York.

In a 2015 study, Zilverstand and colleagues used neurofeedback to treat women with a phobia of spiders. Patients in the scanner saw a series of spider images. The pictures got progressively scarier—from a tiny spider on a green leaf, to a larger, hairier one on a computer keyboard, to a giant iridescent spider crawling on a man's face. The subjects in the active treatment group were also shown an image of two thermometers: a blue one that reflected the activity of the dorsolateral prefrontal cortex (dlPFC), which helps to regulate emotions, and a red one that signified activity in the insula, which is implicated in sustained anxiety. They were told to enhance the activity of the dlPFC and dampen the activity of the insula by using cognitive strategies, such as describing the physical attributes of the spider or imagining it as small and powerless. The control group saw the same spider photos and were told to use the same reappraisal strategies but didn't get the neurofeedback. At the end of the treatment, the women who received the active training had lower anxiety scores. They also had lower insula activity during the treatment.

In another study, researchers at Yale tested two sessions of neurofeedback in people with high levels of contamination anxiety. (Now this is a study I wish I could have joined!) The scientists focused on activity in the orbitofrontal cortex, a part of the brain implicated in emotion regulation. Participants saw a series of images meant to induce contamination anxiety: pictures of cockroaches, feces, blood, and dirty needles. "It had to be something where you'd think, 'I could get sick from that, or somebody could get sick from that,'" says Michelle Hampson, an assistant professor of radiology and biomedical imaging at Yale University School of Medicine and a coauthor of the study. The subjects in the active arm of the study got neurofeedback in the form of a line graph. The control group saw so-called sham feedback—activity from another person's brain rather than their own.

Several days after the study ended, the subjects who received active neurofeedback had reduced contamination anxiety. They also showed increased connections in regions of the brain linked to the regulation of emotion and decreased connections in regions linked to the processing of emotions, such as the quick appraisal of whether something is threatening. One exciting message of this study is that the effects of neurofeedback persist, perhaps causing lasting changes in the brain.

The science on neurofeedback for psychiatric disorders is still in its early days. So far studies are very small, and researchers are still figuring out which brain areas to target and how many sessions will be needed. Results are modest, and it is unclear how long the effects of the treatment will last. Also, fMRI scans are expensive, costing hundreds of dollars. Because of this, some researchers believe that neurofeedback will most often be used as an adjunct to medication and talk therapy.

Therapy doesn't only happen with a therapist.

The New York Shyness and Social Anxiety Meetup Group has more than eight thousand registered members. Founded in 2006, the group arranges a dizzying array of activities—from hikes and museum outings to game nights. The events give socially anxious people a safe space in which to pursue friendships and practice social skills. Basically, it is a support group and exposure therapy wrapped together.

I have a tinge of social anxiety, mostly when I'm around someone in authority or someone who I perceive as "cooler" than me. I also consider myself an introvert in that I prefer to spend time with friends one on one instead of in large groups, and I can feel drained by big social gatherings. That said, I'm generally gregarious and comfortable meeting new people, and I don't fit the criteria for social anxiety disorder. Still, I want to understand it better. It is one of the most prevalent of the anxiety disorders and the only one that affects men and women in equal numbers. I'm also intrigued by the idea of anxious people taking charge of their own exposure treatment.

So on a frigid February evening, I join one of Meetup's social anxiety (SA) support groups. When I arrive at the Sony Atrium, an indoor public space in Manhattan filled with metal tables and chairs, about twenty-five people have gathered for the meeting. Nearby a few homeless people, weighed down with bags of belongings, doze.

Most of the SA group participants on this night are in their twenties and thirties, and all but five are men. The organizer, a slightly harried but friendly guy named Steven, divides us into small groups. We go around the table, introduce ourselves, and say a bit about what brought us to the meeting. One aspiring computer programmer says he's "anxious all the time" about making money and someday having to support his parents. A clean-cut young man who works in finance says he's looking to make friends. He tells a sad story about lunchtime during his middle school days. "I would stand in the lunch line, and when I got to the register, I'd pretend that I forgot my wallet in my locker," he says. "I'd go to my locker and then have to wait in line again. It killed time and hid the fact that I was always alone." A veteran of the group, a guy in his forties, says that during his travels around the city, he looks for groups of tourists who appear to be lost and asks if they need directions. "It is a way for me to practice approaching people," he says. "They're usually really grateful, so it makes me feel good."

I'm perplexed as to why one older man is here. He dominates the conversation and repeatedly pounds the table when making a point. "I used to be shy, but I overcame it," he says. I wonder if he's shouting to drown out his anxiety.

We pass around a pile of notecards and are instructed to write down a fear related to social anxiety. Then we share them. The guy who talks to lost tourists says he's afraid of conflict. The aspiring computer programmer says he's afraid of looking incompetent. I write that I'm afraid of saying something stupid.

I'm heartened to see these people bravely sharing their vulnerabilities. There's a real sense of warmth and camaraderie in the room. But I'm also struck by how much pain there is, and how much anxiety has robbed them of.

For months afterward, I receive emails from the SA group about its activities. Then an invitation lands in my inbox that I can't ignore. It comes with a disclaimer: "WARNING: This is high-level exposure, so if you're not ready to be thrown into the pool of sharks then please reconsider coming."

The SA group is doing karaoke.

I'd never visited a karaoke bar. I can carry a tune and like to sing; I was in an a cappella show choir in high school. But I loathed doing solos. The one time I did—during a performance at a senior center—I was so nervous that my voice came out in thin, breathy puffs. But if I am ever going to do karaoke, doing it with a bunch of other anxious people seems like the way to go.

A few days later I'm belting out Madonna's "Holiday" at Planet Rose, a karaoke joint in the East Village. I have a microphone in one hand and a bottle of Brooklyn Lager in the other. "It's time for the good times. Forget about the bad times," I sing, and do a little dance, stamping my boots on the leopard-patterned rug. Members of the SA group lounge on zebra-print couches. The room is mercifully dark, and strings of Christmas lights ring the walls. During the chorus, two guys jump in and sing backup. "Celebrate," we wail.

I feel ridiculous. And exhilarated.

When I'm finished, an SA member, a thin blond man who has spent most of the evening nursing a beer by himself, steps up and sings a Metallica song. Ultimately, about half the group ends up singing. Everyone is friendly and welcoming. "People here are really nonjudgmental," says one woman. While the support group I attended was made up of a lot of new members, this night is dominated by veterans. Several have been coming to SA Meetups for years and have made their closest friends in the group. Steven, the organizer, says the group has been life-changing for him.

I think about the guy I met at the Sony Atrium, the one who pretended to forget his wallet at lunch. In a year or two—after more support group meetings and other outings—maybe he'll be ready for a karaoke outing, too.

5

MAY CAUSE DIZZINESS
MEDICATIONS FOR ANXIETY

After I relapsed during my senior year of college, my therapist encouraged me to take Prozac.

Well, at first she encouraged. But after I kept saying no, she outright begged.

"I'll meet you on campus every day and watch you take it," she said.

No, I told her.

"I'll take it, too," she offered. (In retrospect this seems pretty strange, but maybe she was already taking it.)

Still no, though I let her give me the prescription.

My resistance was largely part of my illness. I still had a tough time eating. I avoided anything that looked or tasted slightly weird (and weird was a very broad category). I was gripped by fears of salmonella, *E. coli*, listeria, or some other nameless bacterium. I worried about out-of-the-blue allergic reactions. When the fear was too strong, I didn't eat at all. More often the fear would surge after I'd swallowed a bite. Then I'd rush to a bathroom, scan for feet under the other stalls to ensure I was alone, and make myself throw up.

There was no way I was going to be okay with taking a psychotropic drug. Whatever grip on reality I had, whatever fragile equilibrium I had found, would never withstand the manipulation of my brain's neurotransmitters. I never even filled the prescription.

Prozac (or its generic equivalent, fluoxetine) is a selective serotonin reuptake inhibitor (SSRI), a class of drugs that also includes Paxil (paroxetine), Zoloft (sertraline), Celexa (citalopram), and Lexapro (escitalopram). Although the SSRIs are best known as antidepressants, if you complain to a doctor about excessive anxiety, you'll almost certainly be given a prescription for one of them. Serotonin is a neurotransmitter, a chemical that transmits signals between neurons in the brain and is believed to play an important role in mood and anxiety. SSRIs block the reabsorption of serotonin. That leaves more of the chemical hanging around the synapses, the spaces between neurons. That action is thought to account for SSRIs' mood-boosting and anxiety-reducing effects.

Serotonin-norepinephrine reuptake inhibitors (SNRIs) like Effexor (venlafaxine) are also used in anxiety disorders. These drugs act on serotonin and on norepinephrine, a neurotransmitter that is involved in the stress response.

Doctors call SSRIs a "first line" treatment, and reams of studies have shown them to be at least modestly effective in treating the various anxiety disorders. But there's one wrinkle: Placebos have been shown to work almost as well. In a 1998 study of panic disorder patients who took either sertraline (Zoloft) or a placebo for ten weeks, those on the drug saw their mean number of panic attacks per week drop by 88 percent. Those taking the placebo had a 53 percent fall in their number of attacks. In a 2004 study looking at escitalopram (Lexapro) for GAD, patients on the drug saw their scores on an anxiety symptom scale drop by about 29 percent after eight weeks. The scores of those on placebo fell by about 19 percent.

Even the relatively lackluster effects of antidepressants are likely overstated. Research on the efficacy of medications is often paid for by the pharmaceutical companies that stand to profit from their drugs' sales. Studies that reveal that a drug *isn't* beneficial—so-called negative clinical trials—are frequently not published. Also, in some positive trials, research results are written up in a way that inflates a treatment's benefits. This reporting bias is evident in write-ups of studies on both depression and anxiety disorders.

If placebos work almost as well as the drugs, and if even those modest effects are embellished, what's the point of taking an SSRI? The real benefit, it turns out, may be not in treating acute illness but in preventing relapses, says Robert Temple, deputy director for clinical science at the Center for Drug Evaluation and Research at the U.S. Food and Drug Administration (FDA). He is a coauthor of a review paper that found that, for people with a history of major depression, continuing on antidepressants cut the risk of relapse in half. Temple says the FDA has unpublished data showing similar results for GAD.

In college, I eventually recovered without medication. CBT, and maybe just the passage of time, got me to some sort of stability. After graduation, I moved to Washington, D.C., and spent a little more than two years working in politics, writing speeches and press releases for a U.S. senator. Then I moved to New York City to take a job as an administrative assistant at the *Wall Street Journal*—answering phones, fetching faxes, and in my spare time, writing brief articles, focused on the dream of becoming a full-fledged reporter there. I worked hard, had eccentric roommates, traveled, dated both appropriate and inappropriate men, and spent lots of time drinking red wine and dancing in dark velvet-walled bars. I was doing the things you're supposed to do in your twenties.

My anxiety didn't disappear. I still had frequent chest pain and episodic fears of heart attacks. I occasionally visited a cardiologist, a family friend of my college boyfriend. He would hook me up to an EKG and tell me I was fine. I'd be reassured until a few months later, when pain and doubt would land me back in his office. I fretted more than most about dating disasters and setbacks at work. But I remember those first six years after graduation as a period of relative health and equanimity.

By the summer of 1998, I had landed a junior reporter position at the *Journal*, writing, ironically, about the pharmaceutical industry. The big story then was the launch of Viagra, the little blue pill to treat impotence. It became a huge seller for Pfizer, its manufacturer, and a controversial cultural story as well. Why were insurance companies paying for an anti-impotence pill when many didn't pay for birth control? Would it unravel marriages? I spent my days talking to Wall Street analysts, urologists, and formerly impotent men, asking them about their new and improved erections. For a story on the burgeoning recreational Viagra market, I visited clubs with names like Hell and the Tunnel and bought rounds of cosmopolitans for groups of men. I was on the lookout for recreational users and for stories of the drug dealers I had heard were peddling Viagra alongside cocaine and ecstasy, the former used to counteract the erection-deflating effects of the latter.

I loved asking people questions and hearing their stories. I did an actual jig each time I saw my name in print followed by the words "Staff Reporter of the *Wall Street Journal*."

I had a new boyfriend, too. Alan was also a journalist, tall, lanky, and adorable with a lack of style and a social awkwardness that was boldly—and refreshingly—out of step with most men I had met in New York. He was a terrific writer and had a background that I greatly admired, having worked as a freelance reporter in Africa covering the aftermath of the genocide in Rwanda. We were in that giddy stage of new love, just five or so months in, and deep in the emotional striptease of joyful declarations and new confidences. And then I began to unravel.

. . .

It is a brilliant warm Saturday in June. I am walking down Seventh Avenue in Greenwich Village, tired and a little exhilarated, heading to a deli to grab a snack. I have just left the gym where I have taken a class in capoeira, a Brazilian martial art, an intense ninety minutes of kicks and spins, and my legs are already starting to ache. I am looking straight ahead at the pavement and pedestrians in front of me. In my peripheral vision I see a whizzing blur of yellow as the taxis head down Seventh Avenue, tender green splotches of early summer leaves on the trees above, and the architectural lines of nearby buildings.

Suddenly a chunk of the landscape disappears. A black smudge with jagged edges appears in my field of vision, blocking out the taxis, leaves, and buildings. I stop in the middle of the sidewalk and rub my eyes. Close them tightly and open them. The smudge is still there, blocking the upper-right quadrant of my field of vision.

Did I get something in my eye? I put a palm over one eye and look up. I change eyes. The splotch is in both eyes.

I know what that means. Something is wrong with my brain. I am having a stroke.

I am having a stroke. And I have to get to a hospital.

St. Vincent's, thankfully, is only a few blocks away. But I can't get there on my own. I may be seconds away from losing the ability to walk. I'll crumble onto the sidewalk. Baffled tourists will dodge the heap of me. A twenty-seven-year-old woman in yoga pants and a ponytail collapses in the middle of the day? She must be drunk.

In a panic, I scan the sidewalk around me and grab the nearest forearm. It is smooth and sinewy and pale. It belongs to a tall, freckled blond guy about my age. He looks surprised but doesn't blanch or shake me off.

My explanation comes out in a rush: "I think I'm having a stroke. I can't see. There's a hospital two blocks away. Can you please walk me there?"

He says okay.

I grip his forearm the entire way there. He deposits me in St. Vincent's ER and disappears. I hope I remembered to say thank you. (I'll say it now: thank you.)

I go up to a man doing intake. "A huge chunk of my vision just vanished. I can't see," I say.

He tells me to sit down in the waiting room. I sit for five minutes, closing and opening my eyes, trying to will the black smudge away.

I rush back to the man. "I need to see someone now. I think I'm having a stroke."

Either my urgency or the word *stroke* sets things in motion. I'm taken inside and put into a bed: White sheets hang from a metal rod to offer some semblance of privacy. A nurse hooks me up to a heart monitor.

Then all hell breaks loose. The nurse starts pulling my shirt apart. She yells for assistance. Someone else rushes in.

"What is it? What's happening?" I plead.

"You're having a hypertensive episode," the nurse says.

The next few minutes are a blur of hands and movement. *This is it. I really am dying.*

Then, abruptly, the activity stops. The nurse begins pulling the cardiac leads off my body. Her helper disappears behind the white sheet.

"What's going on?" I say.

"Your blood pressure is normal. When we measured it again, it was fine," she says.

"So I'm *not* having a hypertensive episode?"

"No."

The initial high reading, the nurse says, must have been an error. It is then that I realize that I can see perfectly again. The black smudge is gone.

I'm discharged from the ER a little while later, with no explanation for the sudden blind spot or its speedy resolution.

Later that day, when I talk to my regular doctor, he says I must have had an ocular migraine, a type of headache where funky visual changes are the primary symptom. "You should have called me instead of going to the ER," he scolds. "I would have told you you were fine." I feel chastised and a bit sheepish but also a little angry. It seems like losing your vision should be an acceptable reason to go to the ER, even by the standards of a nonanxious person.

The migraine episode triggers a swift slide into constant worry about my health—and everything else. What if something really is wrong with my brain? My mind feels sluggish. I think I can feel the neurons stalling. I handwring about my memory and start writing down conversations for fear I'll forget. I feel cut off from my boyfriend and my friends. My body may be at a museum or at a party, but my mind is elsewhere, caught in a loop of dread.

I worry that my worry will scare away those I love.

Unlike in college, I can't retreat to my parents' sofa or drop a few classes until I feel better. I will lose my job. I will lose my boyfriend. I will have to leave New York.

No. I will not hit the pause button on my life.

I call my therapist, Dr. D, and tell her what is going on. I have been seeing her for about a year now. She's a psychologist who practices psychodynamic therapy, which aims to help people understand how their past history and relationships influence their current behavior. I started therapy with the goal of figuring out why I had the breakdowns in college and why I'm so anxious. Now she gives me the name and number of a psychiatrist. It's time for medication.

The psychiatrist, Dr. I, has frizzy, haphazard gray hair and wears colorful ankle-dusting skirts and macramé necklaces. While she speaks with authority about psychotropic drugs, she looks as if she should run a feminist bookstore in Seattle. I'm relieved when she prescribes Zoloft. After years of fear and trepidation, the little pill doesn't look quite so dangerous anymore. Besides, I feel like I have no choice but to take it. The only other option I see is months of infirmity.

So I start taking Zoloft. My head doesn't explode. I don't instantly feel different, but I know better than to hope for that. SSRIs can take anywhere from four to six weeks to work. When they work at all, that is.

I feel the side effects, however, almost immediately.

It is a few days after I've taken my first pill. I'm sitting in the Bubble Lounge, a silly, expensive champagne bar in Tribeca, with friends from work. We're surrounded by finance types, groups of clean-cut men in dark suits and a handful of serious-looking women. Our group of journalists is a bit scruffy in comparison. I'm chatting with friends, a champagne flute in my hand, when I feel a chill run up and down my forearms. I rub my arms with my hands and pull on a sweater, but the chill doesn't stop. It's not a chill exactly. No, it feels like something is moving up and down my arms. Soon it reaches farther, dancing up the back of my neck and across my scalp.

My skin is crawling.

The medical term for this is *formication*. It is a type of paresthesia, a sensation on the skin that can also include tingling,

numbness, and itching. In clinical trials by Pfizer, Zoloft's manufacturer, about 2 percent of people who took the drug experienced
it. (Oddly, 1 percent of those taking a placebo did, too.)

The next day I call my psychiatrist and tell her what I'm feeling. According to her, it's my anxiety and not the drug that is
making my skin crawl. She recommends that I double the dose of
Zoloft. I do what I'm told and pop two tablets.

Within a few hours, my entire body erupts in waves of
sensation—tingling, crawling, and something almost electric. The
tiny hairs on my body feel charged, as though they're standing on
end. My skin seems to move. It is as if an ant farm has been let
loose on my body. My anxiety has never felt like this. Those are
the last Zoloft pills I'll ever take.

I try Paxil next. Even though the SSRIs are all similar, individual patients often react differently to each drug. With Paxil,
my skin doesn't crawl. I don't, in fact, feel much of anything.
But slowly, over several weeks, some space seems to open up in
my brain. Instead of the worry occupying, say, 70 percent of my
mind, it now seems to take up 40 percent. And the volume of my
anxiety is turned down a bit, too. I'm better able to set it aside. I'll
come home from dinner with friends and realize that I was able
to concentrate on a conversation for several hours, that I was truly
present.

If I miss a pill, however, I am light-headed and dizzy. I get a
woozy feeling even if I take my dose a few hours later than I did
the day before. It is a daily reminder that the drug is playing with
my brain chemistry. Though I have ample evidence that this is a
good thing, it makes me uneasy. Other side effects sneak up on me,
taking several months to make themselves known. My sex drive
plummets. Having an orgasm requires Herculean effort. I become
ravenously hungry. It is a needy, demanding hunger, impossible to
ignore. Sometimes I wake up in the middle of the night, starving,

and clandestinely scarf down a bowl of cereal. My weight inches upward. (Both "increased appetite" and "decreased appetite" are among the long list of Paxil's potential side effects.)

Still, I'm lucky that I've found a medication that works for me. At least a third of people with anxiety disorders don't get much relief from the available drugs. Even when drugs do help, there's the lag time before they alleviate symptoms, and patients often have to cycle through multiple drugs before they find the right one.

This may change soon. A flurry of research is looking at whether brain scans or other tests can predict which patients will respond to a particular treatment. The hope is to uncover biomarkers, such as patterns of activity in the brain or levels of hormones in the blood, that can direct patients to the medication or therapy that will help the most. However, the research is still in its early stages, and it could be years before such tests are available. But if it shakes out, biomarkers could save patients time, money, and a lot of misery.

Scientists have homed in on a number of potential biomarkers for a range of disorders, including PTSD, social anxiety disorder, and OCD. Many studies have found distinct patterns of brain activity that can predict how well someone will do with a specific treatment. In one study, fourteen people with GAD underwent fMRI scans while looking at pictures. Some pictures were revolting, showing mutilated bodies or violent scenes; others were benign. Subjects were warned as to whether they were about to see a disturbing or benign picture. The participants then took the SNRI Effexor for eight weeks. The people who had higher levels of activity in the anterior cingulate cortex when they were anticipating seeing either kind of picture had a better response to Effexor. The anterior cingulate cortex is thought to be involved in detecting and resolving emotional conflict.

In another study, researchers in Oxford, England, gave MRI

scans to fourteen patients with panic disorder while they viewed anxiety-provoking pictures of accidents, funerals, and hospitals. The subjects then had four sessions of CBT. The study found that those who had increased gray matter volume in the hippocampus and increased activity in the insula and dorsolateral prefrontal cortex while viewing the disturbing pictures before their treatment had greater reductions in their symptoms.

I was on Paxil for about two years. Since then I've cycled on and off SSRIs. I had another year's stint on Paxil. A few years on Prozac. Most recently I've taken a daily dose of five milligrams of Lexapro, one of the newer SSRIs. They've all worked similarly well for me, but I've switched in a search for the fewest side effects. Paxil, for me, was the worst. Prozac was a huge improvement. Lexapro has gone down the easiest, although I still feel dizzy when I miss a dose. Hopping off and on medication has been fairly easy for me. I know I'm lucky in that regard. The internet is full of horror stories of immediate relapses and awful withdrawal symptoms.

I've been on SSRIs for eight of the past eighteen years. I've usually gone on them during crises, when the anxiety is unrelenting and prevents me from experiencing much else. But they have never cured my out-of-whack anxiety. Even on medication, I'll get the occasional panic attack. And when things are very stressful, drugs seem to be no match for my amped-up amygdala. What they do, however, is give me space and opportunity. They are like an air pocket for a drowning woman. They aren't the solution, but they keep me conscious long enough to figure out my next move.

I keep my childproof bottle of Lexapro in a silver bowl on top of my dresser, but there's another orange-hued bottle I keep much

closer. This one I have with me always, tucked into my handbag.
It is my security blanket, my good luck charm, my talisman.

The bottle is slapped with three warning stickers.

> **May Cause Drowsiness and Dizziness. Alcohol May**
> **Intensity This Effect. Use Care When Operating A**
> **Car Or Dangerous Machines.**

> **If You Are Pregnant Or Considering Becoming**
> **Pregnant You Should Discuss The Use of This**
> **Medicine With Your Doctor Or Pharmacist.**

And this one, in bright, traffic-cone orange:

> CONTROLLED SUBSTANCE. DANGEROUS UNLESS USED AS
> DIRECTED. CAUTION: **Federal law prohibits the transfer**
> **of this drug to any person other than the patient for**
> **whom it was prescribed.**

The bottle is filled with pale orange pills with the letter K cut
out of the center. It's Klonopin. And it's fantastic.

Klonopin can melt my anxiety and many of its annoying accou-
trements—racing heart, shallow breathing, twisted thoughts—in
about thirty minutes. It can even derail a full-blown panic attack
if I take enough. When I wake at four a.m. with a churning litany
of what-ifs and must-dos, half of a .5 milligram tablet eases me
back to blank sleep. It is literally a chill pill.

Klonopin (or the generic clonazepam) is a benzodiazepine,
one of the class of drugs that also includes Valium and Xanax.
Benzos enhance the activity of the central nervous system's main
inhibitory neurotransmitter, GABA (gamma-aminobutyric acid).

Its primary function is to reduce the activity of neurons. Benzos are used not only for anxiety and panic attacks but also to treat seizure disorders and insomnia. Doctors wrote more than ninety-three million prescriptions for benzodiazepines in 2015, according to QuintilesIMS, which tracks pharmaceutical sales. That is up 16 percent since 2006.

Weirdly, I don't remember taking my first Klonopin. I had tried other benzos a handful of times—a Xanax that knocked me out after a nearly sleepless week, a Valium before an MRI. But my life "before K" and "after K" is starkly delineated. Klonopin is a safety net, a panic button. The difference between having it in my purse and not is like the difference between rock climbing with a harness and ropes and free climbing, an insane practice in which climbers use no safety equipment whatsoever.

My dose of Klonopin has always been "p.r.n." or "as needed." Over the years, "as needed" has meant different things. Some instances are clear-cut, like the time I had a terrifying panic attack on an airplane. (Hands down, a metal tube hurtling through space thirty thousand feet above the ground is the absolute worst place to have a panic attack. No escape. Dozens of onlookers.) I fled to the galley near the back of the plane and clutched the arm of a surprised flight attendant. She gave me a cup of water, and we sat in side-by-side jump seats while I tried, pitifully, to breathe deeply and ride the panic out. I gulped down two full Ks, four times my usual dose, and within an hour I was sprawled across three seats and slept until touchdown.

I've used it as a prophylaxis. I'll pop half of a .5 milligram tablet before I go into a high-anxiety situation: a big meeting or interview at work, or a daunting party, or when getting behind the wheel of a car. (A twenty-year resident of New York City, I rarely drive. I'm nearly assured of a panic attack when I have to take a highway.) Many CBT therapists would *tsk tsk* at this approach, saying that I'm not allowing myself to master my anxiety. But hell, sometimes I just need to get through the day—or the next hour.

I've used K to play medical detective. When I'm plagued by weird physical symptoms, I'll take a benzo to see if the feeling—an odd pain or numb limb—goes away. If it does, I'll chalk it up to anxiety.

During times of sky-high anxiety, I've taken K daily for weeks. Sometimes this means I'm headed for a relapse, and it's a sign that I need to return to therapy and go back on an SSRI. Other times there's a clear, time-limited cause. For a few weeks two winters ago, my husband and I thought our daughter might have a brain tumor. She had been complaining of headaches, smacking her hand against her forehead, and whimpering pitifully. A round of antibiotics for a potential sinus infection didn't help. We were sent to a neurologist who saw something worrying in our daughter's exam. (There aren't many things sadder than the waiting room of a pediatric neurologist's office.) The doctor scheduled our daughter for an MRI. During those two weeks of awful uncertainty— until the neurologist called and said the only thing abnormal on the MRI was, in fact, a tenacious sinus infection—I took Klonopin twice, sometimes three times, a day.

Still, it was no match for my terror. I had vivid images of a grim future. I worried constantly and formulated elaborate plans. How I'd take a leave from my job to care for my ailing child. How I'd cope with the divorce that would be the result of my husband's and my eventual grief. I took videos of my daughter chatting, so I could remember her healthy. I had trouble sleeping. How much worse would it have been if my brain weren't being bathed in benzos?

At other times I've used K more casually, even under questionable circumstances. I'll sometimes take it when I have trouble sleeping and have a big day of work ahead. I'll (very rarely) use it as a chaser after a glass or two of red wine, though not for fun. After I turned forty, I found that if I drank a glass of wine, my heart rate would rise, and that night my sleep would be unsettled. A teensy bit of Klonopin counteracts that.

Klonopin can cause a daunting list of side effects: depression, coordination problems, dizziness, and my favorite, "intellectual ability reduced," according to the manufacturer, Genentech. But what makes some doctors skittish about prescribing benzos is the potential for addiction and abuse. Combined with enough alcohol and other drugs, they can be lethal. People can just stop breathing. Benzos were implicated in the deaths of the actor Heath Ledger, the singer Whitney Houston, and the model Anna Nicole Smith.

Benzos can also be hell to withdraw from, especially for people who have taken them regularly for years. Entire workbook programs have been designed to ease benzo withdrawal, with names like "Stopping Anxiety Medication: Panic Control Therapy for Benzodiazepine Discontinuation." The forums on BenzoBuddies .org, one of several online withdrawal support groups, contain desperate descriptions of horror show symptoms: nausea, a burning tongue, ringing ears, crying jags, depression. People's sign-offs are often long litanies of their benzo use and their slow, agonizing attempts to get off them. Some people posting have been on the drugs for more than twenty-five years. There are chronicles of lost jobs and lost relationships because of addiction.

"Absolute hell on Earth" is the title of one recent post from a BenzoBuddies member who had stopped Xanax cold turkey after taking it daily for three years. She says the withdrawal left her with no energy, no appetite, headaches, and a racing heart. She lost fifteen pounds in two weeks. The anxiety has come roaring back, too. "Talk about wanting and feeling DEATH. . . . I could barely take 10 steps without feeling like my heart was going to beat out of my chest," she writes. "I had depersonalization, insomnia, constant tremors, pain in my limbs, tingling in my limbs, felt detached from my body, I couldn't cry or laugh, I couldn't form complete sentences. I was truly a walking zombie."

The number of American adults who filled prescriptions for benzos jumped 67 percent between 1996 and 2013, up from 8.1 million to 13.5 million people. During that same period, the quantity of medication doled out per person more than doubled and overdose deaths involving benzos quadrupled. The most lethal combination is benzos and opioids: About three-quarters of the deaths involving benzos also involved drugs like OxyContin and Percocet.

I've never felt addicted to Klonopin. I often go months without taking it. And most people on benzos for anxiety disorders don't abuse them or develop a tolerance.

However, lately I've become much more conflicted about my Klonopin use. In the last few years, several studies have found an alarming link between benzos and Alzheimer's disease and dementia. One study published in the journal *BMJ* in 2014 found that older people who had taken benzos daily for more than three months were 32 percent more likely to develop Alzheimer's disease. Not only that, the greater the exposure, the greater the risk. Those who took daily doses for more than six months had an 84 percent greater risk. The risk was greater for benzos with a longer half-life, like Klonopin, than for those with a shorter one, like Xanax and Ativan.

I'm reassured by a more recent study, published in the same journal in 2016, that does not support the hypothesis that benzo use causes dementia. Researchers followed more than 3,400 people older than sixty-five. Over approximately seven years, about

800 subjects developed dementia. People who had used benzos lightly (defined as about 120 or fewer daily doses) during a ten-year period before the study were slightly more likely to be diagnosed with dementia in the follow-up period. Surprisingly, those who had the heaviest use during the ten-year period were no more likely to develop dementia than those who didn't take the drugs at all. The researchers conjecture that the slight risk associated with light use may simply reflect the fact that people with early symptoms of dementia, which include anxiety and insomnia, are more likely to be prescribed benzos. But these results, at least, suggest that benzos don't lead to dementia.

So the science is mixed. Which is why, lately, I pause before opening my bottle of Klonopin and do a silent cost-benefit analysis. Is my anxiety that bad? Is easing my mind now worth ruining it later on? Sometimes—though not as often as I wish I did—I put the bottle away.

A range of pharmacological treatments for anxiety was available in the nineteenth century, particularly bromides and chloral hydrate, a popular sedative introduced in 1869. Lily Bart, the tragic heroine of Edith Wharton's *The House of Mirth*, dies from an overdose of chloral hydrate. Just before nodding off for her final sleep, Lily describes the sedative's initial effects, "the gradual sensation of the inner throb, the soft approach of passiveness, as though an invisible hand made magic passes over her in the darkness."

In 1903, the first barbiturate, barbital, was launched in the United States under the brand name Veronal. Barbiturates were safer than the earlier bromides and were primarily prescribed for insomnia and anxiety. In the first half of the twentieth century, sales soared, and dozens of variations flooded the market. The pills' many colors earned them nicknames like blue angels, pink ladies, and yellow jackets. On the street, they were dubbed goofballs, explains medical historian Andrea Tone.

Barbiturates were dangerous and addictive. It was easy to overdose: The same amount of medication that was sleep-inducing and safe for one person could kill another. And you could build up a tolerance; over time people often needed more of the drug to get the same effect. It was tough to get off barbiturates, too. Stopping them suddenly could lead to a host of awful side effects like rapid pulse, high blood pressure, sweating, and convulsions. Marilyn Monroe was found dead in her Brentwood, California, home with an empty bottle of barbiturates by her side. Judy Garland also died of an overdose of barbiturates.

It was not until 1955 that a safer—and revolutionary—antianxiety drug came to market: Miltown.

Miltown was developed by Frank Berger, a scientist from Czechoslovakia. In 1938, he and his new wife fled the Nazis and settled in England, where he began working on methods to boost the production of penicillin, which was desperately needed on the battlefields of World War II. Berger was testing compounds that might serve as a preservative for penicillin and noted something striking about mephenesin, a substance that was typically used, in modified form, as a disinfectant. When he injected mice with mephenesin, their muscles went limp, but the animals remained conscious and alert. Unlike barbiturates, mephenesin didn't induce a zoned-out state.

In 1949, Berger took a job at Wallace Laboratories, a division of Carter Products, in New Jersey. Carter's cash cow was Carter's Little Liver Pills, a laxative. (It also made Arid deodorant and Nair, the hair-dissolving cream.) But Carter wanted to push forcefully into the prescription drug business. Berger's first project at Wallace was to create a version of mephenesin that was long-lasting and could be taken in pill form. He and his colleagues synthesized five hundred compounds and tested a dozen on animals. One of them, meprobamate, made the muscles of mice go limp and made rhesus and Java monkeys docile. Normally the monkeys were vicious and violent, so much so that "you've got to wear thick gloves and a face guard when you handle them," Berger said. But after a shot of meprobamate, they became "very nice monkeys—friendly and alert."

After a few studies in humans found that meprobamate was safe, eased anxiety, and promoted sleep, Berger submitted an application to the FDA to authorize its sale. The new drug, now named Miltown after a sleepy little town not far from Wallace's headquarters, came to market in May 1955. The pharmaceutical behemoth Wyeth bought a license to manufacture meprobamate, too, and a few months later started selling the drug under the name Equanil. It was the first of what are known as the minor tranquilizers. By 1957, a full third of all prescriptions filled in the United States were tranquilizers.

Miltown became a Hollywood sensation. Lucille Ball was a fan, and so was Tennessee Williams. Milton Berle was so enamored of it that he sometimes called himself Uncle Miltown. "Movie stars and television personalities gushed about Miltown," writes Tone, "gossip reporters wrote treatises on it, and at celebrity galas, illicit Miltown was passed around as casually as canapés." People drank Miltinis, a martini garnished with a Miltown pill instead of an olive. The drug was invoked in ads for everything from ice cream to vacations. It was nicknamed "Executive Excedrin" for its popularity among overworked businessmen. Athletes used it to calm precompetition jitters. The team doctors for the Philadelphia Phillies and the Cincinnati Redlegs (as the Reds were known for a time in the 1950s) prescribed it.

Carter and Wyeth aggressively courted doctors, too. One ad published in the *American Journal of Psychiatry* touted Miltown for a broad swath of people, including "the tense, nervous patient," "the agitated, senile patient," "the alcoholic," and "the problem child." Carter hired the surrealist painter Salvador Dalí to create an installation for the 1958 annual meeting of the American Medical Association depicting the experience of being on Miltown. (Dalí's wife took the drug.) The work, titled *Crisalida,* was a silk-walled tunnel weighing two and a half tons and adorned with murals representing the journey from anxiety (depicted as a twisted hollow figure) to tranquillity (a diaphanously dressed woman with a crown of flowers).

With this success, pharmaceutical companies scrambled to find new anxiety-lifting blockbusters. At Hoffmann–La Roche, Leo Sternbach was a Jewish scientist from Eastern Europe who had left Switzerland in 1941 to escape the growing Nazi threat. Instead of creating a me-too drug like Miltown and its ilk, Sternbach wanted to develop an entirely new tranquilizer. He started tinkering with substances called benzheptoxdiazines, which, years earlier, he had explored while searching for new dyes, creating dozens of derivatives. But when he tested them, none worked as tranquilizers. Disappointed, Hoffmann–La Roche tasked Sternbach with researching antibiotics instead. That could have been the end of the story, but a year later a colleague found a sample that Sternbach had failed to test, numbered Ro 5-0690.

Ro 5-0690 was tested in mice and cats. Mice given the drug hung limply when researchers held them by the ear. When medicated mice were put at the bottom of a tilted screen, they slid down. (Normally mice can easily run to the top.) Cats held by the nape of the neck were relaxed and placid. The animals weren't zonked, however, but remained aware and were able to walk normally. Sternbach even tested it on himself. About an hour and a half after taking fifty milligrams (a bit higher than a therapeutic dose today), Sternbach felt, as he wrote in his journal, "slightly soft in the knees." Later that day he felt sleepy, but by dinnertime he was back to normal. Ro 5-0690 seemed to be the holy grail of tranquilizers—less deadly, more powerful, and not as sedating as competitors. The drug was named Librium (for equilibrium). Within three months of its introduction in 1960, it became the bestselling tranquilizer on the market.

While tranquilizers and benzos generated most of the excitement, the drug treatment of anxiety disorders took another, quieter leap forward in the 1960s, too.

In 1961, Donald Klein was working at Hillside Hospital in Queens, New York, which was then a two-hundred-bed long-term psychiatric facility. He worked with Max Fink, who was an expert in shock therapy. Imipramine, the first of the tricyclic antidepressants, had just recently become available for research, and Fink was eager to experiment with it. Hillside began giving imipramine to some of the depressed patients. "You give it to patients, and they slept a little better, they started eating, and three or four weeks into the treatment, some would come into the office and say, 'Doc, the veil is lifted. I'm okay,'" Klein recalls. Some of the depressed patients were also anxious. Klein noticed that imipramine seemed to be easing the anxiety, too. So Hillside started an experiment, giving imipramine to patients with anxiety, including those who were not depressed.

Klein recalls one pivotal case. The man had been staying at the hospital nearly a year, but he was still terrified of being alone. He wouldn't walk anywhere without a chaperone, and about three or four times a day he ran to the nurses' station in a panic, convinced that he was dying. Klein offered the man the new drug.

Each week Klein increased the patient's dose. For a while, things were status quo. The patient kept having several panic attacks each day. During their appointments, the man would tell Klein what a "lousy" doctor he was. After a few weeks, though, one of the nurses remarked that the patient seemed better. He had made no dramatic appearances at the nurses' station that week. Not one. The patient was as shocked as Klein.

The man wasn't totally cured. He was still afraid to be alone, and his amorphous, free-floating anxiety remained. But the imipramine did block his panic attacks.

Klein and Fink published a paper on their work in 1962 in the *American Journal of Psychiatry.* "It became apparent that anxiety was at least two different things," Klein said. "You had these terrible crises of anxiety which drove him to the nurse's station and this anticipatory anxiety that everything is lousy and is going to get worse. And the drug had dissected those things out."

Today Klein lives in a grand building across the street from the Metropolitan Museum of Art in Manhattan. He greets me at the door of his apartment, accompanied by his small, energetic dog, Koko. He has a shock of white hair and is wearing a blue-and-white-checked dress shirt and navy corduroys. His stocking feet are covered in Koko's hair. At eighty-eight, he is still working. Though he retired from the psychiatry department at Columbia in 2003, he still sees private patients one day a week, publishes papers, and consults on grant proposals.

Klein's imipramine discovery revolutionized psychiatric thinking. It showed that anxiety wasn't a single, amorphous disorder and that patients' responses to medication could help science define the boundaries of illnesses. Of his breakthrough, Klein says, "Pasteur had it right. He says for discovery, it is chance and a prepared mind."

Klein's success with imipramine prompted Robert Spitzer, chairman of the task force working on the *DSM*-III, to invite him to join the group.

Today the *DSM* is arguably the most powerful book in the field of psychiatry. Insurance companies use it to determine coverage. The government uses it to allocate benefits. Scientists use it to plan their research studies. Lawyers use it to defend their clients.

But it was not always so influential. The first edition of the *DSM* was published in 1952, primarily so that doctors in state mental hospitals could more easily compile statistics about their patients. It was firmly under the sway of Freudian ideas. In that edition, anxiety was the star. It was thought to fuel all of the so-called psychoneurotic disorders, comprising what we now consider the various anxiety disorders, depression, and somatoform disorders. "The chief characteristic of these disorders is 'anxiety' which may be directly felt and expressed or which may be unconsciously and automatically controlled by the utilization of various psychological defense mechanisms (depression, conversion, displacement, etc.)," it reads. Disorders included anxiety reaction, obsessive-compulsive reaction, depressive reaction, and phobia reaction, among others.

DSM-II, published in 1968, didn't depart dramatically from the original version. The term *reaction* was dropped, and certain historical terms, like *anxiety neurosis*, *hysterical neurosis*, and *neurasthenic neurosis*, came back. But these were largely semantic changes. The illnesses were still considered to be the result of anxiety produced by unconscious conflicts.

Overseen by Spitzer, the *DSM*-III, published in 1980, was revolutionary. Spitzer was a psychiatrist at Columbia. Although trained as a psychoanalyst, he wanted the new edition of the *DSM* to be based as much as possible on empirical data and to include detailed inclusion and exclusion criteria that would be more useful to clinicians than the vague soup of the two earlier editions. The new book jettisoned the idea that disease had its origins in unconscious conflicts.

Klein was part of both the task force and the working group on "anxiety and dissociative disorders." His experiments with imipramine had convinced him that panic attacks were a distinct disorder. With that in mind, he pushed to create a separate entry for panic disorder, which had previously been lumped in with anxiety neurosis. Anxious expectation became generalized anxiety disorder. Social phobia and post-traumatic stress disorder made their first appearances in *DSM*-III, too.

Psychoanalysts pushed back, deriding the new approach as simplistic and dismissive of their work. A heated controversy erupted over the category of "neurotic disorders." Spitzer wanted it gone, saying it was too tied up with the psychoanalytic views on the origin of mental disorders. But for many psychiatrists, neurosis was their bread and butter. It encompassed their most common diagnoses. They worried that if it disappeared from the *DSM*, insurance companies might stop paying for their services. In the end, the task force compromised, keeping neurosis but demoting it to a few parenthetical phrases, such as "phobic disorders (or phobic neuroses)."

Psychoanalysis was under attack elsewhere in the scientific community, too. One study compared two groups of anxious patients: one that underwent psychoanalysis and another that was kept on a waiting list and did not. The rates of improvement for the two groups were the same. It did not help that psychoanalysis was costly and time-consuming and that there weren't enough practitioners for every anxious person. Of course, medications, which offered the potential of a quicker fix, also hastened its decline.

Despite the runaway success of Librium, Sternbach was not satisfied. He was determined to create a stronger benzodiazepine with even fewer side effects. Valium, from the Latin *valere*, "health," was unveiled in 1963, followed by several others. (I have Sternbach to thank for my Klonopin.) In 1968, Librium, the most frequently prescribed medication in the United States, was dethroned by Valium. From 1968 to 1981, Valium was the most popular drug in the Western world.

By the late 1960s, the market for tranquilizers was overwhelmingly composed of women. A 1968 study, for example, found that women were twice as likely as men to use them. In the 1970s, women made up two-thirds of tranquilizer users. A Valium ad published in 1970 in the *Archives of General Psychiatry* introduces a woman named Jan, "35, single, and psychoneurotic." "You probably see many Jans in your practice," the ad tells doctors. "The unmarried with low self-esteem. Jan never found a man to measure up to her father. Valium (diazepam) can be a useful adjunct in the therapy of the tense, over anxious patient who has a neurotic sense of failure, guilt or loss."

It was not long, however, until benzodiazepines were revealed to have a dark side. Throughout the 1970s, scientific research and stories mounted—in complaints to the FDA and articles in the press—of benzo addiction and patients who suffered awful side effects when going off the drugs. In 1978, former first lady Betty Ford went to rehab for her addiction to alcohol and medications, including Valium. The following year Barbara Gordon released a memoir, *I'm Dancing As Fast As I Can*, about her panic disorder and her horrific withdrawal from Valium. In 1979, Senator Edward Kennedy convened Senate hearings on the dangers of benzodiazepines. Federal and state regulations were changed to rein in refills of benzos and stiffen the penalties for illegal use. Sales slid: Valium prescriptions fell from 61.3 million in 1975 to 33.6 million in 1980. Some people returned to older, even more dangerous drugs, like barbiturates, for relief.

Meanwhile pharmaceutical companies kept churning out new drugs. In 1981, Upjohn introduced Xanax, touting it as safer than Valium, in part because of its shorter half-life. Xanax also benefited from being FDA-approved for panic disorder, which *DSM*-III had recognized as a separate disorder a year earlier. Soon sales of Xanax overtook those of Valium.

Then came the SSRIs. While the drugs, including Prozac, Paxil, and Zoloft, were initially approved for depression, manufacturers quickly sponsored trials showcasing the drugs' efficacy in treating anxiety, too. By 1998, major organizations like the American Psychiatric Association began recommending the SSRIs as first-line medications for anxiety disorders.

In the 1990s, consumer advertising of prescription drugs exploded. GlaxoSmithKline won FDA approval for Paxil as a treatment for social anxiety disorder in 1999. The company spent more than $92 million in one year on a marketing campaign to educate consumers about the disorder and sell them on the new drug to treat it. "Imagine Being Allergic to People," ads said. One TV spot featured a businessman leaning against a wall in despair; a student watching TV alone, bathed in blue light; and a woman gazing forlornly out a window. After Paxil, needless to say, the sun was always shining. The student is playing football with friends and graduating from college. The woman is smiling and joining a party. The businessman is being feted at a dinner while his father smiles proudly. "Paxil, Your Life Is Waiting," the ad proclaimed.

In recent years, traditional pharmaceutical companies have scaled back their development of drugs for psychiatric illnesses. In 2009, GlaxoSmithKline said it was shutting down its neuroscientific research into depression and pain. That same year AstraZeneca said it would stop trying to develop medications for anxiety, depression, schizophrenia, and bipolar disorder. With so many patients getting little relief from current drugs, the market—and potential profits—for new medicines for anxiety and depression would seem to be huge. So why the retreat?

It turns out that new psychiatric drugs take a lot more time and money to bring to market than other medications, for a number of reasons. Symptoms of mental illness can be incredibly heterogeneous, and many people have more than one disorder. Early scientific work is usually done on animals such as rats, but rat brains do not mirror the complexity of the human mind. Also, despite advances in imaging, the human brain usually can't be directly observed. In cancer research, for example, scientists can work directly on tumor cells removed from living patients. No one, thankfully, is going to be slicing into an anxious person's brain.

The next hurdle after development is gaining approval from the FDA. Between 1993 and 2004, however, only 8 percent of medicines developed for the central nervous system passed muster. Potential psychiatric drugs have sometimes failed because of toxic side effects, but usually they've been doomed because they didn't work well enough.

A few years ago scientists and drug companies thought they

were on the verge of a breakthrough. A new class of medications for patients with depression and a variety of anxiety disorders was being studied in large-scale clinical trials. The drugs worked completely differently from existing ones, offering hope to people who didn't respond to SSRIs and other available antidepressants. The new medications acted on a receptor in the brain named corticotropin-releasing factor (CRF) receptor 1. CRF is an amino acid peptide that is involved in the body's response to stress: It activates the HPA axis and spurs the release of adrenocorticotropic hormone (ACTH), kicking off the fight-or-flight response. It made sense that blocking the CRF1 receptor could alleviate anxiety, and in a series of animal studies, it seemed to do just that. Rats injected with the CRF1 antagonists spent more time in open spaces, froze less during fear conditioning, and when subjected to shocks, were less likely to try to bury themselves in the wood shavings and fluffy bedding in their cages.

Early studies with people were encouraging, too. But in larger trials, the kind needed to secure FDA approval and bring the medications to market, the drugs faltered. One medication, saddled with the name Pexacerfont, was no better at treating GAD than a placebo. Another, Verucerfont, didn't help patients with depression. Two others were abandoned when they were found to dangerously raise the levels of subjects' liver enzymes.

The book isn't completely closed on CRF1 antagonists. Some scientists think that perhaps the drugs may be better suited to PTSD, panic disorder, and alcohol and drug addiction. In these disorders, anxiety spikes and dips as opposed to being more chronic, as with GAD.

In the hope of jump-starting drug development, the NIMH launched a program dubbed "Fast-Fail." The federal government is funding small trials to test new compounds as well as existing drugs that scientists think could be repurposed for use in psychiatric illnesses. Instead of starting with studies in animals, Fast-Fail will go straight to human trials.

Researchers are also exploring medications that might boost the efficacy of nondrug therapies. In the early 1990s, Michael Davis (the same neuroscientist who had been engaged in a friendly competition with Joe LeDoux, whom we met in chapter 1), then at Yale, found that NMDA (N-methyl-D-aspartate) receptors were critical for extinction, which some scientists believe underlies exposure therapy. NMDA receptors are activated when glutamate, the main excitatory neurotransmitter in the brain, binds to them. In a pivotal study, Davis and colleagues discovered that when they injected an NMDA antagonist, which blocked the receptor's activity, into the amygdalae of rats, extinction learning didn't occur. The rats continued to freeze and startle even when there was no shock.

If blocking NMDA activity prevented learning, then scientists theorized that perhaps something that enhanced NMDA activity would propel learning, recalls Kerry Ressler, a neuroscientist who was a fellow in Davis's lab at the time. The group considered a host of NMDA agonists and partial agonists and quickly zeroed in on D-cycloserine (DCS). Long used to treat tuberculosis, the drug was safe for humans. At low doses, it sticks to the NMDA receptor, changes its shape, and allows more calcium into the cells so that "a little bit more learning happens," says Stefan Hofmann of Boston University.

In 2002, Davis, Ressler, and colleagues published their first study using DCS in rats. They found that injections of DCS indeed enhanced extinction learning. The higher the dose, the greater the effect.

Davis and Ressler then teamed up with Barbara Rothbaum, a pioneer in using virtual reality to treat psychiatric disorders, to test the drug in people with a fear of heights (acrophobia). Two to four hours before each of two exposure sessions, the researchers gave one group DCS and another a placebo. The participants then donned a virtual reality helmet and spent thirty-five to forty-five minutes in a simulated glass elevator gazing over a railing. Every few minutes, the virtual elevator rose. The subjects could control how high it went. After two sessions, the people who got DCS were "much better, as if they'd had six or seven sessions [of exposure therapy] relative to placebo," says Ressler. The improvement was evident even three months later, when researchers put the participants through a battery of tests. Those who had taken DCS said their fear of heights was dramatically diminished. And compared to those who had gotten the placebo, they willingly exposed themselves to heights more readily in their daily life.

When Davis presented preliminary findings of the study during a NIMH meeting on extinction learning, Hofmann was in the room. "Everybody was speechless," he recalled. A drug that dramatically boosted the effectiveness of exposure therapy could slash the cost of treatment and transform the lives of patients. Many people drop out of therapy after just a few sessions because they find it too difficult or don't see the benefits. DCS may bring relief to those people, too.

Hofmann went back to Boston and started a trial with his social anxiety disorder patients. Other scientists tested DCS in panic disorder, PTSD, and obsessive-compulsive disorder (OCD). Davis and Ressler also obtained a patent for the use of DCS in psychotherapy.

But although the results of the early trials were promising, later studies were disappointing. In one trial, DCS failed to help OCD patients. A larger study of people with social anxiety disorder found that DCS sped up improvement with exposure therapy, without boosting the rates of treatment response or remission. One study of veterans who returned from Iraq and Afghanistan with PTSD found that those who got DCS fared worse than those who got the placebo.

Hofmann, who had done the trials in social anxiety, tried to make sense of these results. He went back through his data and found that a patient's experience during exposure therapy was critical to whether DCS helped. DCS worked when participants had a "good" exposure, meaning that their fear rose initially then plummeted during the task. It didn't work, however, when people had a "bad" exposure, meaning that their fear didn't fall during the sessions, or fell only slightly. In some cases, the anxiety got worse with DCS. The timing and dosing of DCS is critical to its efficacy as well. If given in too big of a dose or too long before exposure therapy, it is less likely to work. Now Hofmann is experimenting with administering DCS after therapy, rather than before, and only to patients who had a "good" session.

Scientists are studying other substances that, like DCS, seem to act as cognitive enhancers when combined with therapy. Yohimbine is derived from the bark of a tree typically found in parts of central and western Africa. (It is also used for erectile dysfunction and weight loss.) In a few small trials, it has been found to reduce fear in patients who have undergone exposure therapy. Hydrocortisone, better known as an anti-itch cream, has been shown to boost fear extinction in people with a spider phobia when used in pill form before exposure therapy.

Another promising drug is ketamine, most commonly used as an anesthetic but also known as the street drug Special K, which acts on NMDA receptors as well. Ketamine has been shown to relieve symptoms of depression within hours, and there have already been small positive trials with PTSD and OCD patients. A few scientists are even starting to look at MDMA, better known as ecstasy, as a way to augment treatment, particularly for PTSD. The euphoria and disinhibition the drug induces seem to help people process terrifying memories. In a few small studies, people have taken MDMA and then had daylong therapy sessions. In a small study with PTSD patients, two MDMA-enhanced therapy sessions were much more effective than a placebo, and the benefit was still evident three years later.

Almost as fraught as the decision to go on psychiatric medication is the decision to go off it. There are no fixed rules for when to stop. Psychiatrists I've spoken to generally suggest that people with anxiety disorders stay on an SSRI for at least one year after their anxiety has remitted. That gives patients time to get through one full cycle of stressors: the holidays, the anniversary of a divorce or the death of a loved one, the start of their children's school year. After that "you almost have a muscle memory" of how to handle those experiences without anxiety exerting control, says Beth Salcedo, a psychiatrist in Washington, D.C. She also recommends doing a course of CBT either before or while going off medication.

I had planned to stop taking my daily 5 milligrams of Lexapro almost a year ago, after I finished the first draft of this book. But then I had to write a second draft. And a third. I was also juggling the book writing with my job at the *Journal*. My daughter started a new school. My father's health faltered. Our bank balances dipped. And my to-do list seemed endless. Little things—

like picking up a birthday present or deciding what to make for
dinner—made me panicky.

I simply felt too stressed out. The waters of my life were too
choppy to travel without my chemical life vest. I kept refilling my
prescription.

Stopping an SSRI is always a leap of faith. Without that excess
serotonin floating around my synapses, will I fall apart? And if I
do, and I need to reach for medication again, will it work? There
is no guarantee.

6

COLD CALLS, AIRPLANES, AND INDECISION
ANXIETY AT WORK AND ON THE ROAD

It may seem strange that I've chosen to be a reporter, a profession characterized by deadlines, not to mention one that requires cold-calling sometimes hostile strangers. My job often makes me anxious. During my years covering technology news, I lived in fear of being beaten on a story by competitors. I opened the *New York Times* with dread.

But this kind of anxiety is rooted in reality. And it has helped me to cope with the amorphous anxiety that doesn't seem to have a good reason.

Looking through the data on anxiety disorders and the workplace, I feel extraordinarily lucky. Many people don't fare so well. A 2005 study by Australian researchers found that a staggering 47 percent of those aged fifteen to sixty-four with anxiety disorders were not working. By comparison, about 20 percent of those in a control group (people without disabilities or chronic health problems) weren't in the labor force. People with anxiety disorders were also more likely to work from home, to be self-employed, or to be employed by the government. They also more often said that they "accomplished less" and "took less care than usual" in their jobs during the previous month.

Maybe that study is an outlier. While both anxiety disorders and depression are associated with short-term and long-term absences from work, once people get better, only past depression is still linked to absenteeism. After people's anxiety disorders remit, they don't miss more work than healthy people do. (Of course, many people suffer from both depression and anxiety.)

This reality is reflected in data on disability benefits. Of the more than ten million Americans receiving disability benefits in 2015, less than 3 percent got them because of an anxiety disorder, whereas about 14 percent received them because of mood disorders, and about 29 percent (the biggest chunk by far) for musculoskeletal and connective tissue problems.

In a lot of ways, my work has been like constant exposure therapy. I've used it to get close to what scares me the most: illness, madness, and death. I've sought out stories about hospice patients and spent many hours with the dying. There have been ridiculous episodes, too: me, working on a story about carbon monoxide poisoning, conducting an interview with my head between my knees. It was via phone, thankfully. During the conversation, I could have sworn that I felt every symptom the doctor I was talking to described.

When I was younger, anxiety sometimes flat-out crippled my ability to work. In second grade that took the form of those math-fueled panic attacks. In college, I had to drop classes when I had my breakdown and relapse. The only reason I was able to graduate on time was because I took a couple of classes during the summer and received college credit for AP courses I'd taken in high school.

Anxiety has also had subtler, more insidious effects on my work. During my school years, it fueled procrastination. For me, procrastination seems tied up with perfectionism. Scientists define perfectionism as the will to achieve high standards combined with excessive self-criticism. Perfectionists expect, well, perfection.

Anything less won't do. In their minds, a mistake equals failure. Perfectionists also tend to doubt their actions.

It isn't tough to see similarities between perfectionism and anxiety: the self-doubt, the self-criticism, the fears of catastrophe. Indeed, people with panic disorder, OCD, and social phobia all score higher on certain measures of perfectionist thinking than do people without those disorders. Research shows, however, that anxiety is linked to some aspects of perfectionism but not others. Specifically, while anxious people are concerned about mistakes and doubt their actions, they don't necessarily have superhigh personal standards. Worriers actually tend to lower their standards when stressed out. It isn't that they want to be the best. They just don't want to mess up.

Perfectionism, in my case, is really just the fear of screwing up. And until I get started on something, I can't fail at it. This is not a useful way to go about life.

In eighth grade, my history class had a series of assignments due. I didn't turn them in on time. I don't think I had even started the project by the deadline. A day went by. Then two. Then a week. Every morning I said I would start the assignment, and every morning I made some excuse to myself. I didn't yet know how to tackle it. I was too tired. I was too anxious. I was too ashamed. I didn't tell my parents about my predicament or ask my teacher for an extension. Instead, I quickly slunk out of class each day to avoid an awkward encounter.

One day at the end of class, the teacher announced that he would leave his grade book open on his desk and we could all take a look to see how our projects had fared. "There were a handful of A's," he said. "And one F." My humiliation was on display for the entire class. As my fellow students crowded around his desk, I busied myself putting my books in my backpack. My heart raced, and hot shame rushed to my cheeks. There was no need for me to join the scrum.

As my friend Mark walked by, he said with a bewildered shake of his head, "Congratulations. You got an F."

I wish I could say that this experience cured my problem, but I continued to struggle with it. Although I never outright didn't do an assignment again, I became a crammer, an extreme deadline student. I finished papers in the car on the way to school, desperately trying to steady a shaking pen as my mother drove up the steep hill that was home to Danbury High. I was a good, but not stellar, student, earning A's and B's.

Procrastination is often defined as voluntarily delaying action despite the knowledge of future negative consequences. A review of more than two hundred journal articles and other scientific sources found that one feature of anxiety—fear of failure—was slightly associated with procrastination. And one aspect of perfectionism—the belief that loved ones have high standards for you—was tied to procrastination. Procrastination was much more strongly linked, however, with impulsiveness. Depression also fueled procrastination.

Maybe I was just a typical student. After all, about 75 percent of college students say they are procrastinators. Half say their procrastination is chronic and problematic. Students say they spend about one-third of their day procrastinating (by, say, sleeping and eating instead of studying). Fortunately, procrastination tends to wane with age: Only about 15 to 20 percent of adults say they chronically procrastinate.

Indeed, procrastination became much less of an issue when I hit the working world. Letting myself down was one thing. But letting other people down—bosses, colleagues—was quite another. I couldn't do it.

I still am a deadline writer. I turn in my stories for the *Journal* pretty much exactly when they're due. I need the urgency of a deadline, the clock ticking down, the specter of a disappointed editor or a blank space in the paper's lineup of stories. It is a duel between anxieties, and only my fears of judgment or failure surmount my fears of writing imperfect words and clumsy sentences.

I've loved reading, writing, telling, and hearing stories since I was a child. I was that kid who always had her nose in a book, oblivious to the world. My mother would call from the kitchen, summoning me to get ready for school, to come for dinner, her voice rising until finally I'd tear myself away from *A Wrinkle in Time* or the latest *Sweet Valley High* and answer her with a mumbled monosyllable. I'd walk down hallways holding a book in front of me, once slamming into a concrete pole at the Danbury Fair Mall. My childhood best friend, Kate, and I would call each other and say, "Want to come over and read?" Our play dates consisted of both of us splayed on a sofa, books in hand and boxes of cookies within reach.

I wrote earnestly in diaries, thrived in English classes, and scribbled short stories and poems, but I knew nothing about journalism. Some of my *Wall Street Journal* colleagues idolized Woodward and Bernstein and had quoted *All the President's Men* in junior high. I didn't regularly read a newspaper until college.

By the time of college graduation, my ambitions were still fuzzy. I had a degree in political science and wanted to do something with "writing" and "politics," but what? Sidelined by anxiety, unpreparedness, and the need to earn money, my résumé was skimpy. No fancy internships in D.C. or New York, let alone overseas—just babysitting and waitressing, summers working at a day care center, and filing and answering phones in offices.

My good friend Vanessa was already living in D.C. and had an extra bedroom. It was 1992, and a presidential campaign was going on. That was good enough for me. I piled my books, sorority sweatshirts, and diploma into my red Honda Civic and drove from Ann Arbor to Washington, fending off panic attacks all through Ohio, Pennsylvania, and into Maryland. I'd pull over at rest stops and call my dad from roadside pay phones, crying over the din of eighteen-wheelers. "I'm so scared. I can't do this," I'd say. He'd give me pep talks. "Just breathe. You're doing great," he'd say. I'd be bolstered enough to get back in the driver's seat for another half hour, maybe an hour. And then I'd find another pay phone. The eight-hour drive took me more than fifteen hours.

I found an internship in an office that handled direct mail for political campaigns—those pamphlets of smiling candidates and their families and their promises that flood people's mailboxes at election time. Through connections I made there, I landed a job in the press office for Senator Harris Wofford, an inspiring liberal Democrat from Pennsylvania who had advised Martin Luther King, Jr., and JFK and cofounded the Peace Corps. I worked twelve-hour days, writing press releases and speeches and traveling to little towns all over Pennsylvania—meetings with former steelworkers in Johnstown, rallies with teachers in Altoona. I went to one of Bill Clinton's inaugural balls and watched Bill and Hillary groove to Fleetwood Mac. (You couldn't escape "Don't Stop" during the campaign.) I rode the underground train that whisked senators from their office buildings to the Capitol: Yes, that was Ted Kennedy sitting across from me. In this age of political cynicism, my excitement might sound ridiculous and naïve. But I was twenty-two, and those were my words being quoted in newspapers, my words—one exhilarating time—the senator was speaking on the Senate floor.

I wrote constantly. I loved to experiment with words and phrases, loved the challenge of crafting something clear and compelling. But I quickly realized a truth about political writing. You have to cover the same topics—using essentially the same words—over and over again. It's called "being on message." I was also becoming more intrigued by journalism. I spoke to reporters every day as part of my job. They called for comments from Senator Wofford. I met them at political events in Pennsylvania and saw their bylines in newspapers—the *Pittsburgh Post-Gazette*, the *Harrisburg Patriot-News*. They jumped from topic to topic: They might write about health care reform one day, the State of the Union Address the next. But what really awed me was the simple fact that if they were curious about something—anything—they could call someone on the phone, and most likely that person would talk to them. A job where you got to satisfy an insatiable curiosity and write was, I decided, the job for me.

In November 1994, Senator Wofford was voted out of office, and I was out of a job. I decided to look for a journalism job in earnest. There was just one problem: I had zero experience. I had written reams of press releases and speeches, but I'd never written a news article. Blogs barely existed. Serendipity arrived in the form of a phone call. My boss from Wofford's office had a friend who was an executive at the *Wall Street Journal* in New York. He was looking for an assistant. The job wouldn't be glamorous. I would be answering phones and picking up faxes. I'd even have to take a pay cut. But I'd at least be in the same building with people who were doing the jobs I wanted. Maybe I would get an opportunity to write.

I was offered the job and moved to New York two weeks later. I rented a U-Haul with the boyfriend I was leaving back in D.C., and we argued the entire trip there. I didn't know anyone in New York and had no place to live, so I bounced around on the couches at friends' parents' places until I found a room in Chelsea. My new roommates were a New England prep school boy turned composer and a drugged-out Minnesota girl who worked in a SoHo shop during the day and danced on a box at the Limelight nightclub at night. She often got home just as I was waking to get ready for work.

In many ways, anxiety has fueled my work. Fear of hurting my career was what finally drove me to take medication in my twenties. In college, I could drop classes and make up tests, but there are no time-outs in the working world. Fear of messing up is what drives me to triple-check that spelling and do one last interview. Many reporters are dilettantes, bouncing between disparate topics. We often have to learn new subjects quickly, synthesize the information, and make it understandable to readers. Mistakes are all too easy to make. (For one of my first feature stories as a cub reporter, I thought someone I interviewed had said his name was Kurt. Alas, it was Knut.) Twitter and Facebook have amplified the reach of our stories—but social media also means that a screw-up can be very public. Insecurity and paranoia can be useful qualities.

Anxiety has made me braver and more tenacious. Fear of not getting the story has overridden my other anxieties—about rejection, about bothering people. One story in particular sticks with me. I was still an administrative assistant at the *Journal*, writing stories after my other duties were done, when an editor gave me an idea for an article. His Sunday *New York Times* had included a packet of salad dressing, a promotional giveaway. But the weight of the paper slamming against his front porch had caused the packet to burst, leaving his paper dripping with dressing. Maybe, he said, there was a story in this advertising message gone awry.

I called the circulation department at the *Times*, and a clerk confirmed that the exploding dressing was not an isolated incident. She herself had received several complaints. Now I just needed to find a subscriber with a sticky paper. With the help of our librarian, I got a list of addresses and phone numbers of people who lived near the editor. The salad dressing promotion had gone only to certain subscribers, so I figured the editor's neighbors were likely suspects. Then I proceeded to cold-call strangers, during dinnertime.

"Do you get the *New York Times*?" I asked.

"Did you get a package of salad dressing in your paper last Sunday?"

"Did it explode?"

I was nervous. I knew how absurd this sounded. As I dialed, my hands shook, and my stomach did flip-flops. I recalled prank calls that friends and I had made during preteen slumber parties: "Is your refrigerator running? You better go get it," we'd giggle.

For four hours, I was hung up on and yelled at. Finally, at nearly nine p.m., someone said yes. After I hung up the phone, I did a little dance in my chair.

My story ran on May 7, 1996. "Greg Kauger would like to try the new Hellmann's salad dressing. If only he could scrape it off his newspaper," it began. "Mr. Kauger, of Short Hills, New Jersey, was among the lucky recipients of 170,000 packets of Hellmann's salad dressing tucked into *New York Times* home deliveries last week. And one of the unlucky ones whose samples exploded when the paper landed on the driveway."

Psychologists have long asserted that a certain amount of anxiety can be helpful. More than a century ago, in 1908, the Harvard psychologists Robert Yerkes and John Dodson published the results of an experiment showing that performance on a difficult task is enhanced by anxiety (often referred to as arousal by researchers) but only up to a certain point. Too much anxiety causes performance to suffer. The so-called Yerkes-Dodson law is portrayed as a bell-shaped curve: As arousal increases, so does performance. Until it hits the peak, that is. If arousal continues to rise beyond this point, performance slides.

Yerkes and Dodson's experiments were with mice, but a range of studies in people has supported their conclusions, finding that memory and learning are best achieved when the levels of stress hormones are neither too high nor too low.

But the relationship between anxiety and success remains murky. Some scientific studies show that anxiety interferes with achievement. Others show the opposite. A study of beginning nursing students in Canada, for example, found that those who had more anxious temperaments had higher first-semester grade point averages.

There's an enduring stereotype of the addled, anxious intellectual, but the research into the relationship between anxiety and intelligence is also quite contradictory. Canadian researchers, for example, have found that people who worry and ruminate have higher scores on a verbal intelligence test. Those who tend to process past social events, however—a hallmark of social anxiety disorder—score lower on a test of nonverbal intelligence. A small 2012 study looked at the intelligence of people with GAD compared with controls. Among GAD patients, those with the most severe symptoms had the highest IQs. But among the controls, those with the least anxiety had the highest IQs. The researchers argue that this may make evolutionary sense. Society needs smart, relaxed people, but it needs intelligent, high-strung ones, too.

The high-strung people are the sentinels, says Israeli psychologist Tsachi Ein-Dor, the ones constantly scanning the horizon for danger. They'll sound a warning or mobilize a retreat, thus saving the hides of their more Zen-like neighbors. Ein-Dor and his colleague Orgad Tal conducted an experiment that revealed the role of the sentinel in action. First, the scientists had the subjects fill out surveys that assessed various psychological measures. The subjects, eighty undergraduate students, were then told that they would be rating how much they liked a series of artworks displayed on a computer screen. Each subject was given instructions and left alone in a room with the computer. After a few minutes, the subject was prompted to press "okay." Then a series of frantic error messages flashed on the screen, warning of a virus and stating that the files on the computer's hard drive were being erased. When the subject told a study staffer—a trained actress in on the ruse—about the virus, the staffer pretended to panic and told the subject to go get help from another employee.

During their trek to get help, the subjects encountered several obstacles. A person asked them to complete a survey. Someone else asked for help photocopying a document. Another person dropped a big pile of papers at their feet. This series of events was intended to test how well subjects remained focused on the original goal: to deliver the news about the dangerous computer virus. The researchers found that subjects who scored higher on measures of anxiety were less likely to let themselves be delayed by the obstacles (i.e., they didn't take the survey or help pick up papers). Anxious people were "eager to spread the word of a troubling, socially threatening incident, a tendency that, in many real world situations, might save others from serious threat," the researchers wrote.

It takes a lot of creativity to envision vivid catastrophes and spin doomsday narratives. Worriers often fashion elaborate contingency plans to avoid disaster. They may create cover stories to hide their anxiety. It isn't hard to see that this requires some smarts.

. . .

For many of my years at the *Journal*, our offices were in the World Financial Center, a warren of buildings in Manhattan's financial district directly across the street from the twin towers of the World Trade Center. On the morning of September 11, 2001, I was leaving for work, heading down the stairs of the Cobble Hill, Brooklyn, brownstone where I rented an apartment on the top floor. My landlords, a couple of documentary filmmakers, were heading up the stairs, looking for me.

"Where are you going?" the woman asked.

"To work," I said.

"Haven't you heard the news?" the man asked. "A plane crashed into the Trade Center. You can probably see it from your window."

The three of us raced up the stairs to my apartment. Indeed, the twin towers were perfectly visible from my living room window on that bright, clear day. Thick gray smoke encircled both towers.

I flipped on the television. The next half hour or so was surreal; our heads whipped back and forth between the news coverage and the real thing. Then we heard a rumble, like slow rolling thunder, and one of the towers crumbled, the whole edifice sliding down with a billowing roar. The newscaster's voice turned shrill, unbelieving. It was a weekday morning, and those buildings were filled with offices. How many hundreds, thousands were dead? Then the second tower fell.

I received three phone calls in quick succession. My mother. My ex-boyfriend Alan, phoning from Mexico City. And a new guy I was dating, a photojournalist named Brad who lived in Manhattan, on the Upper West Side. He was already heading downtown on his bicycle to see what he could shoot.

Brad's phone call jarred me. I was a journalist, too, and here was a huge, tragic story. There was actually something I could do. So why the hell was I still sitting in my apartment?

My BlackBerry was buzzing nonstop with emails from my colleagues in the *Journal*'s technology group. I covered wireless telecommunications. Our team started planning stories on how New York's technological infrastructure was holding up during the crisis. It was clear that cell phone service was crippled. I hadn't been able to make a call in hours. I grabbed a notebook and a pen and headed outside.

By then the sky had darkened. The air around me was thick with smoke, ash, and millions of tiny bits of paper. The winds had blown Trade Center debris across the East River and over to Brooklyn. I ran back inside to grab an old T-shirt to cover my face, then walked toward the Brooklyn Bridge. I interviewed a few people lined up at pay phones, asking them when they lost cell phone service and who they had been calling. Then, approaching the bridge, I saw a couple of dazed people covered in gray soot. Then tens more. The Brooklyn Bridge, usually a joyful, cacophonous parade of cyclists, stroller-pushing locals, and tourists, was now a solemn march away from destruction. Volunteers handed out cups of water. One man yelled at me, "You're walking the wrong way." The twin towers were now just a smoky blot on the Manhattan skyline.

I didn't get far into Manhattan. By then police and firefighters had cordoned off the Trade Center site and the surrounding blocks. So I walked back to my apartment, wrote up my interviews, and sent them to my editor. Only hours later did I find out that the *Journal*'s offices were now a toxic crime scene. Weeks later we would learn that more than 2,600 people died in the towers that day.

In the days after the towers fell, I threw myself into work. I wrote a story about New Yorkers who had heard from old lovers, schoolteachers, and even therapists on 9/11. I wrote another about local businesses that weren't sure whether they should remove the Trade Center from their logos. I wrote about residents of the financial district who, having lost access to their apartments, were being put up in fancy boutique hotels. One man had hotel employees remove a picture above the bed that reminded him of the desperate men and women he had seen jumping from the burning towers.

We set up a temporary newsroom in SoHo, and I was asked to join a group of reporters who would continue writing about the aftermath of 9/11. One of my first assignments was to cover the anthrax attacks in New Jersey. I can't think of a story more tailor-made to unhinge an anxious person: an unknown assailant sending white powder through the mail that could be lethal when inhaled.

I spent several days camped out front of one of the target post offices in Trenton in a scrum of other reporters. Periodically a spokesman would appear to deliver a bit of news. There was a 7-Eleven across the street, and one day I picked up a bottle of orange Gatorade, took a swig, and put the rest in my purse. I must not have closed the cap securely because the bottle leaked, sending sticky liquid all over the lip balms, crumpled receipts, and other detritus at the bottom of my bag. And my cell phone. When I pulled it out, it was drenched and dead. A little wave of orange sloshed back and forth within the display like a mini lava lamp. To file my story that day, I had to run back and forth across the busy road between the post office and a pay phone, dictating the words to my editor in New York.

Sometimes I spent the night at a hotel in New Jersey, but usually I'd drive the ninety minutes or so back to my apartment in Brooklyn. I wanted to see Brad. He was also becoming irritated by my constant absence. I'd spend the night in Brooklyn or at Brad's apartment and then drive back to Trenton in my rental car in the morning.

The stresses were mounting. Brad. The driving. Long hours pursuing stories. Anthrax.

It is late at night, after eleven p.m., and I'm driving from Trenton to my hotel in a nearby town after a long day of reporting, when I start to feel breathless. A slight pressure builds in my chest. My heart beats quickly. Spots dance in front of my eyes. My grip on the steering wheel tightens.

I try to breathe slowly, deeply. *You're just having a panic attack,* I say to myself. I keep driving down the dark highway, but the symptoms are getting worse. My hands sweat. The edges of my vision are fuzzy. Every muscle tenses. Then I see a sign with a capital H and an arrow. There's a hospital nearby.

I drive straight to the emergency room, leave the car in the driveway, and race up to the triage nurse on duty. "I'm a journalist, and I've been writing about anthrax," I say in a rush. "I've been at the post office where the letters came through, the ones with anthrax in them. I'm scared that I could have it."

"You think you have anthrax?" the nurse says, looking alarmed. "I'm sorry, but you'll have to wait outside. Someone will meet you there."

I'm hustled out of the hospital and dumped in the driveway. Standing there alone, bathed in the spotlight of the red and white EMERGENCY ROOM sign, I start to feel ridiculous. I haven't actually been inside the post office. I haven't touched any anthrax-laced letters. I haven't touched anyone who has touched an anthrax-laced letter. There's really no way I could have contracted it. I'm just having a panic attack about the very *idea* of having anthrax.

A few minutes later an ambulance appears, and a guy in an orange hazmat suit jumps out. I sheepishly explain that I've been reporting a story on anthrax but don't have it myself. The man gets back in, and the ambulance drives away.

After that I hit a wall. I was working on a feature story about a small-town New Jersey mayor who had become an unlikely force in the anthrax attack response. It was slated for page one, for the coveted "A-hed" center column. (The name *A-hed* has to do with the stars and dashes around the headline.) The A-hed and the "leders" were the most sought-after slots in the paper, reserved for the best stories, and competition was fierce. I had only a couple of days to turn the story around.

For the first time in my career, I couldn't do it. When I sat down to write, I felt strangely lost. I couldn't find my focus, couldn't see how the story should unfold. I'd write a sentence, then delete it, the blinking cursor a pulsing reproach. With the deadline bearing down at me, I panicked and strung together random vignettes. I felt nauseous as I hit the send button on the email to my editor.

It wasn't a surprise when she called, sounding disappointed and confused. I was usually a reliable reporter and writer. "Try it again," she said.

I did. And again I failed. The story was killed.

When my anxiety soars, I have a hard time concentrating. My mind overflows with worries, leaving scant room for information of the nondoomsday variety. For decades, psychologists have theorized that anxiety hijacks some of the brain's cognitive capacity, even in people without full-blown anxiety disorders. The idea is that there's a battle of resources and that worry gobbles up prime real estate. If your attention is focused on potential threats, you have fewer resources to devote to your goal—whether it is getting your point across in a meeting with the boss or, in my case, writing a story about a New Jersey mayor.

Research has not always borne out these theories, however. In fact, the research into anxiety's effects on cognition is mixed and inconclusive. We know that in people with anxiety disorders, planning is generally unaffected. However, they show deficits in spatial navigation and working memory (short-term memory that allows us to process and manipulate information). Working memory is what lets us follow the thread of a conversation and tally a running bar tab. It is critical for reasoning and decision making.

For those without disorders, new research is showing that situational anxiety—the kind many of us feel before a big presentation—may actually enhance working memory when the task is difficult. In a 2016 study, researchers at the NIMH had thirty people with GAD and thirty people in a control group do a working memory task called the "n-back." The task has several versions. In the 1-back, people are given a string of numbers and have to indicate if the one they are seeing is the same as or different from the number just before. In the 2-back, they need to remember the number two places before. As you can imagine, the 1-back is easy and the 3-back is quite difficult. To induce anxiety, subjects are sometimes told they might receive a shock to the wrist. At other times, participants are told that they are safe and that no shock is forthcoming.

In the study, the healthy controls did more poorly during the 1-back and 2-back when they were threatened with a shock. But during the tougher 3-back task, anxiety actually helped them do better. In the GAD patients, however, the threat of shock disrupted working memory whether the task was easy or hard. Another study by the same NIMH research group had people with GAD, social anxiety disorder, and healthy controls do the same n-back task while in an fMRI scanner. The anxious subjects had a markedly different pattern of brain activity than the nonanxious ones, which could explain the difference in performance: They had less activation of the dorsolateral prefrontal cortex. And the wonky brain activity in those subjects was similar whether they were threatened with shocks or not.

The anxiety prone, however, may not be doomed to suffer lack-luster performance. They may not even have to learn to jettison the anxiety. Instead, a simple mind trick could help.

You simply tell yourself that you're excited.

It sounds absurd, but a series of studies by Alison Wood Brooks, an assistant professor at Harvard Business School, has found that when people think of their anxiety as excitement, they perform better on a range of tasks. (True, the subjects in Wood Brooks's studies weren't screened for full-blown anxiety disorders, so it is unclear how well the tactic would work for those of us whose amygdalae are already on overdrive.) Wood Brooks put young people in a variety of stressful situations. For example, some had to sing Journey's "Don't Stop Believin'" in front of a researcher. To ratchet up their anxiety, they were told that they were performing in front of a karaoke expert and would be paid based on how well they did.

In the singing study, some of the participants went right to the task. Others were told to first say "I am anxious" and to try to believe it. A third group was prompted to say "I am excited." It turns out that the participants who said "I am excited" before their performances were better at matching the pitch, tempo, and volume of the song than those in the other two groups. They also said they felt more excited than the other two groups. It wasn't that the excited group wasn't on edge: They reported that they felt as anxious as everyone else, and their heart rates were just as elevated. But simply reframing that anxiety as excitement made them sing better.

Wood Brooks got similar results when she had people give a speech and take a challenging math test. The subjects who were prompted to reappraise their anxiety as excitement scored better on the test and were judged to be more persuasive and confident speakers. In these experiments, she had some participants try to relax by stating "I am calm" before the speech task and "Try to remain calm" before the math task. But doing that didn't seem to help. Wood Brooks conjectures that it is a lot harder to transform anxiety into tranquillity than it is to convert it to excitement. With the former, you have to fight anxiety's effect on the body—the jacked-up heart rate, the butterflies in the stomach—whereas in the latter you have only to change your attitude. She calls it moving from a threat mind-set to an opportunity mind-set.

Thankfully, my blown front-page story was not the start of a professional downward slide. Back in New York, I redeemed myself with a string of solid articles. After another few months, the special post-9/11 group was disbanded, and I soon moved over to write about health for our then-new Personal Journal section.

My new assignment seemed both perilous and therapeutic. A lot of my anxieties revolved around illness and death. If I could somehow overcome my fear of death, or even ease it a bit, I told myself, I would not be so captive to my anxiety. I asked myself what it was about death that I feared so much. Was it the pain? The separation from those I love? The physical erasure, the non-being? I mulled it over, on my own and with my therapist, until I realized that I was afraid of the fear itself. When I envisioned death, I saw terror, pain, and breathlessness. I couldn't imagine a peaceful ending.

Death, I thought, would be the ultimate panic attack.

So I started spending time with people who were dying. I volunteered to write stories about aging, Alzheimer's disease, and hospice—a sort of self-imposed exposure therapy. I spent days with hospice programs in Kentucky, Washington, D.C., and California, shadowing nurses as they made home visits. I expected the

patients to be bedridden, vacant, and gaunt, but many were vi-
brant and brimming with life. I met an elderly man with terminal
leukemia who was joyfully planning a trip to visit his nephew in
California. One man told me that he and his wife, both terminally
ill, went to their favorite restaurant every day to eat ice cream sun-
daes. A nurse relayed the story of a woman dying in an inpatient
hospice unit who summoned each of her family members into
the room to tell them what they meant to her. Dying, it seemed,
wasn't only fear and pain. I was awestruck by patients' generosity
in spending even a few moments of their limited time with a nosy
stranger.

Not all the stories I encountered were uplifting. In an inpatient
hospice unit in California, I met a man in his forties dying of
brain cancer. The nurses were tinkering with his medication in an
attempt to control his searing pain. His exhausted wife by his side,
the man was hoping the nurses could lessen the pain enough so he
could achieve his goal of dying at home. In Lexington, Kentucky,
an elderly cancer-stricken man caring for his wife with dementia
sat in an afghan-strewn chair in his cozy living room. "I never
thought dying would take so long," he said sadly. He wanted to
hasten what I desperately feared.

I met another man, just a few years older than me, dying of
ALS. His face was friendly, with the vague handsomeness of a former jock. He could talk and breathe on his own but was otherwise
completely immobile, lying in a hospital bed. Photos on a dresser
showed him well and smiling with friends, a can of beer in his
hand. I couldn't imagine a worse way to die.

Still, seeing dying patients' regret, acceptance, and vitality gave
me a way to work out some of my fears. I even wrote a story during this time entitled "Negotiating the Terms of Your Death,"
about how advances in pain medication and new hospice practices were giving patients more control over how and when they

died. And just a few weeks before I wrote these words, I received an up-close lesson in a good death when my ninety-three-year-old grandmother passed away from kidney failure. She was lucid up until the day before she died, reminding those of us keeping vigil to eat and telling me—completely seriously—that she didn't want to take pain pills because they are "habit forming." *Hell, now's the time to try heroin if you want to, Grandma,* I thought. She was luckier than most: She got progressively sleepier and then just slipped away.

Why hasn't anxiety derailed my career? I've been lucky, I think. I've never had a relapse serious enough to require me to take a leave from work. I love being a journalist. Medication helps me. For years, I took a Klonopin about thirty minutes before every one of my live TV or video appearances, part of my job as a *Journal* writer.

I also built a support system at the office—always clueing in a few close work friends about my anxiety. Having an ally at work, someone I know I can reach out to, eases my anxiety. I don't feel trapped by my panic. I know that there is at least one person I can be authentic with, can be weak with. It is tough enough to get through a panic attack without the pressure of having to fake composure, too.

For several years, Jeff was one of my closest work friends. He was from Baton Rouge and was blunt and folksy. Newspaper reporters are not known for their fashion sense, but Jeff was in another league. He wore ripped, faded jeans and 1980s-era leather boat shoes held together by duct tape. There was a group of us at the *Journal* then, all thirtyish, no kids, most of us single. We'd hang out after work, meeting up at Fox Hounds, a generic Irish bar with cheap beer and greasy food, to swap stories, gossip about the office, and debate the legacies of dead presidents. (Yes, we were geeks.) Even though Jeff was married with a kid and living in suburban New Jersey, he bounced around with us.

Jeff and I worked for the same section. He covered personal finance and was amazingly prolific, churning out stories at a swift pace and writing books at night. He taught me to be more efficient in my reporting. "You only need one interview to make that point," he'd say. I'd run stories by him, asking him his thoughts about this lead or that anecdote.

When I felt a panic attack coming on, I'd email Jeff: "Let's go walking." Then we'd meet in the lobby to head to Starbucks (always decaf for me) or simply to stroll around the Habitrail-like hallways of the *Journal*'s old office complex. He would walk beside me, talking if I wanted to talk. Or we'd just wander silently, stopping if I needed water to wash down a Klonopin. He'd check in every so often. "How are you feeling?" he'd ask. "You doing okay?" It wasn't that he could relate. Jeff never seemed anxious. He was confident about his writing and didn't even seem to have a very strong sense of self-preservation. While living in California in his twenties, he had broken his neck surfing and kept right on riding the waves. But even if my anxiety was foreign to him, he never made me feel silly or absurd.

When Jeff moved back to Louisiana, I was bereft.

For years, I didn't tell my bosses about my anxiety. I knew I worked in a place with sensitive, caring people. I had seen senior editors rally around colleagues with cancer and other illnesses. One editor was very open about his OCD, and it didn't seem to stop his ascent through the company. Still, I was afraid of being judged and labeled. Of being thought less capable, of having my assignments limited. I didn't want my editors feeling like they had to protect my fragile psyche. In fact, I outed myself to my current editors only when I handed them the proposal for this book. And I could never have done that, or written this book, without the confidence of knowing that I had two decades of work experience and a solid track record.

The majority of anxious people conceal their disorders at work. Only one in four people with an anxiety disorder has told their employer, according to a 2006 survey by the Anxiety and Depression Association of America. People cited various reasons: that the disclosure would limit promotions, would be recorded in their employee file, or would be perceived as a lack of willingness to do the job.

They may have good reason to be tight-lipped. The 1990 Americans with Disabilities Act prohibits employers from discriminating against job applicants or employees with a disability, including psychiatric ones. Still, one study published in 1999 revealed that employers were seven times more likely to consider hiring someone who used a wheelchair than someone taking medication for anxiety and depression. A 1996 survey conducted by Mind, a mental health support and advocacy group in Britain, found that more than one-third of the respondents had been fired or forced to resign from a job because of their illness. Then again, these studies are about two decades old—I would like to think that we have become more enlightened since then.

I can tell how much the cultural climate has changed when I interview college students and they let me use their names, pictures, and the details of their illnesses in my stories. Many of these young people are campus mental health activists involved with advocacy groups like Active Minds and the Jed Foundation. They are driven by the desire to lessen the stigma around mental illness. And they are much braver than I am.

I will never know exactly how anxiety has affected my career. Even if I didn't struggle with it, I probably wouldn't have become a war correspondent. I haven't won a Pulitzer. I haven't been a huge risk taker in my work life. But I love what I do and have built a solid, rewarding career.

Anxious people often have a tough time making decisions. Not just the big ones, like should I quit this job or marry that person, but also the small, quotidian ones, like which email should I respond to first? That's because we are excellent at anticipating and visualizing bad outcomes. We also tend to interpret ambiguous information in a negative way, which psychologists call interpretation bias. On top of that, we also tend to hate uncertainty, which means we are apt to choose the safest option. If, that is, we can choose at all.

Indeed, anxious people tend to be risk averse. A number of studies have looked at the link between anxiety, decision making, and so-called risk taking behavior. Several use a psychological research tool known as the Iowa gambling task. Participants play a virtual card game where they are told they can win or lose money. Anxious players tend to make fewer risky moves.

When my husband, Sean, and I were debating where to take our honeymoon, I was editing travel stories for the *Journal*. I had the inside scoop on the hottest new hotels and destinations. Friends often asked me for vacation advice. Still, I could not decide where Sean and I should go. I spent hours on TripAdvisor, reading hundreds of hotel reviews. I bought guidebooks to France, Greece, and Italy. I quizzed nearly everyone I encountered about their favorite destinations.

We went to Ireland.

Now, I love Ireland. But we had gone there exactly one year

earlier. And stayed at the same hotel, where the same Enya CD was on endless repeat in the breakfast room.

Talk about risk averse.

I don't usually have that much trouble making vacation plans. But this was my honeymoon—the trip I'd be asked about for the rest of my life. In my mind, the stakes were too high to gamble. (As if Provence would have been a gamble!)

Some studies indicate that anxious people also make less optimal decisions. In one gambling experiment, for example, highly anxious subjects lost more money than mellower ones. And when choices are clouded with uncertainty, anxious people fare even worse. It looks like the slothful prefrontal cortex activity that is implicated in anxiety disorders may be to blame for these decision-making difficulties. When scientists at the University of Pittsburgh injected an anxiety-inducing drug into rats, the rodents had more trouble with a task that required them to switch between two rules in order to obtain a reward (a tasty sugar pellet) compared to when they were given a placebo. When the anxious rats were making a difficult choice, certain neurons in the dorsomedial prefrontal cortex actually fired more slowly.

So some numbed neurons may have sent me back to Ireland.

It is no surprise that wanderlust and anxiety do not mix well. Unfortunately, I have both. I love to travel, especially in the developing world, and yet I'm terrified of malaria-carrying mosquitoes, typhoid-infused water, and dodgy hospitals. Here are just a few of the places where I've had panic attacks: on the back of a motorbike in Vietnam; in a basement tango *milonga* in Buenos Aires; along the seaside walkway (the Malecón) in Havana; and on a massage table in Nicaragua. And on airplanes. Many, many airplanes. Anxiety is a thief that steals the present moment. So some of my headiest travel experiences—visceral, beautiful moments of strangeness—have been muted, dulled by a steady drumbeat of anxious thoughts. Still, a tenacious desire for these moments propels me on to new spots on the globe.

I did not come from a family who traveled to exotic locales. My childhood vacations mainly consisted of long car rides to southern Illinois to visit family. My sister and I fought vociferously over inches of backseat space. When our fighting got too loud or went on too long, my mother would reach back and swat the air as my sister and I ducked and weaved to elude contact. We were also big campers, heading to various state parks in Pennsylvania and Connecticut. My family did not travel lightly. Our tent was enormous, with a turquoise-and-white-striped roof, like a circus big top, and room for four sleeping bags and my sister's playpen. Our cavernous blue cooler held seemingly endless supplies—from fixings for s'mores to boxed wine for the grown-ups.

In high school, I was incredibly lucky to go on a couple of week-long overseas school trips, one to Greece and another to France and Spain, but those were mostly about kissing my boyfriends and sneaking sips of ouzo and red wine. But just before my freshman year of college, I spent the summer in England at a study abroad program. I studied British politics, learned to drink tea with milk, and went to plays and antiapartheid rallies in London. In this program, I met kids from all over the United States, many of whom already had dog-eared passports and told me stories about castles and nightclubs in France and concerts and art in the Netherlands. I pined for my own Eurail pass.

But anxiety derailed my travel plans. In college, I was too sick to study abroad. After graduation, I optimistically planned a two-month European backpacking trip with my roommate, Lisa. But I backed out in the end. I still felt too fragile.

It wasn't until a few years after graduation, when I was between jobs, that I was able to start satisfying my wanderlust. I took a three-week trip to Ecuador with my friend Sarah. We had no real plan, just traveler's checks, my high school Spanish, and a *Lonely Planet* guidebook stuffed into our backpacks. We crisscrossed the country in buses and planes and stayed in ten-dollar-a-night guesthouses, visiting Incan ruins near Cuenca, listening to Andean music, haggling in markets in Otavalo, and seeing the haunting paintings of Oswaldo Guayasamín in Quito. I was dazzled by the majestic mountains, the Technicolor reds and blues of the indigenous women's woolen shawls, and the glossy waist-length hair of some of the Quechua men. It was during this trip that I became infatuated with the surprise and discovery of travel, the chance meetings and serendipitous turns. In Otavalo, I wandered into the middle of a water fight between groups of laughing uniform-clad schoolchildren, bumped into a cute Canadian guy, then spent the afternoon hiking with him and his Quechua friends to a remote waterfall. Uncertainty had never been so thrilling.

From then on, I traveled as much as time and money would allow: to volcanoes in Costa Rica, beaches in Spain, and museums in Italy. Between jobs at the *Journal*, I took a month off and went traveling through Turkey with my friend Dave, eating just-caught fish in outdoor restaurants in Istanbul, exploring the fairytale landscape of Cappadocia, and sailing around the Mediterranean in a traditional *gulet* boat, where we slept outside on deck and dove off the bow to swim. Each day—like an apparition—a couple of young boys in a small motorboat would appear wherever we docked to sell us overpriced ice cream. I left Dave, bounced up to Berlin to visit a friend and sample the city's techno scene, then took an all-night train to Copenhagen. When I awoke, we were waterborne: Sometime in the night the train had been loaded onto a ferryboat. I walked upstairs to an outdoor deck and saw the Baltic Sea.

In my early thirties, I started traveling alone. At first it was for only a few days at a time, but even so it was transformative. Without a traveling companion, there was no buffer, no distraction from experience. I met people easily. And perhaps unexpectedly, I was sometimes less anxious on these excursions. If anxiety overwhelmed me, I didn't have to pretend I was okay, because there was no one to disappoint.

I visited an ashram in the Bahamas, one where alcohol, garlic, and onions were banned (too stimulating) and participants did four hours of yoga each day. Yogis dashed to the resort next door for contraband beer and ice cream. Revelers on party boats heckled us as we chanted in Sanskrit near the shore. "Can you believe these people come here to do yoga?" yelled a wrangler. In Buenos Aires, I took tango lessons and ate steak with young Argentines.

As intoxicating as it can be, travel can also make me feel ridiculous and ashamed. The poverty in Chiapas, garbage-strewn roadways in Nicaragua, political oppression in Cuba, begging children in Hanoi—witnessing these things makes me feel self-involved and absurd. My life is so privileged. Do I have the right to be anxious and fearful?

After the relapse in my late twenties, travel became more challenging. For one thing, I was doing much more of it. My boyfriend, Alan, had moved to Mexico City to take a job as a foreign correspondent, and I visited him every couple of months. Eventually I moved there for six months. To me, Mexico City in the late 1990s was fabulous. Yes, the pollution and traffic were terrible. But it was also a riot of delicious food (*chilaquiles*, which is basically cheese-covered Doritos, for breakfast!), welcoming people, and gobsmacking sights. I once saw a man hawking six-foot-tall crucifixes near a highway tollbooth. (*Are those ever an impulse buy?*

I wondered.) But the reports of crime and violence made me uneasy. Several of the foreign correspondents we knew had been carjacked in taxis and then forced—at gunpoint—to take money out of ATMs.

I began to dread flying and missed more than a few flights. I would stand at the gate, panicking, as passengers boarded—sometimes with my confused and, increasingly, frustrated boyfriend beside me—unable to move. I had an overwhelming fear, an absolute superstition that *this* flight, *this* plane would go down.

I continued to fly. I really had no choice. I was writing about technology and often had to be in San Francisco or New York. Alan was reporting stories all over Mexico and Central America, so if I wanted to spend time with him, I had to go along. Eventually each flight got a little easier.

I'm not afraid to fly anymore. If anything, travel is an antidote to my anxiety. Anxiety shrinks my world, but travel expands it. The heightened sensations of travel, the extremes in colors and tastes, can sometimes drown out the worries and obsessions.

7

THE ISOLATION CHAMBER
ANXIETY IN LOVE AND FRIENDSHIP

The most frustrating—actually heartbreaking—fallout from my anxiety is that, when I'm in the thick of it, it separates me from those I love. Anxiety is an isolation chamber where worry and fear elbow out human connection. The frenetic internal monologue of catastrophe blocks out conversation. It is as if the narrative of my life has been dubbed in a language I don't understand.

In college, during one of my breakdowns, I remember talking with my aunt Gail. "I have mitral valve prolapse," I said. "One of the valves in my heart doesn't close all the way." She looked at me strangely, her sunny smile freezing. I was confused. That is, until I realized that I had told her the exact same thing just minutes before. I had anxiety-induced amnesia. I could walk and talk but nothing held. Like booze, anxiety can cause blackouts.

It is not just a matter of forgotten conversations. I can be selfish, deaf to the needs of others. Anxiety can breed self-absorption, and it is tough to nurture relationships when you're only half there. Wracked with my own fears, what help can I be to anyone else?

I literally hide, too. I don't go out. I don't see friends. Parties, dinners, and long conversations come to an abrupt halt. There's simply no room in my head for anything besides worry. I barely have the energy to respond to texts or emails. The anxiety makes me feel so shaky, so weak, so tired, and so inept, that even that tiny effort is overwhelming. I see incoming phone calls—the names of family or friends—and watch sadly, but with a whiff of relief, as they disappear into voice mail. My world shrinks as my emotional defensive crouch becomes a physical one.

And that is with people I'm close to. It is a different kind of excruciating with acquaintances. Wearing a mask is exhausting. I feel like a fraud. I can become socially anxious, too. I'll lie in bed, replaying the conversations of the day, worrying that I've offended someone; berating myself for talking too much, talking too little, or making a stupid comment.

Even when my anxiety is at a lower volume, it is still a pushy neighbor: chatty, intrusive, and often boring as hell.

There is an upside, though. Anxiety has given me incredible moments of intimacy and love. I've been the recipient of enormous kindness and care. My college friend Susie taking me to the ER in the middle of a panic attack and making me laugh. My dear friend Leslie, walking me around the streets of the Mission in San Francisco after I fled a bar, midbeer, with a racing heart. Lovely Amy holding my hand on a bench near my office while I waited for a Klonopin to kick in. My friends' support, sensitivity, and steadfastness make me cherish them all the more.

And when anxiety is at its usual low hum, I feel like my experience with it has given me a point of connection with other people in pain, that it has made me more empathetic. That is especially true now that I'm more open about it. Among friends and colleagues, I've become the go-to girl for anxiety issues.

I've found only one study that has looked at the relationship between empathy and anxiety; Israeli researchers uncovered a link between empathy and social anxiety. However, if we look at it more broadly, a large body of research shows the upside of trauma and pain. Psychologists even have a term for this: post-traumatic growth. It refers to the potential to develop a greater appreciation for life, see new possibilities, and deepen relationships after adversity. Most often it is studied in relation to physical illnesses like cancer or to tragedies like the death of a child. But I'd argue that grappling with mental illness can lead to growth, too.

I rely on my girlfriends more than I do any therapist or doctor. Ianthe and Roe have been my confidantes and cheerleaders for more than a decade. We met at work. Ianthe, a dogged investigative reporter, newly hired from the *Washington Post*, walked up to my cubicle and introduced herself. Roe, who headed up the *Journal*'s book division, sat less than fifty feet away from me.

The three of us have had loads of fun over the years. There have been late nights dancing at East Village clubs, trips to France and Florida, country hikes—and hundreds of long dinners filled with laughter and extreme silliness. We've supported one another through cancer, the deaths of parents, job changes, breakups, and miscarriages. If I ever need to post bail, I'll call them.

They are both beautiful and brilliant. Ianthe, who grew up in New York and Colorado with four sisters, is a whirling dervish of activity and, I'm certain, could convince almost anyone to do her bidding. She can talk her way out of parking tickets and snare discounts on hotel rooms. In a hostage situation, I'd pick her to negotiate. If we're out to dinner and I find a speck floating in my glass of wine (no *way* will I drink that!), Ianthe will simply reach over and swap glasses with me. Roe grew up in a big Italian-American family in Brooklyn. She's an epic cook whose loves are good wine, good stories, her wacky family, and her large, loyal circle of women friends. When I'm anxious, sending her texts with a litany of worries, she is there to comfort me whether it is noon or midnight.

Most research on the effects of anxiety disorders on adult relationships focuses on romantic ones. But one interesting 2013 study looked at relationships with relatives and friends, too. The results make me realize how lucky I am. People with lower quality relationships with friends and relatives, those researchers found, had higher rates of anxiety disorders. And the researchers theorized that there's a bidirectional relationship between anxiety disorders and support and intimacy in relationships: struggling relationships fuel anxiety, and anxiety stresses relationships. In another study, socially anxious women said they reveal less in their friendships.

The scientific literature on anxiety's effects on friendship in childhood and adolescence is much more robust. This makes sense, since friendships are critical to kids' social and emotional development. For anxious kids, having supportive and intimate friendships leads to reduced anxiety over time. Indeed, being part of a group (any group, not just the "popular" one), and having a close and upbeat best friendship, protects kids from feeling social anxiety.

Supportive friendships also seem to prevent anxious kids from becoming depressed adults. In a 2016 study, anxious teens who said they felt loved or part of a group were much less likely to be depressed more than a decade later. By contrast, a paucity of loving relationships and little sense of belonging and being accepted during the teen years led to depression in adulthood. Good friends also enhance treatment for anxious kids: Those with caring friends respond better to cognitive behavioral therapy.

For kids, too, there is a bidirectional relationship between anxiety and the quality of friendships. Anxious kids tend to avoid social situations. But skipping sleepovers and soccer games means they have fewer opportunities to develop social skills. The ensuing social awkwardness fuels more anxiety. And so on.

Anxious kids generally have fewer friends and feel less well liked than their peers. Kids with social anxiety, in particular, tend to have more social challenges. In experiments designed to assess social skills, they've been found to be less assertive and effective. Socially anxious girls report less acceptance and support from peers. Anxious kids more often expect to be rejected. Research has found at least some of the chill they anticipate from peers is well-founded. One study had nine-to-thirteen-year-old kids rate videotaped speeches of other children, some of whom had anxiety disorders. The raters were then asked whether they liked the kids in the videotapes and whether they thought they would make good friends. Kids with social anxiety disorder were rated the most harshly. A study from 1999 found that 75 percent of children with social phobia said they had few or no friends; half did no extracurricular activities.

Anxious kids are more likely to be bullied. In one study, a staggering 92 percent of adults with social phobia said they had been severely teased in the past. Half of the subjects with OCD and 35 percent of those with panic disorder did. Boys with social anxiety may be more vulnerable to bullying than girls, since being quiet and withdrawn goes against traditional gender roles. And in another example of a negative feedback loop, bullying can lead to increased social anxiety. Adolescents who are frequently picked on are two to three times more likely to develop an anxiety disorder, according to one 2014 study.

Anxiety has cost me at least one friend. In my early thirties, I spent a lot of time with a group of five women, all a few years older than me. They were smart and accomplished, opinionated and fun. We'd meet about once a month for potluck dinners, rotating apartments. I bonded, in particular, with a woman named Alice. She was passionate about yoga and had a ballsy way of talking about her emotions and her relationship deal breakers. I was astonished by how assertive and definite she was. Like most young women I knew, I was much more timid, even apologetic, about my desires. She was a veteran of the Landmark Forum, a self-help seminar that was an outgrowth of the 1970s "est" movement. (One of its core goals is "freedom from anxiety.") We'd have long conversations over tea about love, work, and meaning.

One weekend Alice joined me at the country house I'd rented with friends, a spare place in the Catskill Mountains, a couple of hours north of New York City. We hiked, cooked, and talked. One evening we decided to go to the tiny movie theater in a nearby town where an action movie was playing. I remember finding our seats in the already darkened theater to a booming soundtrack of gunfire and explosions.

Ten or fifteen minutes in, my heart rate kicked up, and I felt hot and slightly breathless: the telltale signs of a panic attack. I turned to Alice. "I need to walk around the block. I'm feeling anxious, like I might have a panic attack. Can you come with me?"

"You want to leave the movie right now?" she asked.

"Yes, I need to go," I said.

She did come with me, and she did walk with me. I paced around the block, Alice silent beside me, for a good half hour or so. Then I drove us back to the house. I tried to explain what a panic attack feels like and how I dealt with them.

The next morning I felt embarrassed. I apologized for aborting the movie. "Don't worry about it," Alice said, yet I felt a subtle shift, a new distance. I made an extra effort to be sunny and calm. I took a series of portraits of her next to a blooming magnolia tree, then drove us back to the city.

After that she retreated. There were no more tea dates or long talks. We still saw each other at the potlucks, but it became clear that that was as close as she wanted to get.

The truth is that some people are spooked by out-of-control anxiety. Emotional states, neuroscientists have found, are contagious, and some people don't want to catch what I have. Scientists call this "emotional contagion," based on findings that we tend to automatically mimic the expressions of others. Making a particular expression can actually induce that emotion, which means that being around an anxious person can make you feel anxious, too. In fact, it can cause levels of the stress hormone cortisol to spike.

When the anxious person is someone you love, this emotional contagion is even more pronounced. In a 2014 study, researchers in Germany and Boston had subjects perform stress-inducing tasks while they were watched via a one-way mirror or live video feed by someone of the opposite sex. In some cases, the observers were strangers; in others, the observers were the subjects' romantic partners. The tasks—giving a short speech and doing some difficult math problems—made the participants stressed and anxious; most of them saw their cortisol levels at least double. That was no surprise. But about 26 percent of the *observers* had significant increases in cortisol, too. If they were watching a romantic partner rather than a stranger, the number jumped to 40 percent.

This might be one reason why adults with anxiety disorders are more likely to be single. With dating, the goal is usually to present your best, most confident, most alluring self, and anxiety is no aphrodisiac. Those with anxiety disorders who do marry are more likely to divorce.

I've had boyfriends who were caretakers and others who were much less supportive or indulgent. Some were clearly afraid of my fear, worried they'd be sucked into a vortex and that their lives would become as constrained and small as my own sometimes was.

When I was sixteen, I met Scott at Images, a nightclub in Brewster, New York. It was teen night, an evening for kids who were into New Wave music to flirt, dive into mosh pits, and see bands with names like Cerebral Meltdown. We got to talking, and our two groups of friends ended up at the Windmill Diner, a cheap, brightly lit twenty-four-hour spot. Scott said he was charmed by the way I ate pancakes with my fingers. I thought he was ridiculously cute.

We were an unlikely pair. Six feet tall, handsome, and dark-haired, Scott was a sports star—starter on the football team, ace pitcher in baseball—at the Catholic high school in town. He was confident and popular but an average student. I was a bit of an oddball. While I was in honors classes, ran track, and sang in an a cappella choral group, I also bought my clothes at the Salvation Army (five dollars for a grocery bag full of vintage stuff) or dressed in flannel pajama bottoms and one of my dad's suit jackets, his silk tie wrapped around my ponytail. I defined myself by the music I listened to: the Smiths, Love and Rockets, Siouxsie and the Banshees. In 1987 western Connecticut, this was not mainstream: Boston, Def Leppard, and AC/DC dominated the mixtapes of most of my schoolmates. When someone in my sociology class hissed at me, "I bet you like U2," it was not a compliment.

But it was summer, and we went to different schools, and so our disparate places in the high school pecking order didn't seem to matter. We had an idyllic few months, roaming the streets in my little Chevy with a carload of friends, singing along to music, swimming in the lake, and drinking wine coolers in assorted fields and backyards.

Then Scott left for college. I moved to Michigan, and Scott and I broke up. But by the following year, I was a freshman at Michigan, and Scott had transferred to Michigan State. We started dating again, off and on. When I got sick, Scott became the "nocturnal life raft" I described in the first chapter of this book, when my panic disorder hadn't yet been diagnosed.

Looking back, I'm astonished by his unwavering support. He was twenty years old and a full-time student at what was known as an epic party school. He had pledged a fraternity. He liked to drink, smoke pot, and hang out with his friends. I would not have pegged him as a steadfast partner in the face of mental illness.

When I got sick my senior year, Scott came through once more. What's remarkable is that by this time we weren't even dating. In fact, I had another boyfriend, although that relationship was long distance. My parents had moved to Texas, and Scott was one of the only people nearby I could count on. He was, once again, my anxiety car service, taking me to therapy appointments, doctors' visits, and the ER. I spent many weekends in his room in the beat-up apartment he shared with several of his fraternity brothers. I'd lie huddled in his bed—really just a mattress thrown on the floor—as a party swirled in the apartment beyond Scott's closed door. I'd hear girls giggling, boys boasting, and music blaring and hunch farther under the covers, feeling embarrassed and fragile.

I became physically weak. I was barely eating, and the churning anxiety zapped my energy. One episode from this time is seared into my memory. I'm in Scott's bathroom, leaning against the white-tiled wall and clutching the towel bar. I need to take a shower but I'm too wobbly to stand on my own. Tenderly, as if I'm a child, Scott undresses me and leads me under the water. Keeping a steadying grip on my elbow, he shampoos my hair, cupping a hand at my forehead so the soap doesn't run into my eyes.

I'm certain that I would not have stayed in school if it weren't for Scott. His support and care kept me from phoning my parents in Texas and demanding that they let me come home. When things got too tough in Ann Arbor, he'd whisk me back to his darkened bedroom, a cocoon where I felt safe. Scott was one of the few people with whom I could be truly authentic. No matter how scared or self-involved I was or how much of an invalid I became, he stayed. I don't remember him ever criticizing me or telling me to toughen up.

I had the immense good fortune in college to move from one understanding boyfriend to another. I met Joel during spring break of my junior year. This spring break was unusual. I still felt shaky and anxious. I did not want a repeat of the prior year's truncated and disastrous trip to Cancún, so I had a strange hybrid vacation. Several of my sorority sisters planned to travel to South Padre Island, Texas. My parents lived in San Antonio, about a four-hour drive away, so I convinced them to stay a few days in South Padre, too. That way I could hang out with my college friends during the day but retreat to the safety of my family at night or when I got too anxious.

I was on the beach when my friends and I noticed a group of guys smiling our way and generally trying to get our attention. We engaged in a volley of whispering and glances but didn't actually meet. Later that night, though, I was at a bar, one of those open-air fishing-themed spots with plastic starfish on the walls and Jell-O shots on the menu. One of the guys from the beach—tall and cute, olive-skinned with sandy brown hair arranged in an artful bedhead—walked over to me and told me his name was Joel.

He bought me a Coke. We danced to "Just Like Heaven" by the Cure. He asked for my phone number. Joel was twenty-five and an MBA student at Michigan, and we began seeing each other as soon as we got back to Ann Arbor. I fell in love with his goofiness and kindness. But Joel graduated just a few months after we met and left for a job in San Francisco. I flew to see him every few months—as often as I could pay for plane tickets with the money I made at my part-time job in a clothing store. I was still struggling with anxiety, but I remember our early relationship as light and fun, filled with dance parties with friends and meandering strolls around the Marina district.

Joel, however, recalls that anxiety reared its head as early as our third date. We were at his grad student apartment in Ann Arbor, and I started to feel panicky. I told him I needed to get some air, and we walked around the triangle-shaped block outside about ten or twenty times. "I thought it was a little weird, but okay," he told me recently.

After my December relapse, Joel bought a pager so that I could reach him anytime. (This was 1992, before cell phones were ubiquitous.) I was the only one with the number. He left the device on all night, sitting on the nightstand, so he'd wake if I needed him. I'd buzz him mid-panic attack, and he'd call and calm me down, telling me I'd be okay, that he loved me and wouldn't let anything happen to me.

Joel researched my various physical symptoms and always made sure we were close to an emergency room. One day I called him and told him my legs felt tingly and numb. He walked to a bookstore across the street from his office and began paging through a medical reference book. "Everything just kept coming up MS," he says. "That was the scariest incident, thinking that you'd have this progressive downward spiral."

It is spring break 1992, a glorious blue-sky day in San Francisco. I'm lying on Joel's bed struggling to breathe. There's a weight on my torso. Pushing my chest out to inhale seems to take formidable effort. Then I exhale in a big rush. At the time, I'm in therapy at the Anxiety Disorders Clinic, but I still think it might be something terrible. Joel has been trying to reassure me for days. "You've been able to have sex," he points out. "You couldn't do that if you were dying." But my doomsday forecasts have spawned a seed of doubt. Could it be a pulmonary embolism? Joel finds a well-regarded pulmonologist at a local hospital and gets me an emergency appointment. I lie on a cold, metal table, and a technician injects a radioactive substance into a vein in my arm.

There's no blood clot. Joel drives me to a bed and breakfast in Santa Barbara to celebrate. We drink wine and eat chocolate in bed.

Years later Joel says my anxiety sometimes made him feel helpless and scared. But it was never a drag to him, he says. "It actually drew me closer to you," he says. "I felt very protective. You were going through something really hard, and I wanted to help in any way I could."

Joel and I broke up not long after I graduated from college and moved to Washington, D.C. During my twenties, I had several boyfriends. While my anxiety was mostly under control during those years, I still felt its effects. I stayed in some relationships—like one with a controlling and belittling editor thirteen years older than me—too long. I became emotionally dependent on, and romantically entangled with, my best male friend. The relationship—marooned in that awkward gray zone between friend and boyfriend—was unfair to him and ended painfully. The friendship was destroyed. I was like a trapeze artist flinging myself from one relationship to another, sometimes keeping my grip on one guy while transitioning to another.

The thing was that I was awful at making decisions. I was petrified of making the "wrong" choice. It wasn't, I don't think, that I was afraid of being alone. I was more afraid of regret. I didn't trust myself not to change my mind about someone.

Numerous studies have shown a link between mental illness and problems in romantic relationships. While depression seems to dampen relationship quality the most, anxiety wreaks its own havoc, contributing to a glass-half-empty view of relationships. In one 2012 study of heterosexual couples in which one or both partners suffered from panic disorder or GAD, the partners with anxiety disorders judged their relationships to be of lower quality than those without disorders. This was especially true of women. Men with anxiety problems judged their relationships harshly only if their female partners also had anxiety disorders.

Some anxiety disorders seem to cause more relationship turbulence than others. In one study, men whose wives had panic disorder reported lower-quality marriages than men whose wives had other anxiety disorders. Relationship issues exacerbate anxiety, too. A 1985 study following people with agoraphobia found that those with marital problems didn't respond as well to treatment for their anxiety.

Of all the anxiety disorders, social anxiety tends to be most disruptive to relationships. Women with high levels of social anxiety say they both give to and receive from their partners less support. They say they disclose less and tend to be less satisfied in their relationships, too.

As I entered my late twenties, anxiety seemed to be more of an occupying force in my relationships. While I wasn't debilitated as I'd been in college, these relationships were more serious. They were the ones that might conceivably lead to marriage and children. The stakes were higher.

I met Alan at a nondescript restaurant on the Upper West Side during lunch with a mutual friend who was not so subtly trying to set us up. The lunch was awkward, filled with long pauses. Alan had just moved to New York from Africa, where he had been living and working as a freelance journalist for several years. He was having a tough time making the transition to New York and the seeming frivolity of life in such a peaceful, affluent place. "People here talk about going to the gym," he grumbled.

We met again, at a party a month later, and the conversation flowed more easily. A few months after that, he called and asked me out. We ended up going to an awful play and having dinner at a cheap Italian joint, now long gone, in the West Village. We laughed and talked late into the night. On our second date, we wandered around the Metropolitan Museum of Art and kissed in a hammock on the rooftop of his apartment building. A few weeks after that, he shyly asked if he could call me his girlfriend.

I fell hard for him. We bonded over reporting and writing. We read each other's stories and gave each other advice. I was wowed by his fearlessness, how he had flown to Africa with a laptop and almost no journalism experience and made his way as a freelance reporter. He told me of grim experiences: seeing bones at a church in Rwanda, seeing a mass grave of Tutsis who had been slaughtered in the country's genocide. He joked about the various parasites he'd contracted in Africa, about the worm he'd passed during a fancy dinner with diplomats. He put it in a film canister so that a doctor could identify it later. He had done things I wished I were brave enough to do.

But he wasn't cocky about it. In fact, he was often wracked by self-doubt. It was that combination of fearlessness and vulnerability that hooked me.

In New York, we threw parties, saw bands, and lounged around in Central Park. Alan taught me how to Rollerblade and rock climb, helping me pick out a bright orange harness and purple climbing shoes. But five months into our relationship, he was offered the job in Mexico City.

I told him he had to do it, but there was never any doubt that he'd go. He was miserable as an office-bound editor. He wanted to travel and cover stories. He asked me to come with him to Mexico, but at the time I was close to being made a staff reporter at the *Journal* and felt I'd being saying goodbye to a journalism career if I left New York. We decided we'd stay together and have a long-distance relationship. After all, we still had six months before Alan had to make the move.

Within weeks of Alan accepting the new job, I had a relapse, spawned by the episode of blind spots while walking down Seventh Avenue. While Alan was throwing himself into Spanish lessons and Mexican history, I was swiftly sliding back into hypochondria. Because my doctor thought the blind spots were an ocular migraine, he had me see an ophthalmologist. The eye doctor said he thought he saw some "bulging" behind one of my eyes. (This can be a sign of a brain tumor.) He sent me to a neurologist, who did an MRI. (Was this the third—no fourth—brain MRI I'd had in my not-yet-three decades of life?) There was no tumor.

Even with the clean MRI results, I became fixated on the idea that something was wrong with my brain. I worried especially about my memory. I furtively wrote down conversations shortly after they happened, then tested myself at night to see how much I could remember. I'd wring my hands when I discovered a lapse. I tried to keep most of these worries from Alan, but I wasn't that successful. "We would be out, and you'd say 'I have a headache' or 'I feel weird, I think I have a brain tumor,'" Alan recalls. "I'd think, 'Seriously? You had one last week.' You were often imagining that you had a terminal illness."

I felt ridiculous and ashamed. Alan had seen some truly horrible things in his work. My own concerns seemed petty and small. So I did my best to hide emotionally. Between that and Alan's impending move, I felt increasingly cut off from him.

The anxiety built all summer. That August Alan and I planned a trip to Maine. We'd spend three days hiking along the Appalachian Trail, traversing three mountains more than four thousand feet high, and a few days relaxing at a rustic cabin on a lake. This would be my first real backpacking trip—carrying my gear, drinking water from streams (after adding a dose of iodine), and sleeping in a tiny tent or bunking in primitive lean-tos.

The trouble started with my tortured attempt to buy a sleeping bag for the trip. I could not do it; in my addled mind, selecting the "right" bag would magically protect me from dehydration, broken bones, homicidal bears, and other sinister scenarios. Choose the wrong bag, and I was screwed. I bought two bags and laid them out in Alan's bedroom, climbing into one and then the other over and over again. "Just pick one," Alan said, growing frustrated and confused.

My experience of that trip was like a split screen. On one side, I worried about having an asthma attack and dying. I thought about how far we were from a hospital and how long it would take help to arrive. On the other side, I marveled at a moose drinking from a pristine mountaintop lake. Alan and I made love on top of a picnic table. We laughed about the "thru-hikers" we met (people who had been hiking the trail for months) with trail names like Mousetrap and Stickman. One guy was proud that he was still wearing his original boots, now held together with duct tape. The thru-hikers dubbed Alan and me "the Weekenders." There's a photo of me from that trip: topless with khaki shorts and brown leather hiking boots, triumphant on the apex of a mountain. I look healthy and strong.

Several days later Alan and I are eating at a fish shack in Bar Harbor. Chattering sunburned families, red plastic baskets of lobster tails and crab claws in front of them, are all around us.

Suddenly I feel a lump in my throat. I cough. Take a swig of water. The lump is still there.

My skin feels hot. My heart beats faster.

I'm having an allergic reaction to the shellfish, I decide. My throat will close up. My throat will close up, and I will die.

"I feel like I can't breathe," I tell Alan. "I think I'm allergic to the crab. I need to get to a hospital."

He asks whether I'm sure, and when I say yes, he grabs my hand, and we run to the car. Mount Desert Island Hospital is a twenty-minute drive away.

It is getting dark. Alan is speeding along the twisting roads, glancing worriedly over at me, his arms taut on the steering wheel. I am motionless in the passenger seat. My entire focus is on moving air through the viselike grip of my constricted throat.

"Please don't let me die. Please don't let me die," I beg.

"We're almost there. You'll be okay," Alan says. He does not sound convinced.

As we pull up to the small hospital, a tiny doubt pierces the fear: *Maybe I'm having a panic attack.*

The building is almost entirely dark. The few visible lights point the way to the emergency room. Alan is breathing fast, too, hopped up on adrenaline. I lean into him. "Maybe I'm just having a panic attack," I say.

My doubt grows. When I check in with a nurse, I tell her my symptoms but also that I'm prone to panic attacks. Instead of seeing a doctor right away, I pace around the waiting room. My symptoms begin to subside. Alan is quiet, shoulders slumped. He looks drained. Later he tells me that during the drive he was making plans. If I stopped breathing, he'd pull over to the side of the road and jam a hole in my trachea with one of the tools on his Leatherman, which is something like a Swiss Army knife.

My anxiety shrouds the rest of the trip. It is now an uncaged thing, ready to land on any uncertainty. On the drive home, the lump in my throat returns, and my skin feels itchy. I make Alan exit the interstate to stop at another emergency room, where I get a shot of Benadryl.

. . .

Back at home, I started taking Paxil, and my anxiety abated somewhat. Alan left for Mexico a few months later. For the next year and a half, we had a long-distance relationship. In some ways it was idyllic. We traveled all over Mexico. We met up for road trips to California and Nevada and Mississippi and Louisiana, fishing for crawfish off the deck of a rented house on a bayou. We visited Culebra, an island in Puerto Rico, just in time for a hurricane. We raided the grocery store for food along with the locals and huddled around a battery-powered radio in a cinder-block-walled hotel with new friends.

My anxiety waxed and waned. Alan, for the most part, tried to ignore it. He told me recently that he hadn't known what to do. "I think my instinct and the instinct of a lot of men is to solve problems, and this one didn't seem like a solvable problem. Usually, I just tried to pretend it didn't exist," he said. He did sometimes try to talk me out of my anxiety, to convince my revved-up amygdala to listen to logic. Like during the Oreo Incident.

During our vacation in Culebra, we were staying in a small wooden bungalow near the beach. I was in the kitchen eating Oreos, a treat I'd loved since childhood. I had eaten maybe two or three and reached my hand into the bag for another.

That's when I saw them.

Ants. Dozens—no, hundreds!—of ants. A mob of ants. They were swarming inside the bag, crawling on the cookies, their wiggling black bodies stark against the white filling. An intrepid few had started the trek up my hand.

I shrieked and dropped the bag. I grabbed a paper towel and spat out the cookie sludge in my mouth. But I knew it was too late. I had definitely already eaten some. Ants were now making their way down my esophagus. They were moments away from my bloodstream.

"Oh, my God, there are ants in here. I've eaten ants!" I wailed to Alan. "I need to throw up."

Alan looked inside the bag. "Okay, maybe you've eaten a couple of ants. But it doesn't seem like such a big deal. They're protein."

"No, I need to get rid of the ants. I could get sick. They could be carrying some awful disease," I said, and moved toward the bathroom.

"Look, I'll prove it to you. I'll put myself at the same risk." He reached into the bag, grabbed an ant-covered cookie, and popped it into his mouth. "Mmm, that was tasty," he said, chewing.

He swallowed and reached in and grabbed another one. "That was good protein," he said, downing the second ant-strewn Oreo. "These are really good," he said as he ate a third cookie.

I laughed. "You really are crazy."

Still, Alan's antics weren't enough to defeat my anxiety. I went to the bathroom, stuck my finger down my throat, and made myself vomit.

The time apart—me in New York, him in Mexico—was a strain. There were anguished email exchanges, flirtations with other people, and angry silences during our brief times together. Our emotional bond frayed. Finally I got permission from the *Journal* to work from Mexico City for six months. I arrived with a six-foot-long blue duffel bag stuffed with clothes and books and moved into Alan's house in the lovely Coyoacán neighborhood, not far from the onetime home of Frida Kahlo and Diego Rivera. I was twenty-nine, and it was the first time I'd lived with a boyfriend.

I loved Mexico City. The early morning call of the tamale carts: "*Tamales, tamales.*" The circus acts—acrobats, flamethrowers—

performing on the streets during red lights. The riot of colors in the plaza during the Day of the Dead celebration. Even the catcalls—*gringa, gringa, rubia, rubia* (blondie)—I heard en route to my favorite coffee spot. And always the lilt of Spanish.

I wasn't blind to the poverty and corruption. And I did notice that people with darker skin were more likely to wear the cheap blue uniforms of nannies and housekeepers, while the lighter-skinned shopped at Gucci and Zara in the tony Polanco neighborhood. Because of the pollution, I had to stop running. My asthma was kicked up by Mexico City's air, and I didn't have the money to pay for access to one of the pricey health clubs that circulated filtered air.

When Alan and I were in Mexico City, we did normal things: We rented movies, went grocery shopping, and worked in our side-by-side offices. I loved being able to pop next door to see him, still in my bathrobe, and run part of a story by him. We also kept traveling. To Panama. To Cuba. To the pyramids of Teotihuacan and the Mayan ruins of Palenque. The frenzied travel was partly anxiety-driven. I had promised the *Journal* that I would return in January, and the specter of my departure was on my mind. Alan and I didn't talk much about what my return to New York would mean for our relationship. In hindsight, I wish I had been less focused on ticking off destinations in my *Lonely Planet* guidebooks and rooted myself a bit more, made my own friends, and carved out more of a routine in Mexico City.

At the same time, Paxil's side effects mounted and took a toll on my relationship. My sex drive ebbed. Alan was frustrated, saying he felt rejected. I went off the medication.

When I moved back to New York, Alan and I had a vague understanding that I would stay for a few months to fulfill my commitment to the *Journal*, then quit and move back to Mexico

City. I'd freelance. We'd get engaged. But a few weeks later, during a phone call, he broke up with me. He wasn't ready for a big commitment, he said. He wanted to date other people.

Years later he told me that my anxiety was a big part of why he ended things. "I wanted an adventurous life," he said. "I worried that your issues would hold us back, that our lives would be controlled by your fears and anxieties." Because I was scared of driving on highways, Alan thought we'd be limited in where we could live or that I would be too dependent on him. He also worried that I wouldn't be able to handle the pressures of motherhood, that I'd "freak out in moments when I needed you to be in charge with a kid."

I was devastated by the breakup. My emotional whiplash quickly devolved into the rom-com version of grief. I wrote pleading letters, dialed Alan's number, and hung up. I cried to my friends. I drank too much. I kissed cute strangers. I lost weight. (The misery diet is just as effective as the anxiety diet, I discovered.)

What I didn't do was have a relapse.

In some ways, heartbreak is antithetical to anxiety. Anxiety is all about the future, about the tragedies around the corner. Grief is about the awful thing that has already happened. I sank deeply into my messy present. (Years later I cyberstalked Alan on a dating website. In the section that asks "What have you learned from past relationships?" he had written: "How to diagnose panic disorder.")

I did obsess some about the past, about all the ways I'd failed as a girlfriend. The next time, I vowed, I'd be the most loving, the most patient, the most giving girlfriend around. That vow must have been why I ignored the endless red flags about Brad.

I had met Brad several times during my relationship with Alan, but it was not until a party for a mutual friend, just a month or two after I arrived back in New York, that we had our first real conversation, filled with light teasing and easy verbal volleys. He was thirty-five, with sandy brown hair, sexy crow's-feet, and impish blue eyes. A freelance photographer and avid rock climber, he was funny and wry and smart, with a quiet confidence. But I also found him emotionally opaque. His expressions and inflections could be tough to read. Despite that (or maybe because of it), I was instantly, wildly attracted to him.

The day after the party, I emailed my friend Anne, who was Brad's roommate, to debrief about the evening. "It was so nice to see your roommate Brad again," I wrote. "He's adorable, by the way." She wrote back saying that, funnily enough, Brad had said I was adorable, too. "Actually 'lovely' was the word he used," she wrote. Later that afternoon, my phone rang at work. It was Brad, calling to ask me out.

On our first date, I was nervous. I hadn't been on a first date in more than three years, and I was still wobbly from the breakup with Alan. I drank too much and talked too much, firing off probing questions like "Do you believe in God?" We kissed good night, but Brad didn't call me again.

Over the next few months, we saw each other at parties and emailed a little. In one exchange, he reminded me that we had promised to get together over dessert. We made another date.

We started seeing each other casually, meeting up for a bike ride, an outdoor movie, or a drink. The dates were fun, but he deflected personal questions. He was stingy with compliments and gave me few clues as to how much he liked me. Each time we parted, I wondered if he'd call again.

Then September 11 happened.

Brad hopped on his bike and rode to the twin towers with his cameras immediately after the attack. His photographs from that day—of the wreckage, the firefighters, the soot-covered survivors—were featured in magazines and newspapers. Meanwhile I was writing about the aftermath for the *Journal*. We'd work all day in a frenzy and meet up at night. The tragedy around us, the shared purpose, and the disruption of any normal routine shredded any resistance. We fell into a war zone romance.

We were sitting in his bathtub when he looked at me and said: "I love your eyes." He paused. "I love you," he continued. I was elated. "I love you, too," I replied.

Still, even in those first few months, I noticed something distressing. He was nit-picking and critical. He admonished me for clanging my spoon against my cereal bowl, for laughing at my own jokes, for talking about work too much. He criticized the way I ate and the way I kissed. One night after a dinner party, I confronted him. "I know I have a lot of issues, but the way I eat my cereal isn't one of them," I began.

He apologized. "I know I have a problem."

I stayed.

But the criticisms continued. We'd be having a good time, laughing and chatting, and then he'd pull away and get quiet. "What's wrong?" I'd ask.

I used the word *basically* too much. I kicked his shin. I spoke too loudly. Brad seemed to seethe with a quiet anger. "It must be hard to be so annoyed by so many little things," I said. The digs fueled my anxiety, which just made me clumsier, more unnatural, and I'm guessing, romantically unappealing. I'd oscillate between fury and despondency, between anger at his unreasonableness and shame at my own flaws.

Then I moved in with him.

This may sound crazy, but there was a strange logic to my actions. I had a strong suspicion that this relationship wasn't good for me and that it had to end. But I knew I couldn't quit him yet. There was too much physical attraction, and I clung to the misguided belief that if I just tried harder and was more loving, he would be less critical. Part of me couldn't believe that someone could truly be so hung up on silly and inconsequential things. It must signal something else, some core unhappiness. If I could get to the bottom of that unhappiness, he would change.

So I held out a slim hope that things would get better. But I also figured that if we moved in together, things could get much, much worse. So bad, in fact, that I would have to leave. Moving in with him, in this scenario, would actually be a huge time-saver. Instead of frittering away several more years of my life, I would sacrifice only months.

I put almost all my furniture in storage and brought nothing to Brad's apartment in Gramercy Park other than some clothes, books, and a couple of bookcases. My first week there, Brad barely spoke to me. Did he regret asking me to move in? Did he feel ambushed by my stuff? (Living together had been his idea, I reminded him.) He wouldn't tell me. Instead, he complained to his sister: My towels didn't match. My bookcases were cheap.

Over the next several months, we did have some fun. We went dancing in East Village dive bars, had friends over for dinner, and went for long, beautiful hikes in the Catskills. But Brad was icy and aloof much of the time. And without my own apartment to retreat to, I had little respite from his moods. I became increasingly nervous. After waking, my heart would race for several hours. I lost weight. I became consumed with my relationship troubles and spoke with friends about little else. My panic attacks returned with a vengeance.

I had one in the kitchen of a Catskill rental house. My heart rate shot up, my arms went numb, and my breath came in gasps. I was convinced I was dying and asked Brad to call 911. (He did. I was loaded into an ambulance and checked out at a tiny country hospital.) I had another during an ocular migraine. Brad and I had spent a long day rock climbing. On the drive home, a chunk of my vision disappeared. Yes, this had happened before, but I still panicked. Maybe this time it really was a stroke. We passed a fire station, and I asked Brad to stop so that I could wait out the symptoms within arm's reach of medical help. Two sympathetic young firefighters sat me in a metal folding chair and chatted with me until my vision returned.

The attacks became more frequent. I was a repeat visitor to the ER at NYU Hospital. It wasn't often that I actually went inside and saw a doctor; I felt safer just being on the sidewalk out front. I could frequently be found skulking around the ER entrance mid-panic attack. I'd pace up and down First Avenue, trying to breathe deeply and talk myself down from whatever medical emergency I thought I was having.

With each panic attack, Brad retreated a little further. The warm moments between us became increasingly rare, and it was only when we were with friends that I saw the funny, charming guy I had fallen for. "You hardly ever smile anymore," I said to him one morning. Brad looked at me, stone-faced, and flashed an aggressive, over-the-top grin. "Is that better?" he barked.

It is September, and I'm on the top of a mountain in New Hampshire. It is a glorious early evening. Dark shadows shift as clouds dance above the rolling green vista. My worn-in leather boots dodge the delicate white wildflowers along the rocky trail. Brad and I are on day one of a three-day hiking trip in the White Mountains. We've hiked steeply uphill all day.

I've been nervous about this trip for weeks. By now, I love backcountry backpacking—the quiet, the beauty, the physical exertion—but I'm still afraid of it, too. There's always the potential for broken bones, snakebites, and asthma attacks, all of it miles from hospitals and help. And my anxiety has been so much worse lately.

We drop our packs off at the hut where we'll stay that night and continue farther along the trail to catch more mountaintop views. I start to feel a little woozy. The rocks under my feet rear up; the undulating mountains flatten. I stop walking. "Wait," I call to Brad. "I don't feel well."

Brad stops. "Maybe you need some water," he says. He opens the top of his Nalgene bottle and hands it to me. I tell him I want to go back to the hut.

Then my dizziness turns into a full-blown panic attack. My heart gallops, and my breath shortens. *You're okay, you're okay, you're okay,* I repeat silently to myself, like a mantra.

It's dinnertime back at the hut. Fleece-clad families sit at long wooden tables and young staffers cheerfully pass out platters of freshly baked bread. While hikers eat hungrily, the staffers sing camp songs and act out silly skits. Brad and I sit across from each other in silence. He looks exasperated. My heart thumps wildly.

We sleep in bunk beds in a room with several others. All night I huddle in a ball on my top bunk, swallowing bits of Klonopin every few hours. But this time it fails me. It doesn't calm my racing heart. Brad disappears. I don't see him for hours.

In the morning, I tell him that I just can't continue the trip to the next hut, as planned. We hike down the mountain. As I descend, the anxiety eases. By the time I reach the trailhead, I feel almost fine.

A few nights later Brad and I were sitting on the sofa in our apartment. "You lost me on top of that mountain," he said.

A few weeks later I started looking for an apartment of my own. I signed a lease. Then I told Brad I was moving out.

The days leading up to my move were both banal and surreal. We didn't fight. Nor did we talk about what was happening. Finally I asked Brad, "Do you want to process this with me at all?"

"I'm sad you're leaving," he said.

Settling into my new apartment in an old brownstone in Fort Greene, Brooklyn, I was relieved but emotionally exhausted. I went on my own version of a relationship detox. I fell asleep early on Saturday nights. I binge-watched the entire six seasons of *Sex and the City*. I painted my bedroom walls a sprightly chartreuse. I found a new therapist, whom I have seen off and on ever since, the fabulous Dr. L. I went back on Paxil. And I took stock of what I wanted in a relationship. To my usual criteria of smart, funny, and cute, I added several more must-haves: kind, emotionally available and consistent, and able to handle my anxiety.

From then on, I made it a policy to tell every man I dated—no later than the second meeting—about my anxiety. I treated it almost like having an STD.

Because the reality is that anxiety affects partners. One study followed thirty-three heterosexual couples in which the women had anxiety disorders. On the days when the women experienced high levels of anxiety, the men reported less positive relationship quality (measured by things like "partner showed concern" and "partner was dependable") and more anxiety, anger, and depression. The more the men accommodated their wives' anxiety, the angrier they were. On women's highly anxious days, they reported higher negative relationship quality (measured by, among other things, "partner was demanding" and "partner was critical").

I met Sean online, on Nerve.com. It was 2005, way before Ok-Cupid became popular and aeons before Tinder. In the mid-2000s, Match.com and Nerve.com were the online dating behemoths. Match was more mainstream. Nerve, which was initially founded as a racy online magazine that covered sex and relationships, was where you could find musicians, film editors, and graphic designers, many of whom had a penchant for artful eyewear.

Sean and I joke that it was his hat that hooked me. Among the pictures he posted on his profile was one of him wearing a Tibetan knit hat that fanned out in an enormous black yarn Mohawk. (There was no false advertising. Another photo revealed his completely bald head.) His note to me was sweet, complimentary, and clever. But it was the slightly weird, goofy photo that compelled me to answer and make a date.

We met at a café in Nolita. He had lovely blue eyes, strong features, and a slim gym-going build. While he had the look of the hipster Brooklyn artist/professor he in fact was (black jeans, green leather jacket, black wool beanie), he was also warm, funny, and direct. He exuberantly talked up his lifelong obsession with the Beatles and chastised me for suggesting that the Rolling Stones were in the same league.

On our second date, at a wine bar in Williamsburg, I told him about my panic attacks and my college breakdowns. I did not put a rosy spin on things: I told him that my anxiety was chronic and would likely return. Sean was empathetic; he didn't seem put off at all. And he had a secret of his own to tell me that night. Although he had listed himself as "single" on his profile, he had been married before. Six years earlier his first wife had collapsed suddenly of a heart arrhythmia brought on by a long struggle with anorexia and bulimia. She died in his arms. They were both thirty-three.

At nearly every date that spring and summer—to museums, galleries, and concerts—Sean brought me roses. Actually, they were drawings and screenprints he made of roses. "For beautiful Andrea," they were inscribed. He called when he said he would. He showed up on time. He told me how much he liked me, then how much he loved me. He drove me to IKEA when I wanted bookcases, then put them together for me. When my father was diagnosed with cancer and given a grim diagnosis, he researched treatment options. He could also be refreshingly unself-conscious and silly. I knew I loved him when I saw him sitting in his underwear eating a huge bowl of grapes and guffawing to the movie *This Is Spinal Tap*. I admired his certainty, steadfastness, and directness. And it freaked me out, too.

It is fall, and Sean and I are hiking up Mount Monadnock in

New Hampshire. (Yes, it seems that the pivotal moments in all my relationships happen on mountains.) We're close to the summit when I trip on a tree root and go down. As I fall, I brace myself with my left hand. My wrist bends back alarmingly when I hit the ground, and my forehead bounces off a rock. Sean reaches out to steady me as I stand up. My arm and head throb. Within minutes, my wrist and hand turn red and swell. A large bump erupts on my forehead.

Sean is calm. "Let's get you back to the car," he says.

We walk quickly down the mountain. As we descend, I start to panic. I'm not so worried about my wrist. But the bump on my head really hurts. I feel dizzy. Maybe I have a head injury. Maybe my brain is bleeding right now. I focus on my feet, dodging rocks and fallen tree branches. The car seems so far away.

The trail begins to level off. My breath comes in sharp gasps. My arms tingle. "My arms feel numb," I say. "I think something is really wrong with my head."

When we get to the car, Sean calls 911. An ambulance picks us up and takes me to a small hospital. Sean sits beside me, stroking my hair the whole way. Crutches and casts line the exam room wall. (A nurse tells us that hiking injuries on Mount Monadnock keep them in business.) My head is fine. My wrist, however, is broken. I leave with a plastic splint and instructions to see a hand specialist when I return to New York.

On the drive home, Sean stops and gets me ice cream. When we get to my apartment, he heads to a grocery store to pick up milk and other essentials, then props me up in bed, placing a pillow under my sore wrist and a bottle of Tylenol and a book within easy reach.

A year later Sean proposed to me at the Metropolitan Museum of Art, his favorite place in New York, in front of a Van Gogh painting of white roses. We married six months later.

8

WORRIES ABOUT MY DAUGHTER
THE EDUCATION OF AN ANXIOUS PARENT

A couple of months after our wedding, Sean and I started trying to get pregnant.

I had always yearned to have a child. I thought it would be fascinating to have a ringside seat as a little person developed. And I wanted to feel that kind of immersive, unconditional love. You could abandon any other relationship, it seemed: with friends, boyfriends, a spouse, even with siblings or parents. But not with a child. That was eternal. I was awed by the thought of it.

I didn't, however, think I would actually be able to do it. After all, pregnancy is basically a ten-month dive into uncertainty. The scary tests, the strange symptoms, and the deep unknown of first-time childbirth can rattle even women without anxiety disorders. And there was a bigger question, too: With my marked genes, would it be fair to potentially doom a child to a life of anxiety and depression?

I am now a mother. These days I often think of my genetic albatross at the playground, while goofing around with my daughter, Fiona, who is now seven. Fiona is a delight—funny, bright, and kind. She loves to draw and read (*Pippi Longstocking* is a favorite) and play elaborate pretend games with her friends. She can also be shy and sensitive. She's petrified of many kids' movies. Play-dates have sometimes ended with her in a heaving heap because of some perceived slight. I try not to see every personality quirk through *DSM*-colored glasses, as some sort of burgeoning psychiatric illness, but I'm not always successful. I've read the research. Studies of preschoolers have shown that young children who are clingy and don't explore their surroundings—who are behaviorally inhibited—are three times more likely to develop an anxiety disorder by adolescence than kids with other temperaments.

Anxiety is a disease of doubt. Pregnancy and new motherhood are almost defined by uncertainty and unease. I did not have an easy time of it. Almost as soon as I knew I was pregnant, my anxiety soared. I worried about everything from amnios to autism. I'd wake suddenly at three or four in the morning, my mind overflowing with catastrophe. *This is the week when neural tube defects occur,* I'd think. *Is it happening to my baby now?* I was obsessed with miscarriage. I'd run to the bathroom to scrutinize my underwear for blood. My heart rate was constantly elevated. My breathing was quick and shallow. I was both exhausted and jittery—as though I had pulled several all-nighters in a row but was jacked up on a pot of coffee. I lost weight when I should have been gaining.

My bottle of Klonopin was still tucked into my bag, but I couldn't take any. My psychiatrist had told me it was too dangerous, that benzodiazepines during pregnancy were linked to birth defects. So I took walks in Fort Greene Park. I tried the breathing exercises I had learned in cognitive behavioral therapy. I weighed the evidence of my worries, telling myself that most babies are healthy, that most women get through pregnancy without dying or going crazy.

It didn't work. I called my psychiatrist on his cell phone. "How am I going to get through the next nine months like this?" I wailed.

At one point my husband was so concerned, he said, "We don't have to go through with this."

And we didn't.

I was ten weeks pregnant and getting an NT scan, a detailed ultrasound. The technician, a smiling middle-aged woman, was chatty as she wielded the wand and looked at a screen. I heard the even *whoosh, whoosh, whoosh* of the baby's heartbeat.

Then her brow furrowed, and she fell silent. She stared intently at the screen while moving the wand around.

"Is everything okay?" I asked.

"I'll have to get the doctor," she said, taking off her rubber gloves.

"Please, can you tell me? Is everything okay?" I asked again.

"I need to talk to the doctor," she insisted.

I pressed further. "Can you just tell me if it's something bad? I'm here alone. My husband is working out of state. Should I tell a friend to come meet me here? If it's bad news, I don't want to be alone."

"I'm sorry. I can't give any results. The doctor will see you shortly, I promise," she said.

It was bad. I knew it. I'd seen enough hospital shows and movies to know that this is how it goes: the silence, the look of concern, the wait for the doctor, the awful news. I sat in the waiting room and texted my husband and my friend Ianthe. "Something is wrong with the baby," I wrote.

I was ushered into a small windowless room with a doctor. "Your fetus has a cystic hygroma," the doctor said flatly. "This can mean a genetic disorder or some other defect." I began to cry hard, catching tears and snot on my sleeve. *Couldn't they have put a box of tissues in this room?* I thought angrily.

Later that afternoon another doctor, this one softer and kinder, explained that cystic hygromas are fluid-filled cysts caused by a blockage in the lymphatic system. My baby's case was severe: Many cysts lined the neck and spine. The doctor drew me a chart. Fifty percent of fetuses with a cystic hygroma have some chromosomal abnormality. Of the other 50 percent, one-third have a major structural birth defect, such as a heart anomaly. Some pregnancies end in miscarriage or stillbirth. Babies who survive might have cerebral palsy and developmental delays. In the far right corner of the chart, in small letters, she had written 17 percent. That was our chance of having a healthy baby.

But no test she or any other doctor could order would ever tell us for sure. Even if our baby's chromosomes, organs, arms, and legs were normal, there could be some stealth syndrome. The what-ifs were endless. It was uncertainty writ large.

We terminated the pregnancy.

Weeks later I started corresponding with a woman I met on a "pregnancy loss" online message board. Her fetus had recently been diagnosed with a severe cystic hygroma. She was told that the baby would likely die before birth. Deeply religious, she decided to carry the baby to term. I followed the blog she kept about her pregnancy. She wrote about the clothes she picked out for her son's funeral, about the memorial service she was planning, even as the baby was kicking inside her. Her son lived less than an hour after delivery.

Even though I wholeheartedly wanted a child, I was relieved not to be pregnant anymore. But I felt guilty about my relief. Had my anxiety somehow caused the cystic hygroma? I wondered. Was it the Prozac? I was taking 10 milligrams daily.

Studies have indicated that about 10 percent of pregnant women in the United States receive prescriptions for SSRIs. On the advice of my psychiatrist, I had switched from Paxil to Prozac before I got pregnant. In the mid-2000s, studies had linked mothers' Paxil use during pregnancy to heart defects in their babies. At the time, many doctors considered Prozac to be the safest SSRI during pregnancy. It had been around the longest, and thousands of babies had already been exposed to it.

However, Prozac was no match for my anxiety during my own brief pregnancy. I went to see a reproductive psychiatrist, one of a growing number who specialize in treating depressed and anxious pregnant women and their vulnerable fetuses. She reassured me that Prozac was safe to take during my next pregnancy. She told me I should take Klonopin, too, if my anxiety escalated again; the risk to the baby was minimal, she said. What I shouldn't do, she said, was try to go off meds. "She merits long-term prophylaxis with an SSRI to minimize the risk of relapse including during pregnancy and lactation," the psychiatrist's report read. "Many patients require a dosage increase during pregnancy to maintain remission."

I stayed on the Prozac and hoped for the best.

Later studies emerged showing that Prozac, too, was linked to a higher risk—about double—of heart defects and skull malformations in babies exposed to the drug during the first trimester of pregnancy. There were reports of birth defects among babies whose mothers took other SSRIs as well, but more recent research seems to exonerate Zoloft and Lexapro. There is a small increased risk of neural tube defects with Celexa. Some studies have shown that babies exposed to SSRIs in utero are more likely to be born prematurely and at lower birth weights. They are also more at risk of facing a serious lung condition called pulmonary hypertension.

However, the risks of all these outcomes are very small. Most women will have unaffected babies. And studies conflict, too. One 2016 analysis involving more than 2,700 women who took SSRIs during pregnancy found that their babies were no more likely to have heart defects than women who didn't take the drugs.

After my termination, my doctor had some of the fetal cells

tested to see if there was a genetic reason for the cystic hygroma. The chromosomes were normal. Although I hadn't wanted my doctor to tell me the gender, there it was, typed on the lab report: XY. A boy.

The road to getting pregnant again was not smooth. I was thirty-seven at the time of my D&C, a uterine surgery commonly performed after a miscarriage or to terminate a pregnancy. My doctor told me to wait until my period returned and then try again. I was exhausted, emotionally drained, and terrified of another pregnancy, but I had no time to waste. I still wanted a baby. About a month after my D&C, my period returned. It was light and short. I called my doctor, who said this was typical, that it might take a while for my body to heal and my cycle to return to normal. Another month went by. The next period was similar, barely there, this time accompanied by intense cramping. I called my doctor again. She reassured me again. I made an appointment with another gynecologist. And another. They, too, said I had to be patient. It could take several months for my body to reset.

But I wasn't reassured. I posted questions on an online pregnancy loss support group and Googled "light periods after D&C." Eventually I found my way to Ashermans.org, a site devoted to Asherman's syndrome, a condition characterized by scar tissue in the uterus. The symptoms? Light—or absent—periods and cramping. The cause? Usually a D&C or other uterine surgery. I read haunting entries from desperate women made infertile by the scarring. I posted questions, describing my periods in gory detail. Kind, helpful women wrote back, advising me on the exact tests to request to secure an accurate diagnosis. I called one of the doctors

I had seen and asked for an HSG, a type of X-ray where a dye is injected into the uterus.

Sure enough, the test revealed scar tissue nearly blocking my cervix. The cause of Asherman's—uterine surgery—is, ironically, also the cure. Sean and I traveled to a specialist in suburban Boston recommended by the Ashermans.org ladies. After three surgeries and a month on estrogen pills, I was cleared to try to get pregnant again. It was early June.

By July, I had a positive pregnancy test.

I braced myself for a resurgence of anxiety, but it didn't happen. During my first trimester, I was queasy and exhausted. In my third, I was achy and had trouble sleeping. But I wasn't extraordinarily anxious. I don't know why this pregnancy was different. The bout with Asherman's, I think, overrode some of my earlier fears. I had spent months desperately afraid I wouldn't get pregnant again. I had started to research surrogacy and adoption. So this time the positive test was a relief. Part of me also wonders if my body knew on some primitive level that my first pregnancy was doomed.

As my due date approached, I became scared of birth itself. My husband and I hired a doula. Many couples employ a doula to help them have an unmedicated birth. My own sister gave birth twice at home with no drugs. My goal, however, was much more modest: I just wanted to survive the ordeal without losing my mind.

I went into labor three days after my due date. It was a warm March day, and Sean and I walked the streets of our Brooklyn neighborhood. I paused and leaned on him during contractions. The pains were close together but not particularly intense. Our doula met us at home, and the three of us drove to the hospital together. For several hours, I wandered the halls of the labor and delivery unit, climbed in and out of the shower, and at one point took my husband's hand and banged it against my forehead to distract myself from the pain.

I got an epidural, and the pain vanished. Unfortunately, this opened up space for anxiety to come roaring in. Without the pain to focus on, I worried. Was the baby okay? Was I okay? I had heard about women having strokes after delivery. Would that happen to me? My legs felt heavy and numb from the epidural. Would it leave me paralyzed? I heard a *beep, beep, beep*. An alarm rang notifying the nurses that my heart rate was markedly high. I lay motionless in the hospital bed, staring at the clock. Worrying. Worrying. My husband and my doula dozed in straight-backed chairs.

My labor stalled. The doctor gave me Pitocin to try to kick-start it. Two hours went by, then four. Nothing was happening. My doctor decided that I needed a cesarean section.

I know women have C-sections every day, but for me, the surgery was horrifying. My epidural was upped so far, it felt difficult to breathe. My arms were strapped down to padded supports on either side of me. A blue plastic sheet went up in front of me, and a team of blue-cap-and-gown-shrouded doctors and nurses milled about. There was a jarring juxtaposition between my whirring mind and my paralyzed body. I've never felt so out of control.

"I don't think I can do this," I said to my husband.

"Help me," I said to the doctors.

The anesthesiologist bent down. "We can give you a sedative," he said. "But we want to get the baby out first."

I wish I could say that I felt a rush of love or awe when I saw my daughter's wriggling, blood-streaked body emerge above the blue sheet. "It's a nine pounder!" I heard someone exclaim. But I just felt desperation. I looked to the anesthesiologist. He was pushing a syringe into my IV. I felt the balled-up muscles in my neck ease a bit. The sedative was in.

Fiona was healthy and beautiful. She was also a tough baby. For the first few months, we had feeding challenges. She wouldn't latch onto my breast. When I tried to nurse, she would ball up her hands into fists and put them in front of her face. I took to yelling "hands" to my mother, mother-in-law, and husband, a signal for them to come over and pull the baby's hands away so I could push her mouth onto me. I had rounds of painful clogged milk ducts. My daughter and I passed thrush, a yeast infection in my breasts and her mouth, back and forth. I visited a lactation consultant, who ordered me to drink raspberry leaf tea (good for milk production), stop eating dairy, and do various mouth exercises with my daughter. (Smooshing her cheeks together to make a fish face was one.)

Almost as soon as we got the feeding thing down, the crying escalated. Fiona was colicky, which is just a euphemism for what seemed like nonstop screaming. We swaddled her, shushed her, and held her while bouncing up and down on an exercise ball. Still, she cried five, six, seven hours a day. Nothing seemed to work except for Marvin Gaye's "What's Going On" on endless repeat. It was her aural pacifier.

I joined a group of new moms and met up with them and their newborns at neighborhood cafés and, sometimes, bars. Early evening at one was dubbed "Nappy Hour" because of all the diaper-clad infants and pilsner-sipping moms. The other women chatted as their babies slept, nursed, or lay passively in baby slings. It seemed as though I was always on the periphery, bouncing and swaying in a futile attempt to stop Fiona from bawling.

Since I was breastfeeding, Fiona was still getting a daily dose of Prozac. But when she was nearly three months old, we were in Florida, at my parents' house. I had run out of Prozac, and my psychiatrist had called in a prescription to a nearby Walgreens. When I got the bottle, there was an orange warning label, one I had never seen before: "Do not take this medication while breastfeeding." I stopped taking Prozac that day.

As with the emerging evidence about heart defects, scientists were finding that SSRIs had varying degrees of safety during breastfeeding. Prozac, it turns out, is found in breast milk in much higher levels compared to other drugs in its class. There have been some reports of excessive crying, irritability, and feeding problems in nursing infants whose moms were taking it. Other studies link Prozac to slow weight gain in infants. Paxil and Zoloft, which are nearly undetectable in infants' blood, are considered a safer choice.

More worrisome are the potential long-term effects on kids exposed to antidepressants in utero. The science is decidedly mixed: Some studies have found an increased risk of autism and ADHD. A 2016 study, for example, found that children born to women who took SSRIs during the second and/or third trimester of pregnancy were twice as likely to develop autism as those who weren't exposed to the drugs. Other studies have found no link between antidepressants and autism.

Another set of studies has found that exposure to SSRIs can lead to behavior problems and subtle defects in motor function and language development. In a 2016 study of preschoolers, some whose mothers had taken SSRIs during pregnancy had more behavioral issues and lower scores on an assessment of expressive language. Other studies, however, found no long-term effects. One 2015 study compared children exposed to SSRIs in utero with their unexposed siblings. When it came to certain measures of intelligence and behavior, there was no difference between them.

Some doctors say that the mixed findings should be reassuring to women who take SSRIs during pregnancy. "If there was a definite problem, it should show up consistently," says Marlene P. Freeman, associate director of the Perinatal and Reproductive Psychiatry Program at Massachusetts General Hospital.

Still, some recent research has raised new concerns. A large study published in 2016 found that adolescents whose mothers took SSRIs while pregnant with them are more than four times as likely to become depressed by age fifteen, compared to children whose mothers had psychiatric disorders but didn't take SSRIs during pregnancy. The study is one of very few to follow children beyond the age of six. And it is the first to link SSRI exposure in utero to a later risk of depression.

The results are "a bit worrisome," says Heli Malm, an obstetrician at Helsinki University Hospital and lead author of the study. She notes that the oldest children in the study are just entering the ages when mood disorders tend to arise, so the number of them with depression could increase. She also cautions that the results are preliminary.

The impetus for the study was work that researchers at Columbia University had done on rodents. Mice who were given Prozac during the first week or two of life exhibited anxious and depressed behavior when they became adults. (The first few weeks of the life of a mouse are roughly equivalent to the second and third trimesters in utero for human babies.) For example, normal mice run away when mild shocks are delivered to their feet. But the Prozac-exposed mice moved very slowly or didn't escape at all when shocked. The mice "look perfectly normal until they reach the mouse equivalent of adolescence," says Jay A. Gingrich, a psychiatry professor at Columbia University Medical Center, who led the rodent research.

The early-life exposure led to slowed firing of neurons that respond to serotonin in the prefrontal cortex. In mice, higher doses and exposure during the equivalent of the second and third trimester were linked to the most severe behavioral effects. Gingrich is exploring whether non-SSRI antidepressants lead to the same problems. Most distressing to Gingrich was that administering antidepressants to the adult mice didn't reverse the anxious or depressed behavior. "That is what keeps me awake at night," he says.

After I got off the phone with Gingrich, I walked to a quiet corner of the *Journal* newsroom and cried. By treating my anxiety, had I sentenced my daughter to depression? I felt waves of guilt and regret. I tried to reassure myself: Fiona is not a mouse. I took a small dose—only 10 milligrams—while pregnant. (The mice were given the equivalent of 40 milligrams.) Still, wouldn't it have been more logical simply not to take antidepressants during pregnancy?

But it isn't so simple. Mothers' anxiety and depression during pregnancy have been linked to problems in babies and kids, too. And many of those are the same conditions that are associated with exposure to SSRIs in utero. Some studies have shown that depression during pregnancy increases the risk of autism. It is also linked to preterm birth and lower birth weight in babies. And high anxiety during pregnancy has been linked to ADHD symptoms in children. It can be tough to tease apart the effects of the disease and the effects of the medication.

It wouldn't be ethical to conduct a randomized-controlled clinical trial with pregnant women, choosing some to get treatment and others to go without, which means that all this research is "observational." It is impossible to control all the factors that might confound the results. It could be, for example, that women who take SSRIs during pregnancy have more serious and more chronic illnesses than women who don't take SSRIs—illnesses that are likely to persist after their babies are born. Being exposed to a parent's depression during childhood ups the risk of developing mood and anxiety disorders.

The Belgian researcher Bea Van den Bergh has been studying the long-term effects of anxiety during pregnancy since the late

1980s. She initially recruited eighty-six pregnant women and has followed them and their children ever since. None of the mothers were being treated for anxiety disorders, but some were highly anxious. In a series of studies, she and colleagues found that the children of women who were highly anxious during pregnancy were more likely to be difficult babies, with more fussiness and sleeping and eating issues. By age eight or nine, they had higher rates of anxiety, aggressive behavior, restlessness, and difficulty focusing their attention.

When the children reached their teens, the ones whose moms had been anxious during pregnancy showed an atypical pattern in their levels of the stress hormone cortisol. In girls, that was associated with higher rates of depression. When the kids were seventeen years old, mothers' high anxiety during pregnancy was linked to specific cognitive issues in both boys and girls: These offspring had a tougher time on tasks that measured "endogenous cognitive control," a way of processing information that allows you to successfully adapt your behavior to changing goals without the help of external cues.

Van den Bergh found that babies were particularly vulnerable to their mothers' anxiety during the second trimester—from about the twelfth to the twenty-second week of pregnancy. High anxiety later in pregnancy didn't seem to affect children much. Researchers at the University of California at Irvine have found that mothers' anxiety during the nineteenth week of pregnancy (yes, that specific week) might actually reduce the volume of parts of the brain related to working memory and language processing. Since the women in this research weren't being treated for psychiatric illnesses, the negative impact could be even more severe for children of women with actual anxiety disorders.

Scientists in Dresden, Germany, are following more than three hundred women and their babies to see the effect of women's anxiety disorders and depression on themselves and their children. They've found that women who had an anxiety disorder anytime during their lifetime are more likely to have babies that cry excessively. (By excessive, they mean more than three hours per day, at least three days per week and for three weeks or more.) The researchers have also found a link between mothers' history of anxiety disorders and feeding problems in their babies.

This research bolsters what is known as the fetal programming hypothesis. There's growing evidence that the uterine environment can alter the development of the fetus, especially during certain particularly sensitive time periods. This means that children of anxious moms don't just have a genetic predisposition to anxiety; anxiety may actually be transmitted to them in utero.

"Normally a child is pretty protected" during pregnancy, says Hans-Ulrich Wittchen, a coauthor of the Dresden studies. "But in the later developmental months, there are stronger environmental factors. The unborn child is very sensitive to learning."

How does the transmission occur? Researchers think that one way is that high levels of cortisol in anxious or stressed pregnant women can cross the placenta and affect the developing fetal brain. There's also evidence that anxiety can restrict blood flow to the fetus. In a fascinating study by Columbia University researchers published in 2016, stress during pregnancy was found to turn off a gene in the placenta that helps to deactivate a mother's cortisol before the stress hormone reaches the fetus. This genetic change in the placenta had effects on the fetus: The offspring with the change had lower synchronicity between their movements and heart rates, which is known as fetal coupling. Increased fetal coupling is a marker of healthy neurodevelopment.

Ideally, babies would not be exposed to either SSRIs *or* anxiety and depression while in utero. But that can be difficult to achieve.

One study found that about two-thirds of women with a history of depression who stopped their medication just before getting pregnant or early in pregnancy relapsed. Women need more choices for treatment, and doctors need to encourage women to try nondrug therapies. (The reproductive psychiatrist I saw did not mention alternatives to me.) Perhaps women could do a course of CBT while tapering their drugs before trying to become pregnant and continue therapy during their pregnancies to deal with symptoms and prevent relapse.

During the early months of Fiona's life, I don't think I was more anxious than any other new parent. I had quotidian worries: Was she eating enough? Was she warm enough? Too warm? Was that bottle really BPA-free? Is that a choking hazard? Should I let her gnaw on that toy that says "Made in China"? My circumstances, it seemed, had finally caught up with the natural workings of my mind. It is socially acceptable, even encouraged, for new parents to worry: The "new mom" message boards I visited were a marketplace of anxiety and reassurance.

I only had one ER visit with Fiona during her first year. Desperate to use the bathroom, I had left her asleep in the middle of our queen-size bed. A minute later I heard a thump and a cry. She had fallen onto the floor, a distance of maybe a foot. With thoughts of head injuries and brain bleeds, I scooped her up, grabbed her car seat, hustled out to a cab, still in my pajamas, and took her to the ER at Columbia University Medical Center. I had heard that they had the best pediatric neurosurgery department in the city. She was fine.

My daughter seemed to hate sleep. For the first seven months of her life, nearly every daytime nap was taken on someone's body, usually mine. I held her on my lap or wore her in a baby carrier while she dozed. I'd drape a napkin over her head while I ate but still found crumbs and the occasional blueberry in her hair. At night, I could usually get her to sleep in her crib, at least for a few hours. She would fall asleep on me, and then I would gently, gently lower her to the bed, holding my breath and willing her eyes to stay shut. Yet too often she would wake and cry as soon as her body brushed the mattress. Even after the newborn sobbing abated, Fiona seemed chronically pissed off. Until just before her first birthday, she had the air of a disgruntled old man.

Sean and I were fried. We had no family nearby to help and, with me on unpaid maternity leave, little money to hire a babysitter. We argued. If one of us stayed minutes too long in the laundry room or in the shower, we'd be welcomed back with an accusing, "Where *were* you?"

There's a rash of new studies looking at the ill effects of sleep problems in children, such as insomnia and chronically insufficient shut-eye. Poor sleep has been linked to aggressive behavior, learning and memory problems, and obesity. It also appears to increase the risk of the later development of mental illness, including anxiety and depression: There's some evidence that sleep deprivation weakens the connection between the amygdala and the prefrontal cortex.

Like so many parents, I read the baby sleep guides and periodically tried to "sleep train" Fiona. That invariably meant hours of screaming (the baby) and knocked-back glasses of wine (me). When as a two-year-old, she wouldn't nap outside the stroller, I wheeled her back and forth in the hallway of our apartment building until she nodded off and then parked her in the bedroom.

As Fiona grew into a toddler, she became sunny, affectionate, and funny. Parenting became much less of a grind when it was accompanied by giggles, hugs, and silly impromptu dancing.

As a preschooler, Fiona was spirited and joyful, obsessed with Mary Poppins and her hot-pink scooter. She was also reserved and cautious. She hovered along the perimeter of birthday parties and music classes. At the playground, if there were more than a few children on the jungle gym, she wouldn't budge from my side. At school, she struggled when making mistakes. "I'm terrible at G's," she'd wail when practicing her letters. She took rejection hard. At her fourth birthday party, she collapsed in sobs. "Leila told me not to look at her," she cried, her mouth still ringed with chocolate frosting.

I fretted and wrung my hands. Was this evidence of an anxiety disorder in the making? The future isn't exactly rosy for anxious kids. In a 2007 study, young people ages fourteen to twenty-four who had social anxiety disorder were almost three times as likely to later develop depression than those without anxiety. Another study, published in 2004, followed children ages nine to thirteen who had been treated for an anxiety disorder. Those who still had the disorder seven years after treatment drank alcohol more frequently and were more likely to use marijuana than those whose disorders had resolved.

New research shows that serious anxiety disorders can likely be prevented if they are caught and treated when kids are still young. Children can be taught to cope so that they don't later self-medicate with drugs and alcohol or screw up plans for college and careers.

There are also new therapy programs specifically designed for healthy kids with a genetic predisposition like my daughter's. Researchers at the University of Connecticut Health Center and Johns Hopkins University School of Medicine tested an eight-week program for 136 healthy kids ages six to thirteen who each had at least one parent with an anxiety disorder. During the following year, 31 percent of kids who didn't receive the therapy developed an anxiety disorder, whereas only 5 percent of the kids who received treatment developed one.

With evidence like that, how am I going to feel if I don't do something now and my daughter falls apart when she's a teenager?

Psychology professor Ronald Rapee began treating behaviorally inhibited preschoolers more than a decade ago, with the aim of forestalling anxiety disorders. More accurately, he began treating the *parents* of behaviorally inhibited kids. Many parents of shy, skittish children fall into the trap of being overprotective of their emotionally fragile progeny. While understandable, this just reinforces kids' burgeoning feelings of vulnerability and inadequacy, which leads to more anxiety. In a six-session program called Cool Little Kids, Rapee teaches parents to reverse that pattern by fostering "bravery." Parents are told to resist the urge to allow their kids to avoid stressful situations or rescue them when they're afraid. Moms and dads are taught to deal with their own anxieties, too, since children model the behavior they see. (Parents are the only ones seen in the program. Children aren't treated directly.)

The program started at Macquarie University, where Rapee is the founder of the school's Centre for Emotional Health. I traveled to Sydney, Australia, to meet him. The Macquarie campus, a sprawling, leafy space dotted with buildings in a cacophonous hodgepodge of architectural styles, was quiet. Most of the thirty thousand students were on their summer break. I saw only a few slightly scared-looking young people with adults in tow, perhaps prospective students.

Rapee, who is fifty-five, is soft-spoken, with little of the swagger often encountered in world-renowned scientists. His office contains a shrine to his now-teenaged daughters' childhood. A bulletin board on one wall is filled with their preschool artwork: a painting of a rainbow, a drawing of butterflies, and a portrait of their father. A note says "I love my dad."

We speak candidly about the efficacy of Cool Little Kids. There's evidence that the program does prevent some anxiety disorders, particularly in girls. One study followed 146 behaviorally inhibited preschoolers. Half the parents attended six ninety-minute sessions of the Cool Little Kids program; the other half did not. The children were assessed again eleven years later, when they were, on average, fifteen years old. Thirty-nine percent of the teenage girls whose parents had gone through Cool Little Kids had an anxiety disorder, versus 61 percent of girls in the control group. The program didn't, however, make much of a difference for boys.

Technically, Rapee's work isn't prevention. Most of the children in the Cool Little Kids program, even the three-year-olds, were already clinically anxious. "The overlap between temperament and diagnosis is all just a big messy blob," he tells me.

Talking to Rapee is sometimes disorienting. He vacillates. Parenting matters when it comes to anxiety. Parenting doesn't matter. I feel as though I am seeing scientific uncertainty—or maybe scientific rumination—up close. His latest thinking seems to boil down to this: Parenting doesn't generally make kids anxious. But if a child is already anxious, then controlling, overprotective parenting can fuel and maintain kids' anxiety.

Over the years, Rapee has become more inclined to see the controlling hand of genes. The notion scares me. My genes, my grandmother's genes, may determine my daughter's trajectory. And there may not be much I can do about it.

Six preschoolers sit in a circle, legs crisscrossed on colorful foam mats. It is the final meeting of the Turtle Program, an intervention for behaviorally inhibited preschoolers. A shiny gold sign exclaiming CONGRATS GRAD! hangs on the wall.

"Can anyone remind us about some of the new things we've learned in circle time?" asks Danielle Novick, one of the program's leaders.

Marie, a little girl with curly brown hair and silver sneakers, shyly raises her hand. "Being brave," she says.

"Good job," replies Novick. "Thank you." She leans over and puts a sticker on Marie's knee, a reward for speaking up. "And we learned something about our eyes. What did we learn about our eyes?" Novick continues.

"Eye contact," says a little girl with honey-blond hair and a blue skirt.

"Yes, it's good to look in someone's eyes when you're talking to them," Novick says. "They can tell that you're listening to them and that you're being friendly."

I'm watching this exchange from an adjacent room via a one-way mirror. The program is actually a study conducted by researchers at the University of Maryland on the efficacy of an eight-week treatment to prevent anxiety disorders in behaviorally inhibited preschoolers. The children in this group have all scored in the top 15 percent on a scale of behavioral inhibition. Many already have difficulties making friends, going to birthday parties, and speaking up in preschool.

In the group, the children learn social skills. They practice introducing themselves, asking another kid to play, and asking and answering questions. They learn to express their emotions and to negotiate conflict—first using puppets, which can be less stressful. The children also learn deep breathing, or what the program calls "balloon breathing," to help cope with anxiety. Ken Rubin, one of the lead investigators of the study, says that even as early as age four, behaviorally inhibited kids often have poor social skills, are being rejected by their peers, and are internalizing negative feelings about themselves. "We're trying to interrupt that whole process," says Andrea Chronis-Tuscano, the other principal investigator.

While the children are in circle time, their parents are in a room across the hall, where they are taught to ignore anxious and avoidant behavior and to praise brave behavior. The treatment is based on parent-child interaction therapy, an approach originally created for kids with behavior problems. Parents first learn child-directed interaction (CDI), a form of play where children lead. This aims to strengthen the parent-child relationship, bolster the kids' self-esteem, and combat some parents' impulse to control situations with their inhibited children.

Parents are also taught to create a fear hierarchy for their children consisting of incremental steps culminating in an ultimate goal. (Rapee's Cool Little Kids teaches this, too.) For example, if the ultimate goal is to ask another child to play, a first step might be to say hello to another child. The idea is for each step to be achievable, so that children have success and can gain confidence. The parents are coached on how to set up bravery practice (which is basically exposure therapy). They help their children to practice things like talking to a teacher or doing show-and-tell during the group. Therapists coach parents in the moment via earpieces, secret service style.

On this day, nine parents and two program leaders are preparing for the scavenger hunt that will be today's bravery practice. Each family is assigned an animal. Group leader Christina Danko passes out a piece of paper with pictures of six animals; the goal is to find all the critters shown. To do that, the children will need to approach each of the other families to ask the name of their animals so that they can check them off. For these kids, the task is going to be difficult. It will be the first time that all the parents and kids have been together, and each child will be exposed to ten new adults.

The parents—with help from Danko—decide on goals for their children. One mother says that she thinks her son will be able to say "Hi," and then "Monkey" when asked which animal he has. But Danko doesn't think the child is quite ready to ask other families a question, so Mom will make the inquiries. Kids who aren't ready to respond to questions verbally are allowed to point to the pictures of their animals instead.

The parents file across the hall and into the children's room, where they tell their kids the goals and role-play interactions. Then Danko calls for the hunt to begin. The noise volume in the room rises. Soon kids are covered in stickers: IST RATE, COOL, TOP NOTCH, they say. Marie has one in her hair. Another little boy has one on his forehead.

The din is joyful.

Then, crying.

One boy has tears running down his face. He's hiding behind his mother, clinging to her leg, "Mommyyy. I want to leaavvee!" he yells. His mother looks panicked, as if she'd love nothing more than to escape, too. Danko stands beside her, coaching her. "Tell him to stand next to you," Danko says. "Stand next to me," the mom says to her son. When the boy does as he's told, Danko reminds the mom to praise him for it.

After a snack of mini donuts, the wailing little boy calms down. Danko congratulates the parents for hanging in there. By not leaving, they've communicated to their son that they won't back down and that he can survive uncomfortable situations.

Ultimately, the Maryland study will include 150 kids. Half will be enrolled in the Turtle Program and half, the control group, will do Rapee's less-intensive Cool Little Kids. The study is gathering physiological data on the children, like heart rate variability. And researchers are observing parents and kids together to assess such aspects of parenting as overcontrol, warmth versus negativity, and fostering independence. The kids will be observed at school, too. The study hopes to discern which kids benefit most from the program and whether a parent's anxiety, parenting style, or the child's own physiology affect how much the kids improve.

The researchers take pains to emphasize that they are not trying to change these kids' personalities—to turn shy and introverted children into extroverts. "Impairment is really the key," says Chronis-Tuscano. "We know how important social relationships are to people's happiness and success in life, and we don't want their inhibition to hold them back from doing anything." In an earlier small pilot study, the Turtle Program reduced anxiety symptoms in behaviorally inhibited kids. Before the treatment, nearly three-quarters of the kids met criteria for social anxiety disorder. Afterward less than a third did.

Marie's parents, Nancy and Brandon, say they knew they needed to get help for their daughter after a birthday party for another child. Marie, who was three at the time, was excited for the party and looking forward to seeing her friends in her playgroup. But during the celebration Marie spent the entire time clinging to her mother's leg. "She loves other kids. But she just freezes and gets very scared. The fear and anxiety were really holding her back and preventing her from being herself and enjoying her life," Nancy says.

This behavior was typical. At home, Marie sang and danced and chattered nonstop, but around other people she was painfully shy, almost silent. Once when Nancy had a friend over who Marie had met before, Marie hid under the dining room table and cried. Nancy and Brandon were worried about the future, too. Both describe themselves as socially anxious. Nancy had been diagnosed with social anxiety disorder in her thirties; she had a tough time mingling at parties and says her anxiety limited her friendships. Medication and therapy helped tremendously. "I didn't want Marie to struggle with it for decades like we did," Nancy says.

On Nancy and Brandon's fear hierarchy, the top spot—their main goal for Marie—was to attend a birthday party and play with the other children. Nancy and Brandon broke that goal down into small steps: making eye contact with a new child, saying hello, saying her name. At their weekly excursion to the farmer's market, Marie's parents told her if she waved to three other kids, they'd buy her a Popsicle. "She started waving to everyone," Nancy says.

Nancy and Brandon changed their own behavior, too. They used to apologize for Marie's silence or answer for her. They'd pull her out of situations where she was uncomfortable. They let Marie quit a ballet class when she had trouble separating from them at drop-off. Now they push her to be brave and have stopped using the word *shy* in her presence. Recently, she has taken to calling herself Brave Marie. The program has made a real difference, the couple says. Indeed, Marie made a triumphant appearance at a birthday party just the week before. Now four, Marie clung to Nancy at the party at first, but soon she was doing crafts with the other kids and playing with the birthday girl. Although she didn't engage with kids she didn't know, Nancy and Brandon say this is huge progress.

Back in the Turtle Program the graduation ceremony begins. Novick calls each child forward to receive a diploma. CERTIFICATE FOR BEING BRAVE, it reads. One little boy skips across the room and beams as he shows his mom his diploma. Then he turns to me—an adult he doesn't know—and waits for me to congratulate him, too.

. . .

These days I'm much less worried about my daughter. In the last couple of years, she's become markedly more confident. She's still sensitive to shame and rejection, but she's more likely to stand up for herself. At her kindergarten graduation performance, she even stepped in and delivered the lines of another little girl overcome by stage fright. And when her class decided to sing "Happiness" from *You're a Good Man, Charlie Brown* at the first-grade talent show, she volunteered to be Charlie Brown.

In a funny twist, it has become clear to me that my husband, Sean, is sometimes the more anxious parent. He's the one who panics when Fiona has a fever and admonishes her to be careful on the playground. If there's anything that worries me, it's Fiona's outsize fear of many kids' movies. Is it the equivalent of my childhood clown phobia—an omen of greater anxiety to come? Since prevention programs now exist for a range of mental health issues (not just anxiety disorders, but depression and psychosis, too), and since we know that mental illness is at least partly genetic, am I being neglectful by not enrolling Fiona in an intervention while she's still young?

While I was in Sydney, I tried to get some free advice. I told Rapee about my daughter's fears—that she's not only petrified of movie monsters and villains but also hates it when anyone in a movie is nasty or mean. We got through only a few minutes of *The Wizard of Oz*, I told him. She made me turn it off at the appearance of Miss Gulch, the nasty woman who snatches Toto and later transforms into the Wicked Witch.

I told Rapee that I wanted to take my daughter to see *Paddington*, a movie about the talking bear that loves marmalade, so I showed her the trailer. It was frenetic. Paddington floods the bathroom and whooshes down a staircase in a bathtub. "I'm not seeing that movie," Fiona said. "It's too scary." I asked Rapee whether I should push her to see it. If the *Paddington* avoidance was part of a bigger picture, I could work on it, he said. "Will it scar her?" I asked. The only downside, he said, was that she might have nightmares afterward.

So a couple of weeks after I returned to Brooklyn, during a frigid Presidents' Week when Fiona didn't have school, I took her to our local theater, a beat-up old place where the screens don't seem much bigger than some TVs. When I told her where we were headed, Fiona said she didn't want to go. "We can leave if it's too scary," I promised.

I could feel Fiona bracing for fear from the movie's first scenes. By the time an earthquake leveled Paddington's home in "darkest Peru" and killed his uncle, she had left her seat and scrambled onto my lap. When the villain, an icy Nicole Kidman, captured Paddington and threw him into a black van with TAXIDERMIST on the side, Fiona began to sob uncontrollably. "We can go," I said, and moved to get up. "No," she wailed, tears and snot running down her face.

We stayed. But Paddington's escape was drawn out and perilous. He nearly fell into a fiery pit. He was almost shot. Fiona's sobbing escalated, then abated. I asked her again whether she wanted to leave. An emphatic no. "Paddington will be okay," I whispered to her. And he was.

When the lights went up, I heard another mother say, "That poor kid got so scared." I felt awful and embarrassed, like I was a terrible parent. I told Fiona how proud I was of her.

That night and the next day Fiona talked incessantly about the movie. Not the scary parts but the parts she liked. Paddington making marmalade. And especially about the villain's eventual comeuppance: The taxidermist played by Kidman is arrested and sentenced to community service at a petting zoo, where a monkey she had planned on stuffing gets his revenge. He pushes a button, and hay and manure fall on Kidman's head. Fiona tells that part of the story over and over.

But when my husband asks her if she liked the movie, Fiona shakes her head. "It was too scary."

I'm still not sure what, if anything, I accomplished. As with everything else in parenting, I'm winging it.

9

STAYING GROUNDED
LEARNING TO LIVE WITH ANXIETY

After more than twenty-five years of living with anxiety disorders, I know better than to hope for a cure. I have easy years and tough years. When things are rough and anxiety threatens to derail my life and keep me from my family and work, I reach for medication (now Lexapro and my ever faithful Klonopin). I see my longtime psychologist. I try new forms of therapy.

Even when things are going smoothly, I'm careful. I arrange my life so I can sleep eight hours a night (sometimes nine). I rarely drink. I do yoga and take walks in the park.

I had always worried that when something truly terrible did happen (and if you live long enough, it always does), I wouldn't be able to handle it, that it would paralyze me. But that hasn't happened.

Ten years ago my father called to tell me he wasn't feeling well. He was achy and tired. Maybe he had the flu, he said. My mother was away visiting my sister, and my father often falls into a slight funk when he's alone, so I wasn't worried. A few weeks later, though, my mother called to say that my dad was in the hospital with kidney failure. I flew to Florida, where my parents had moved years earlier.

After a few days of tests, we learned that Dad had multiple myeloma, a virulent and incurable cancer of the blood.

He was put in the ICU and immediately began an intense regimen of chemotherapy. The hospital also tried an experimental course of continuous dialysis. It was terrible and surreal to see him so pale and supine in that hospital bed. At fifty-seven, he had been biking and Rollerblading just weeks before.

Back in New York, I put on my reporter's hat and researched his condition and its treatments for hours each day. While at work one evening, I stumbled upon one study that gave the life expectancy for patients with multiple myeloma that presents with kidney failure: three months. I broke down and called Sean. He drove to pick me up and held me while I cried.

After that I pulled myself together. I pushed my father to get a second opinion at the University of Arkansas for Medical Sciences in Little Rock. Data I found showed that their aggressive approach—which then involved two stem cell transplants—seemed to yield the longest survival rates.

We have no idea whether moving my father's treatment to Little Rock made a difference. But after many grueling months of treatment and one nearly fatal bout of sepsis, he has been in remission ever since.

I had my own cancer scare four years ago after I noticed that a mole on my cheek looked a little funny. What had been a flat brown spot was now raised and tinged with red. I went to my dermatologist, who said it was nothing, but I couldn't shake the feeling that something was off. I obsessively checked it in the mirror. I went back to the dermatologist. Still fine, she said. Still not reassured, I decided to see a more senior partner in the practice. She biopsied it and, a few days later, called me. "It's melanoma," she said, with urgency in her voice. "It has to be removed now."

Thankfully, the cancer seemed to be contained. Still, I got a second opinion. And a third. And a fourth. The problem was that the doctors didn't agree on a course of treatment. A few thought I could get away with cutting out just the spot. Others recommended a more aggressive approach that would involve removing a larger patch of skin. I decided to be cautious and then developed a huge crush on the plastic surgeon who dug a two-inch hole in my face.

The cancer dramas were overwhelming and nerve-wracking, but they didn't crush me. Real peril, I have found, galvanizes me. I make decisions and get stuff done. It's fear—not danger—that shuts me down.

I take some solace in the fact that anxiety may dissipate as we get older. Indeed, the rates of anxiety disorders dip as people enter their fifties. Is it wisdom or the growing awareness of our mortality that causes us to chill out? "Anxiety disorders have a tendency to burn out. You just can't stay anxious your whole life," says Harvard's Ron Kessler.

But after all my reporting and all my interviews with scientists, one major question still nagged at me: Why do the rates of anxiety disorders seem to be rising among young people? The numbers are particularly troubling for college students. Between 2008 and 2016, the number of college students diagnosed with or treated for anxiety problems jumped from 10 to 17 percent. Are we facing some generational mental health apocalypse?

I went back to the site of my own college breakdowns—the University of Michigan—to try to find out. I arrived in Ann Arbor in late April, in the middle of finals, which seemed a fitting time to be asking questions about anxiety. The libraries and cafés were filled with students hunched over laptops and scribbling in notebooks.

I met with student mental health advocates in the local Starbucks. Grant Rivas and Shelby Steverson are nineteen-year-old first-year students. Anna Chen is twenty-three and a graduating senior. All three are articulate, passionate, and slightly formal, rebuffing my offers to buy them coffee.

I asked them why they thought their generation seemed so prone to anxiety. They felt, they said, a relentless pressure to succeed academically. Their middle and high school years had been filled with talk of the recession, they told me, and a bachelor's degree is no longer any guarantee of a job, so they and many of their friends were gunning for graduate school and competitive internships. Every class, every test, every paper is high stakes. Rivas, who was wearing a yellow T-shirt that said MAIZE RAGE, said he was planning to apply for a spot in the undergraduate public policy program. "You've got to be really on top of your game from day one," he said. "If you get a B plus instead of the A minus, that little GPA difference can matter." He said a friend applying to the undergrad business program was so stressed out about an economics grade that he landed in the hospital with a panic attack. He could think of at least a dozen friends who were on psychotropic medications.

Steverson, who grappled with anxiety, depression, and ADHD, started feeling the pressure in middle school in Crystal Lake, Illinois, when students were first put on academic tracks. If you weren't in the top level in middle school, you wouldn't qualify for honors classes in high school, which meant that you wouldn't be prepared for Advanced Placement tests. And competitive colleges want to see AP classes. "If you want to get into these top schools, all of a sudden your résumé for college is gone," Steverson said. "So in sixth grade, kids were freaking out."

The students said social media has only amplified the stress. They knew that Facebook and Instagram were highlights reels—

the party photos and boasting only a sliver of real life. But when they're feeling lonely or down, "it can be easy to compare the bad day you just had to everyone's smiling pictures," said Chen, the president of Michigan's chapter of Active Minds, the national student mental health advocacy group.

"You know how you can edit your education on Facebook, and it shows up in people's news feed? And people will like or comment on it and congratulate you?" Chen asked the group.

"You're going to so-and-so university," chimed in Steverson.

"Or you're going to intern at Microsoft," said Chen.

"And you get one hundred likes on it," said Steverson.

"And you feel really good about yourself," finished Chen.

Unless, of course, you're the one staying home and scooping ice cream for the summer.

Rivas argued that the culture of social media self-promotion has infected real-life interactions. "There's a very big push to seem like you have it all together," he said. Studies looking at the relationship between the use of social media and psychological well-being are mixed, but some do show a link to anxiety and depression. And certain types of behavior—like passively scrolling through Facebook news feeds without posting status updates—appear more likely to lead to feelings of loneliness.

The Michigan these students describe is a Darwinian pressure cooker, with kids obsessed with grades and routinely pulling all-nighters. This is not how I remember it. But the school is a lot harder to get into—and a lot more expensive—than when I went there. When I was a student in 1990, in-state tuition at Michigan was $3,502 a year. Now it's $16,218 for juniors and seniors. Even taking into account inflation, tuition has jumped nearly two and a half times. Adding room and board and books pushes the in-state cost to about $30,000 a year. The out-of-state cost is more than double that. In the United States, the average college senior who has taken out student loans will graduate with about $29,000 in debt, a figure that has jumped more than 50 percent in a decade.

"I see a lot more stress and anxiety and striving for perfectionism," said Todd Sevig, a psychologist and the director of Michigan's Counseling and Psychological Services, known as CAPS. Because of all the pressures in middle school and high school, "they are pretty fried when they get here. Sometimes I think students feel like they can't fail."

I met with Sevig and Christine Asidao, CAPS's associate director of community engagement and outreach education. CAPS provides individual and group therapy to Michigan students. Since arriving in Ann Arbor, I had heard several students grumble about wait times to see a therapist and about the pressure to end treatment before they're ready, but they universally had good things to say about Sevig, noting his commitment and approachability. Soft-spoken, gray-bearded, and bespectacled, Sevig has been working at CAPS since 1989, the year I had my first breakdown.

I posed the same question to Sevig and Asidao that I had to the students: Why are young adults now so much more anxious?

"When I was here, getting a B wasn't the end of the world," I told them.

"But it is now," said Asidao.

Besides the increased pressure to get good grades, Sevig and Asidao said students also might be more anxious because their parents didn't allow them to fail or flounder earlier: Some young adults face their first real defeats only after getting to college. But they also believe that much of the apparent rise in anxiety issues is an illusion. Reduced stigma around mental health issues is leading to an increase in help-seeking behavior, they said, and the success of their own outreach is causing more students to ask for assistance, too.

Starting in about 2008, CAPS dramatically ramped up its

prevention programs. A year earlier, Seung-Hui Cho, a senior at Virginia Tech with a history of mental health problems, had shot and killed thirty-two people and wounded seventeen others. Then in February 2008, a graduate student at the University of Illinois killed five people and injured twenty-one in a lecture hall at Northern Illinois University. He, too, had previously been treated for psychological issues. All of a sudden, the mental health of college students and the responsibilities of universities were heavily covered by the media.

CAPS became a robust and highly visible presence on campus. It now does dozens of "tabling" events at university gatherings and festivals; staff members talk to students and hand out pamphlets about anxiety, depression, and stress. It jazzed up its website, adding quick screening questionnaires for GAD, depression, PTSD, and other psychiatric illnesses, and a series of videos of students talking about their own mental health issues. It created a YouTube channel and Facebook and Instagram accounts, and launched a Stressbusters app with inspirational quotes and relaxation exercises. It hosts a biannual Play Day, with balloon animals, chair massages, and Legos, to encourage students to take breaks and relax.

CAPS staffers are also trying to boost resilience among students, teaching them that it is okay to mess up, that obstacles will come up and they can learn how to cope with them. To that end, CAPS launched the "Wellness Zone" in 2011—a darkened room with three massage chairs, a light therapy machine, and meditation cushions. Between 3,000 and 4,000 students use the zone each year.

Around campus, I noticed small wooden plaques hanging from trees. DO SOMETHING: STOP STUDENT SUICIDE, they read. Underneath students wrote uplifting or imploring messages. "I lost someone to suicide. I've wanted to commit suicide. They both suck. Please don't," one pleaded. This was a CAPS effort, too.

When I was a student, I didn't know anyone who had visited CAPS. I didn't even know it existed. "When you were here, we primarily stayed in our offices and did a lot of individual therapy, along with the occasional workshop with RAs or student groups," said Sevig. Back then CAPS had one training program and one psychiatrist who came in for only a few hours a week. Now it has eight training programs and three psychiatrists working full-time. The increase in staff is a necessity: During the fall of 2015, CAPS faced an unprecedented 40 percent increase in the number of students visiting over the previous year. Between 2009 and 2016, demand for CAPS services increased by 36 percent.

"Previous generations would never touch the door of a therapist, that was the worst thing in the world," says Sevig. "That has really changed, and that's a beautiful thing."

CAPS sees many students who have already been treated for mental health problems in middle school or high school. By 2009, about 22 percent of students arriving on campus had had some previous counseling. Some students have had IEPs, or independent education plans, and received various types of services, so they feel comfortable asking for similar help in college. Indeed, like many other colleges, Michigan has seen soaring numbers of students formally requesting academic accommodations—like extra time to take tests, or permission to take exams in a smaller, separate room—because of psychiatric illnesses. Of course, not all students who seek help at CAPS have a psychiatric diagnosis. Plenty of students come in looking for support after an event like a fight with a boyfriend or girlfriend. But since 2008, anxiety has been the number-one issue for students visiting CAPS.

To accommodate larger numbers of students, CAPS does more group therapy. During the school year, they run thirty groups on topics from social anxiety to eating disorders, and for specific communities like women of color and LGBT students. CAPS has also added after-hours phone counseling. Students can call at three a.m. if they need to talk to someone. In tandem with these changes, the number of student advocacy groups devoted to mental health has skyrocketed over the last year at Michigan, from two to ten. The last few student government presidents have made mental health a center of their platforms, too.

I wish I could say that Michigan is typical, but in fact it has more mental health resources than many other colleges around the country. Almost 30 percent of schools don't provide psychiatric services to students, only referrals to outside practitioners.

The student mental health advocates I met say there is still stigma in some corners of campus, especially in the Greek system, among certain groups of international students, and in some communities of color. But most said they felt incredibly supported by friends, family, and the larger university community. Indeed, in a 2015 survey, 60 percent of young adults said seeing a mental health professional is a sign of strength; only 35 percent of adults older than twenty-five did.

I admit that I am nervous for these young people. I wonder what will happen when they leave this cocoon and enter the working world. Will their openness about their mental illnesses limit their career prospects?

I asked Cheyenne Stone, a freckled, smiley twenty-two-year-old senior who is heading to graduate school at Michigan. She is the executive director of the Wolverine Support Network, a student organization that runs peer support groups. (Students talk about everything from social anxiety to failing a test.) She's dealt with depression, OCD, and substance abuse and has written blog posts about her experiences.

"Mental health is a huge part of who I am. I would need an employer who understands that," Stone said. "I think if there is an employer who has a problem with the facts of my advocacy work, I don't want to work there anyway."

Anna Learis, an eighteen-year-old freshman, is equally unapologetic. She told me that when she decided to speak publicly about her panic attacks, her mother tried to dissuade her. "She's like, 'One day your possible employers are going to Google your name, and they're going to see that and then they're not going to want to hire you,'" Learis said. "I was like, 'Mom, the whole point of it is to address the stigma of mental health so people don't do that.'"

Learis, who says she's been anxious since she was about five years old, performed at Michigan's yearly *Mental Health Monologues*, a show that features about a dozen students talking about mental health. She spoke about how her anxiety affects her boyfriend, whom she summons when she has panic attacks and who took her to the psychiatric ER a few months ago. When Learis has an attack, she scratches her arms until they bleed. "My skin feels like it's crawling. I don't notice I'm scratching until afterward when I see my hand bleeding," she says. On her wrists, jagged purple scars peek out from the long sleeves of her black-and-white-striped dress.

Learis, an engineering major, has an academic scholarship, which means she has to maintain a 3.0 grade point average. The stress fuels her anxiety. "If I don't do well on a test, I could fail a class. I'll lose the scholarship. We'll have to find the money to pay for it. I'll have to transfer schools. All about one test." She's trying to get approval to take tests in a smaller, quieter room. One of her friends who had a broken arm got to take a test in the smaller room. (The seats were bigger.) Learis doesn't see why her anxiety should be treated any differently.

I can't help but wonder—enviously, if I'm honest about it—

what my college years would have been like if I had known about CAPS, if I had gone to the Wolverine Support Network meetings, if I had been able to participate in the *Mental Health Monologues.* These young people are energetic, passionate, and fearless. They, along with the adult leaders who support them, have transformed their campus into a place where mental health is a priority and mental illness isn't shameful. I have no doubt that in the years ahead, they'll revolutionize our workplaces, too.

Since my own college days, I've done two more rounds of CBT. I pursued the last one a couple of years ago, after spending months dealing with a strange tingling on the left side of my body. The tingling ran from my thigh to my knee, from my shoulder to my wrist, and sometimes from my cheek to my forehead. I worried about strokes and rare cancers. I visited a neurologist and had MRIs of my brain and my neck. I spent far too much time with Google.

It wasn't the first time I'd had weird neurological symptoms, but my new psychiatrist, Dr. S, gave me two new diagnoses: conversion disorder and somatic symptom disorder. Conversion disorder is characterized by medically unexplained neurological symptoms, coupled with "significant distress or impairment," according to the *DSM.* (Freud would have called it hysteria.) It often occurs alongside panic disorder and depression. Somatic symptom disorder involves distressing physical symptoms and significant worry about them. People with somatic symptom disorder "appraise their bodily symptoms as unduly threatening, harmful or troublesome and often think the worst about their health," says the *DSM.*

Medically unexplained symptoms are strikingly common. One

study of primary care patients in Germany found that mystery symptoms made up two-thirds of all symptoms. For most people, however, the reassuring words of a doctor or a negative test result are enough to ease their minds.

The goal of CBT this time was not to make the weird symptoms go away but to teach me to live with them, to see them as benign and ignore them. I wrote down my irrational fears: that I was having a stroke, that I had ALS. Then I wrote down the evidence that these thoughts were likely false. (All my test results had come back normal.) I was given relaxation exercises and encouraged to meditate. (A confession, Dr. S: I didn't meditate.) I compiled lists of things that made me happy—reading to my daughter, calling a friend—and picked one to do when the symptoms surged.

The CBT worked. After several months, I was less worried. And while I still get a tingly leg or arm every once in a while, the symptoms are largely gone.

When people ask me which therapy they should choose for anxiety, I always recommend CBT. But I've also dipped in and out of psychodynamic therapy, a school that views anxiety as originating from relationship experiences. I did a stint in my twenties, and I've seen my most recent therapist, Dr. L, who practices a mix of psychodynamic therapy and CBT, off and on since my early thirties. We've talked about how, as a child, I yearned for more rules and guidance. About how I struggled to be comfortable with anger, both my own and others'. She's helped me navigate relationships with friends and family.

Psychodynamic therapy may sound like self-indulgent navelgazing, but there is some evidence that it is beneficial for anxiety disorders. A 2014 meta-analysis found that after a course of psychodynamic therapy almost half of patients had their anxiety disorders go into remission. And it has had a monumental impact on me. I've gotten better at noticing my feelings and figuring out where they come from. I've gotten to know my emotional mine-fields and become braver and more authentic in relationships. Psychodynamic therapy has helped me grow up. And when anxiety hits, I feel less sideswiped. I have an emotional home base.

Grounding myself in the present moment also helps to keep anxiety at bay. Even dusting or scrubbing the toilets can quiet my worrying. (Yes, I am becoming my mother.)

Baking is one of my favorite soothing activities. The tactile pleasure of kneading flour into butter. The focus, but also slight mindlessness, of following a recipe. The wonderful alchemy of transforming a collection of ingredients into a pie or cake. And of course the accolades from family and friends. The closest I've ever felt to being a celebrity was when I rode the New York City subway with a still-steaming blueberry pie on my lap, my hands in oven mitts. "Can I have a piece?" passengers shamelessly asked.

Healthy habits—getting enough sleep, eating well, reducing stress, exercising regularly—aren't especially novel, and they are decidedly unglamorous. But they are critical to keeping my anxiety in check. The leeway for neglect is very slim.

Insomnia and other sleep problems are common in people with anxiety disorders. Sleeping fewer hours than normal is associated with anxiety in teenagers. Going to sleep late, not getting enough sleep, and being drowsy during the day is linked to anxiety in kids. Depressed or anxious people who sleep too much (ten hours or more) or too little (six hours or less) are at greater risk of having more chronic illnesses.

Some studies have found that difficulty sleeping is a precursor to a bout of anxiety or depression. There's evidence that sleep problems increase the risk of developing PTSD after trauma. Poor sleep may also weaken the effects of CBT: Research indicates that good sleep is critical for consolidating memories in extinction learning.

Various theories explain the relationship between sleep and anxiety. Scientists have discovered that when people without psychiatric disorders are deprived of sleep, their amygdala activity in response to negative stimuli increases and the connections between the amygdala and the medial prefrontal cortex are weakened. Since an anxious person already has a revved-up amygdala, it could be that sleep problems turn up the volume even further.

So I go to bed early enough to make sure I get my eight hours. But that doesn't mean I stay asleep. I'm prone to waking up—and staying up—at two a.m. or three a.m., dark, solitary times that are ripe for anxiety. Without the tethers of the day's routines, my mind hopscotches: I must remember to call my niece to wish her a happy birthday. How will I possibly get all my work done before my next deadline? Am I spending enough time with my daughter? My friend Amy never responded to my email. Have I done something to upset her? Should I cook fish or chicken for dinner tomorrow? How will we pay for college? Is the tightness in my belly cancer?

My husband and daughter are still and asleep. I skulk around the apartment, from bed to sofa to bathroom.

Exercise seems the easier fix, though it took me a while to figure out what I enjoyed and how to fit it into my life. I'm not keen on running or lifting weights. I love yoga but I rarely have time to schlep to a studio for a ninety-minute—or even an hour-long—class. Then I found online yoga. Now I do anywhere from fifteen minutes to a half hour in the morning before my daughter wakes. I feel stronger. And I've noticed that, since starting it, my Klonopin use has taken a nosedive. I don't think it's a coincidence.

Cardio is important for me, too, and not just because it's good for my body. A lot of my anxiety has involved worries about my heart. So I take the stairs and use a seven-minute workout app on my phone. They are short bursts of exposure therapy. Indeed, this interoceptive exposure, or exposure to feared bodily sensations, is a core element of CBT for panic disorder. In scientific studies, exercise is modestly effective at reducing anxiety symptoms. It is best at reducing so-called anxiety sensitivity, or the fear of the bodily sensations caused by anxiety. There are many theories about why exercise helps. Some scientists have pointed to exercise's ability to boost brain-derived neurotrophic factor (BDNF), a protein important for maintaining mood that is sometimes reduced in people with anxiety disorders. Regular aerobic exercise also lowers activity in the HPA axis.

It's even better if I can get that exercise in a park. Spending time in nature can reduce stress and even improve cognition. It may also calm anxiety. Researchers at Stanford and the University of San Francisco had people take a fifty-minute walk. One group walked in a grassy park; the other along a busy street. After the stroll, the people who spent time in the park had decreased anxiety compared to those who walked along the street.

One meta-analysis found that rates of anxiety disorders were 21 percent higher in urban areas than in rural ones.

I'm not ready to move to the country yet. I'm also convinced that there is no one best way to deal with anxiety. Everyone finds his or her own salves. A neighbor with GAD finds solace in music and meditation apps. For Cheyenne Stone, it is sleeping eight hours a night and surrounding herself with supportive friends. For Anna Learis, it is spending thirty minutes doing her makeup in the morning, a ritual she finds calming.

Since my anxiety often seems to manifest itself in weird physical symptoms, I've needed to find some way to discern when I need an MRI versus a dose of Klonopin. I've been down the rabbit hole of specialists and expensive tests before. I need a guide to interpret my noisy body. My primary care physician, Dr. G, does this. She's warm, thoughtful, and supersmart. She doesn't dismiss my concerns out of hand or use my anxiety as a knee-jerk scapegoat, but she's not an alarmist either. And she doesn't kick the can by immediately sending me to a specialist, leaving the problem for someone else to figure out. Most important, I trust her. She helps me manage my hypochondria. She asks me specifically what my worst fear is about a particular symptom. Then she'll tell me why she's ruled that out.

A few months ago I had a persistent burning feeling in my lungs. It lasted for weeks. Dr. G first had me use my asthma inhaler. When that didn't help, she had me try Klonopin for several days to see if reducing my anxiety level would lessen the symptom. Only when that didn't work did she send me to a pulmonologist. His assessment? Probably a postviral syndrome that would go away within a few weeks. And it did.

Another time I called her with a frantic question. "I think I have a leptomeningeal carcinomatosis," I said in a rush. "I'm dizzy sometimes. I have that tingling on the left side of my body."

"That is a very rare cancer," she said. "Where did you hear about it?"

I blushed and stammered. "I was looking at People.com and read that this actress Valerie Harper has it. I looked up the symptoms, and I have a bunch of them."

"You had a normal neurological exam the last time I saw you," she said. "We would have seen some abnormality if you had this type of cancer."

This kind of hand-holding takes time. And it isn't cheap. Dr. G doesn't take insurance. I pay out of pocket and then hope my insurance company will reimburse me. Unfortunately, this quality of care is not available to many.

As I've conducted the research for this book, I've been mulling a question. If I could wish my anxiety away, would I?

I certainly don't see my anxiety as a gift. And I don't buy the platitude that everything happens for a reason. When my anxiety is at its worst, it's deeply painful, erasing love and life. Even when it's more moderate, anxiety is a huge energy and time suck.

Still, I've come to realize that the question is unanswerable. When I try to envision my life without all the experiences anxiety has given me—as well as the ones it has taken away—I don't recognize myself. At this point, anxiety and I are too tightly bound. Take my struggles with anxiety away and I'm someone else.

Anxiety has been good to me, too. Without it, I might have listened to the first doctor who told me that the spot on my cheek was nothing.

Anxiety is a great bullshit detector. Reams of studies have looked at the mind-body connection. In anxious people, that link seems amplified. When my marriage feels off-kilter, when I'm avoiding some necessary confrontation or saying yes to too many superfluous obligations, I feel it in my hopped-up amygdala. Weirdly, anxiety makes me live a more authentic life. And a more empathic one. Anxiety has made me ask for help, made me vulnerable, and thereby deepened my friendships.

A background hum of uneasiness has motivated me to work harder, travel farther, speak more honestly, and curiously, take more risks than I might have otherwise. People who have a brush with death often talk of how it has given them a sense of what really matters. An omnipresent fear of disaster, a constant bracing for catastrophe can do that, too. Time takes on more urgency.

Anxiety means I'm simply not mellow enough to take things for granted. And that has made my life all the richer.

NOTES

I. THE ANTICIPATION OF PAIN

6 **estimated number of people:** Ronald C. Kessler et al., "Twelve-Month and Lifetime Prevalence and Lifetime Morbid Risk of Anxiety and Mood Disorders in the United States," *International Journal of Methods in Psychiatric Research* 21, no. 3 (2012): 169–84.

6 **about 40 million American adults:** "Facts and Statistics," Anxiety and Depression Association of America, https://www.adaa.org/about-adaa/press-room/facts-statistics.

6 **anxiety disorders cost the United States:** Paul E. Greenberg et al., "The Economic Burden of Anxiety Disorders in the 1990s," *Journal of Clinical Psychiatry* 60, no. 7 (1999): 427–35.

7 **According to a spring 2016 survey:** American College Health Association National College Health Assessment, *Spring 2016 Reference Group Executive Summary* (American College Health Association, 2016).

7 **up from about 10 percent:** American College Health Association National College Health Assessment, *Fall 2008 Reference Group Executive Summary* (American College Health Association, 2008).

7 **Depression may get most of the headlines:** In 2015 the National Institutes of Health spent $156 million for research on anxiety disorders and $390 million on depression. *Estimates of Funding for Various*

Research, Condition, and Disease Categories, National Institutes of Health, https://report.nih.gov/categorical_spending.aspx.

7 **In people with a history:** Ronald C. Kessler, "The Global Burden of Anxiety and Mood Disorders: Putting ESEMeD Findings into Perspective," *Journal of Clinical Psychiatry* 68, suppl. 2 (2007): 10–19.

7 **doesn't often lead to suicidal acts:** Matthew K. Nock et al., "Mental Disorders, Comorbidity and Suicidal Behavior: Results from the National Comorbidity Survey Replication," *Molecular Psychiatry* 15, no. 8 (2010): 868–76.

7 **Someone who develops an anxiety disorder:** Ronald C. Kessler, Harvard Medical School, interview by author.

8 **"the dizziness of freedom":** Søren Kierkegaard, *The Concept of Anxiety* (Princeton, NJ: Princeton University Press, 1980), 61.

9 **varies by culture:** American Psychiatric Association, *Diagnostic and Statistical Manual of Mental Disorders,* 5th ed. (Washington, DC: American Psychiatric Publishing, 2013), 216. Cited hereinafter as *DSM-5.*

9 **studies show that, in Japan:** Ronald C. Kessler et al., "The Global Burden of Mental Disorders: An Update from the WHO World Mental Health (WMH) Surveys," *Epidemiologia e psichiatria sociale* 18, no. 1 (2009): 23–33.

22 **Andreas of Charystos:** Allan V. Horwitz, *Anxiety: A Short History* (Baltimore: Johns Hopkins University Press, 2013), 27.

22 **pantophobia:** I can't read the word *pantophobia* without thinking of the scene in *A Charlie Brown Christmas* when Charlie Brown consults Lucy's "Psychiatric Help, 5 cents" booth. Trying to get to the bottom of his despair, Lucy asks him about a litany of phobias, including fears of crossing bridges (gephyrophobia) and of the ocean (thalassophobia). "Do you think you have pantophobia?" she finally asks. "What's pantophobia?" says Charlie Brown. "The fear of everything," Lucy says. "That's it!" Charlie Brown yells, sending Lucy somersaulting back across the snow.

22 **In the Classical period:** Andrea Tone, *The Age of Anxiety: A History of America's Turbulent Affair with Tranquilizers* (New York: Basic Books, 2009), 6–7.

23 **"It was as if a light of relief":** Quoted in Horwitz, *Anxiety*, 37.

23 **emerging concept of nervous disorders:** Ibid., 48–49.

23 **In 1869, George Miller Beard:** Ibid., 64–66.

23 **The Greek physician Hippocrates:** Cecilia Tasca et al., "Women and Hysteria in the History of Mental Health," *Clinical Practice and Epidemiology in Mental Health* 8 (2012): 110–19.

24 **"irritable heart syndrome":** Andrea Tone, "Listening to the Past: History, Psychiatry and Anxiety," *Canadian Journal of Psychiatry* 50, no. 7 (2005): 373–80.

24 **a groundbreaking paper:** Sigmund Freud, *Collected Papers* (London: Hogarth Press, 1953), 1:76–106.

25 **he abandoned this theory:** Horwitz, *Anxiety*, 85–91.

26 **When that response is initiated:** Harvard Medical School has done a nice write-up of the stress response and the HPA axis. "Understanding the Stress Response," Harvard Medical School, http://www.health.harvard.edu/staying-healthy/understanding-the-stress-response.

27 **In his experiments, LeDoux:** Two major papers detailing LeDoux's 1980s lesion work are Joseph E. LeDoux et al., "Subcortical Efferent Projections of the Medial Geniculate Nucleus Mediate Emotional Responses Conditioned to Acoustic Stimuli," *Journal of Neuroscience* 4, no. 3 (1983): 683–98; and Jiro Iwata et al., "Intrinsic Neurons in the Amygdaloid Field Projected to by the Medial Geniculate Body Mediate Emotional Responses Conditioned to Acoustic Stimuli," *Brain Research* 383 (1986): 195–214.

27 **one of two routes:** Joseph LeDoux, *The Emotional Brain: The Mysterious Underpinnings of Emotional Life* (New York: Simon & Schuster, 1996). Also see LeDoux's most recent book, *Anxious: Using the Brain to Understand and Treat Fear and Anxiety* (New York: Viking, 2015).

29 **The part of the cow that most:** Ibid., 11.

30 **Studies have found that the amygdala:** Shmuel Lissek et al., "Classic Fear Conditioning in the Anxiety Disorders: A Meta-Analysis," *Behaviour Research and Therapy* 43, no. 11 (2005): 1391–424.

31 **In many studies, those with anxiety disorders:** Here's a good summary of the attention bias literature: Yair Bar-Haim et al., "Threat-Related Attentional Bias in Anxious and Nonanxious Individuals: A Meta-Analytic Study," *Psychological Bulletin* 133, no. 1 (2007): 1–24.

31 "intolerance of uncertainty": Dan W. Grupe and Jack B. Nitschke, "Uncertainty and Anticipations in Anxiety: An Integrated Neurobiological and Psychological Perspective," *Nature Reviews Neuroscience* 14 (2013): 488–501.

31 Researchers at the University of California: Alan Simmons et al., "Intolerance of Uncertainty Correlates with Insula Activation During Affective Ambiguity," *Neuroscience Letters* 430, no. 2 (2008): 92–97.

32 In Davis's lab: Michael Davis et al., "Phasic vs Sustained Fear in Rats and Humans: Role of the Extended Amygdala in Fear vs Anxiety," *Neuropsychopharmacology* 35, no. 1 (2010): 105–35.

33 In the 1990s, Christian Grillon: Christian Grillon, "Models and Mechanisms of Anxiety: Evidence from Startle Studies," *Psychopharmacology* 199, no. 3 (2008): 421–37.

34 In one critical experiment: Christian Grillon and Michael Davis, "Fear-Potentiated Startle Conditioning in Humans: Explicit and Contextual Cue Conditioning Following Paired Versus Unpaired Training," *Pschophysiology* 34 (1997): 451–58.

34 Using the new equipment: Salvatore Torrisi et al., "Resting State Connectivity of the Bed Nucleus of the Stria Terminalis at Ultra-High Field," *Human Brain Mapping* 36 (2015): 4076–88.

35 As researchers Dan Grupe: Dan W. Grupe and Jack B. Nitschke, "Uncertainty and Anticipations in Anxiety."

2. SCARY CLOWNS AND THE END OF DAYS

38 more likely to develop a wide range of disorders: Renee Goodwin et al., "Panic Attack as a Risk Factor for Severe Psychopathology," *American Journal of Psychiatry* 161, no. 12 (2004): 2207–14.

38 four out of thirteen possible: *DSM-5*, 208.

38 Children who experience fearful spells: Eva Asselmann et al., "Associations of Fearful Spells and Panic Attacks with Incident Anxiety, Depressive and Substance Use Disorders: A 10-Year Prospective Longitudinal Community Study of Adolescents and Young Adults," *Journal of Psychiatric Research* 55 (2014): 8–14.

40 *Sesame Street* segment on YouTube: "*Sesame Street*: A Clown's Face," https://www.youtube.com/watch?v=Vs5VYOnpMrw.

40 **These are all typical:** For an excellent chart detailing normal fears in childhood and adolescence, see Katja Beesdo et al., "Anxiety and Anxiety Disorders in Children and Adolescents: Developmental Issues and Implications for DSM-V," *Psychiatric Clinics* 32, no. 3 (2009): 483–524.

40 **Specific phobia is one of the earliest:** Ronald C. Kessler et al., "Age of Onset of Mental Disorders: A Review of Recent Literature," *Current Opinion in Psychiatry* 20, no. 4 (2007): 359–64.

40 **phobia of buttons:** Lissette M. Saavedra and Wendy K. Silverman, "Case Study: Disgust and a Specific Phobia of Buttons," *Journal of the American Academy of Child and Adolescent Psychiatry* 41, no. 11 (2002): 1376–79.

40 **The most common involve animals:** National Alliance on Mental Illness, *Specific Phobias*, fact sheet.

40 **these fears developed over millennia:** Randolph M. Nesse and George C. Williams, *Why We Get Sick: The New Science of Darwinian Medicine* (New York: Vintage, 1994), 210.

41 **A 2010 study of about fifteen hundred:** Julia Trumpf et al., "Specific Phobia Predicts Psychopathology in Young Women," *Social Psychiatry and Psychiatric Epidemiology* 45, no. 12 (2010): 1161–66.

43 **the prediction set forth:** John R. Gribbin and Stephen H. Plagemann, *The Jupiter Effect* (New York: Walker & Co., 1974).

44 **early maltreatment can alter the HPA axis:** Carlo Faravelli et al., "Childhood Stressful Events, HPA Axis and Anxiety Disorders," *World Journal of Psychiatry* 2, no. 1 (2012): 13–25.

44 **When researchers at the University of Wisconsin:** Ryan J. Herringa et al., "Childhood Maltreatment Is Associated with Altered Fear Circuitry and Increased Internalizing Symptoms by Late Adolescence," *Proceedings of the National Academy of Sciences* 110, no. 47 (2013): 19119–24.

44 **physical illness and economic adversity:** Jennifer Greif Green et al., "Childhood Adversities and Adult Psychopathology in the National Comorbidity Survey Replication (NCS-R) 1: Associations with First Onset of DSM-IV Disorders," *Archives of General Psychiatry* 67, no. 2 (2010): 113.

44 **A study that surveyed nearly seven hundred:** Nicholas B. Allen et al., "Prenatal and Perinatal Influences on Risk for Psychopathology in Childhood and Adolescence," *Development and Psychopathology* 10 (1998): 513–29.

46 **a history of asthma:** Michelle G. Craske et al., "Paths to Panic Disorder/Agoraphobia: An Exploratory Analysis from Age 3 to 21 in an Unselected Birth Cohort," *Journal of the American Academy of Child and Adolescent Psychiatry* 40, no. 5 (2001): 556–63.

46 **adults with asthma, emphysema, and bronchitis:** See, for example, R. D. Goodwin et al., "A 10-Year Prospective Study of Respiratory Disease and Depression and Anxiety in Adulthood," *Annals of Allergy, Asthma and Immunology* 113, no. 5 (2014): 565–70.

46 **A 2008 study showed that those:** Renee D. Goodwin et al., "Childhood Respiratory Disease and the Risk of Anxiety Disorder and Major Depression in Adulthood," *Archives of Pediatrics and Adolescent Medicine* 162, no. 8 (2008): 774–80.

46 **There's some evidence:** Jordan W. Smoller et al., "The Human Ortholog of Acid-Sensing Ion Channel Gene ASIC1a Is Associated with Panic Disorder and Amygdala Structure and Function," *Biological Psychiatry* 76, no. 11 (2014): 902–10.

47 **In the UCLA and New Zealand study:** Craske et al., "Paths to Panic Disorder/Agoraphobia."

48 **Researchers in Australia wanted to see:** Jennifer L. Hudson and Ronald M. Rapee, "Parent-Child Interactions and Anxiety Disorders: An Observational Study," *Behaviour Research and Therapy* 39 (2001): 1411–27.

48 **In a big 2007 review:** Bryce D. McLeod et al., "Examining the Association Between Parenting and Childhood Anxiety: A Meta-Analysis," *Clinical Psychology Review* 27 (2007): 155–72.

55 **In a small study using this paradigm:** Jennifer Lau et al., "Fear Conditioning in Adolescents with Anxiety Disorders: Results from a Novel Experimental Paradigm," *Journal of the American Academy of Child and Adolescent Psychiatry* 47, no. 1 (2008): 94–102.

55 **Another larger study published in 2013:** Jennifer C. Britton et al., "Response to Learned Threat: An fMRI Study in Adolescent and

Adult Anxiety," *American Journal of Psychiatry* 170, no. 10 (2013): 1195–1204.

3. MY GRANDMOTHER'S MADNESS

59 **genes are responsible for 30 to 40 percent:** John M. Hettema et al., "A Review and Meta-Analysis of the Genetic Epidemiology of Anxiety Disorders," *American Journal of Psychiatry* 158, no. 10 (2001): 1568–78. In twin studies, scientists compared the similarities of a trait (which could also be an illness such as anxiety disorders) in pairs of identical twins to those of fraternal twins. Since both kinds of twins grow up in similar environments, the greater similarity in the trait among identical twins can be largely attributed to genes. Jordan Smoller's *The Other Side of Normal* (New York: HarperCollins, 2012) has a nice explanation of twin studies on page 63.

59 **For schizophrenia, Gladys's diagnosis:** Ming T. Tsuang et al., "Genes, Environment and Schizophrenia," *British Journal of Psychiatry* 40, Suppl. (April 2001): s18–s24.

59 **Having a first-degree relative:** Jordan W. Smoller et al., "The Genetics of Anxiety Disorders," in *Primer on Anxiety Disorders: Translational Perspectives on Diagnosis and Treatment*, ed. Kerry J. Ressler et al. (Oxford: Oxford University Press, 2015), 61.

59 **In a 2013 study, genetic:** Cross-Disorder Group of the Psychiatric Genomics Consortium, "Genetic Relationship Between Five Psychiatric Disorders Estimated from Genome-Wide SNPs," *Nature Genetics* 45, no. 9 (2013): 984–94.

62 **insulin coma therapy:** There's a terrific description of ICT by Max Fink, the former head of an ICT unit at a New York mental hospital, on the website for the documentary *A Brilliant Madness*. The film tells the story of the mathematician John Nash, who was treated with ICT for schizophrenia: http://www.pbs.org/wgbh/amex/nash/filmmore/ps_ict.html. Also see Edward Shorter and David Healy, *Shock Therapy: A History of Electroconvulsive Treatment in Mental Illness* (New Brunswick, NJ: Rutgers University Press, 2007).

63 **In Mendota's 1955 annual report:** Mendota State Hospital, *Report to State Board of Public Welfare*, March 23, 1955.

63 **divided into "quiet" and "disturbed":** Mendota State Hospital, *Report to State Board of Public Welfare*, June 14, 1961.

64 **a movement to provide more freedom:** Mendota State Hospital, *Report to the State Board of Public Welfare*, May 14, 1958, and May 27, 1959.

65 **Antipsychotic drugs were instant hits:** Mendota State Hospital, *Report to the State Board of Public Welfare*, May 23, 1956.

65 **staff members were complaining:** Mendota State Hospital, *Report to State Board of Public Welfare*, May 25, 1960.

66 **Electroconvulsive therapy was first employed:** Edward Shorter, *A History of Psychiatry* (Hoboken, NJ: John Wiley & Sons, 1997), 218–24.

67 **During the 1960s, a movement arose:** In 1963, President John F. Kennedy signed the Community Mental Health Act, legislation that aimed to build a network of community mental health centers. The goal was for people to receive treatment at home; many patients would no longer have to spend years in crowded psychiatric institutions, some of which were rife with abuse and neglect. But only half the community centers were built and most were not fully funded. See "Kennedy's Vision for Mental Health Never Realized," Associated Press, October 20, 2013.

70 **The vast majority:** "Mental Health Reporting," fact sheet, University of Washington School of Social Work, http://depts.washington.edu/mhreport/facts_violence.php.

76 **One of the most extensively researched is the SLC6A4 gene:** For a nice, clear write-up of the serotonin transporter story, see Smoller, *Other Side of Normal*, 68–70.

78 **Women are about twice as likely:** Carmen P. McLean et al., "Gender Differences in Anxiety Disorders: Prevalence, Course of Illness, Comorbidity and Burden of Illness," *Journal of Psychiatric Research* 45, no. 8 (2011): 1027–35.

79 **girls "catch" fear more easily:** Michelle G. Craske, *Origins of Phobias and Anxiety Disorders: Why More Women Than Men?* (Oxford: Elsevier, 2003), 176–203.

79 **In one study, mothers presented two toys:** Friederike C. Gerull and Ronald M. Rapee, "Mother Knows Best: Effects of Maternal Modelling on the Acquisition of Fear and Avoidance Behaviour in Toddlers," *Behaviour Research and Therapy* 40, no. 3 (2002): 279–87.

80 **In a University of California, Berkeley study:** Patricia K. Kerig et al., "Marital Quality and Gender Differences in Parent-Child Interaction," *Developmental Psychology* 29, no. 6 (1993): 931–39.

81 **Morrongiello had a hunch:** Barbara A. Morrongiello and Tess Dawber, "Mothers' Responses to Sons and Daughters Engaging in Injury-Risk Behaviors on a Playground: Implications for Sex Differences in Injury Rates," *Journal of Experimental Child Psychology* 76 (2000): 89–103.

81 **Morrongiello and her colleague:** Barbara A. Morrongiello and Theresa Dawber, "Parental Influences on Toddlers' Injury-Risk Behaviors: Are Sons and Daughters Socialized Differently?" *Journal of Applied Developmental Psychology* 20, no. 2 (1999): 227–51.

82 **girls tended to see it as riskier than boys:** Barbara A. Morrongiello and Heather Rennie, "Why Do Boys Engage in More Risk Taking Than Girls? The Role of Attributions, Beliefs, and Risk Appraisals," *Journal of Pediatric Psychology* 23, no. 1 (1998): 33–43.

82 **When girls engage in risky behaviors:** Barbara A. Morrongiello et al., "Understanding Gender Differences in Children's Risk Taking and Injury: A Comparison of Mothers' and Fathers' Reactions to Sons and Daughters Misbehaving in Ways That Lead to Injury," *Journal of Applied Developmental Psychology* 31 (2010): 322–29.

82 **By late elementary school, girls:** Craske, *Origins of Phobias and Anxiety Disorders*, 185.

83 **Surprisingly, men's *physiological* reactions:** Ibid., 194–95.

84 **In one study, thirty-four women:** Mohamed A. Zeidan et al., "Estradiol Modulates Medial Prefrontal Cortex and Amygdala Activity During Fear Extinction in Women and Female Rats," *Biological Psychiatry* 70, no. 10 (2011): 920–27.

84 **Men generally encounter more traumatic events:** Naomi Breslau et al., "Trauma Exposure and Posttraumatic Stress Disorder: A Study

of Youths in Urban America," *Journal of Urban Health: Bulletin of the New York Academy of Medicine* 81, no. 4 (2004): 530–44.

84 **more likely to be the victims:** Craske, *Origins of Phobias and Anxiety Disorders*, 179–80.

85 **Studies by Kagan and others:** K. A. Degnan and N. A. Fox, "Behavioral Inhibition and Anxiety Disorders: Multiple Levels of a Resilience Process," *Development and Psychopathology* 19 (2007): 729–46, referred to in Lauren M. McGrath et al., "Bringing a Developmental Perspective to Anxiety Genetics," *Development and Psychopathology* 24, no. 4 (2012): 1179–93.

85 **Twin studies have found:** Jordan W. Smoller et al., "Genetics of Anxiety Disorders: The Complex Road from DSM to DNA," *Depression and Anxiety* 26 (2009): 965–75.

85 **Kagan started his temperament work:** Kagan details his studies in the following books, among others: Jerome Kagan, *Galen's Prophecy: Temperament in Human Nature* (New York: Basic Books, 1994); and Jerome Kagan and Nancy Snidman, *The Long Shadow of Temperament* (Cambridge, MA: Belknap Press of Harvard University Press, 2004). Also see Robin Marantz Henig, "Understanding the Anxious Mind," *New York Times*, September 29, 2009.

89 **only those BI kids whose mothers were overcontrolling:** Erin Lewis-Morrarty et al., "Maternal Over-Control Moderates the Association Between Early Childhood Behavioral Inhibition and Adolescent Social Anxiety Symptoms," *Journal of Abnormal Child Psychology* 40, no. 8 (2012): 1363–73.

89 **BI kids who are put in day care:** Nathan Fox, interview by author.

89 **who have an attention bias to threat:** Koraly Pérez-Edgar et al., "Attention Biases to Threat Link Behavioral Inhibition to Social Withdrawal over Time in Very Young Children, *Journal of Abnormal Child Psychology* 39, no. 6 (2011): 885–95; and Koraly Pérez-Edgar et al., "Attention Biases to Threat and Behavioral Inhibition in Early Childhood Shape Adolescent Social Withdrawal," *Emotion* 10, no. 3 (2010): 349–57.

90 **Kids with BI who are adept at attention shifting:** Lauren K. White et al., "Behavioral Inhibition and Anxiety: The Moderating Roles

of Inhibitory Control and Attention Shifting," *Journal of Abnormal Child Psychology* 39, no. 5 (2011): 735–47.

4. FROM CBT TO KARAOKE

95 **This was called cognitive reappraisal:** David H. Barlow and Michelle G. Craske, *Mastery of Your Anxiety and Panic* (New York: Oxford University Press, 2007).

95 **About half of anxiety disorder patients:** Amanda G. Loerinc et al., "Response Rates for CBT for Anxiety Disorders: Need for Standardized Criteria," *Clinical Psychology Review* 42 (2015): 72–82.

95 **a meta-analysis of twenty-seven studies:** The effect size was .73. Effect size is a statistical definition that allows scientists to compare the results of many different studies. In general, an effect size of .2 is considered small, .5 is medium, and .8 or greater is large. In the studies included in the meta-analysis, the placebo conditions involved contact with therapists and education about anxiety—things that alone can help patients and skew research results—but excluded other treatment that scientists thought could be effective. See Stefan G. Hofmann and Jasper A. J. Smits, "Cognitive-Behavioral Therapy for Adult Anxiety Disorders: A Meta-analysis of Randomized Placebo-Controlled Trials," *Journal of Clinical Psychiatry* 69, no. 4 (2008): 621–32.

96 **CBT actually shrank:** K.N.T. Månsson et al., "Neuroplasticity in Response to Cognitive Behavior Therapy for Social Anxiety Disorder," *Translational Psychiatry* 6 (2016): e727.

96 **have a colorful history:** Edward Shorter, *A History of Psychiatry* (Hoboken, NJ: John Wiley & Sons, 1997), 119–36.

96 **John Watson, an American psychologist:** Edward Shorter, *A Historical Dictionary of Psychiatry* (Oxford: Oxford University Press, 2005), 57, 102–3.

98 **Freud claimed:** Ibid., 113.

99 **In 1971, psychiatrist Manuel Zane:** Kate Stone Lombardi, "Phobia Clinic, 1st in U.S., Offers Road to Recovery for 25 Years," *New York Times*, November 24, 1996.

99   **psychiatrist Arthur Hardy:** "Arthur B. Hardy, 78, Psychiatrist Who Treated a Fear of Going Out," *New York Times*, October 31, 1991.

99   **These iconoclasts:** Dr. Martin Seif, interview with the author.

100 **People with panic disorder wait:** Philip S. Wang et al., "Failure and Delay in Initial Treatment Contact After First Onset of Mental Disorders in the National Comorbidity Survey Replication," *Archives of General Psychiatry* 62 (2005): 603–13.

100 **This is particularly true of African Americans:** See, for example, Joshua Breslau et al., "Lifetime Risk and Persistence of Psychiatric Disorders Across Ethnic Groups in the United States," *Psychological Medicine* 35, no. 3 (2005): 317–27, and Joseph A. Himle et al., "Anxiety Disorders Among African Americans, Blacks of Caribbean Descent, and Non-Hispanic Whites in the United States," *Journal of Anxiety Disorders* 23, no. 5 (2009): 578–90.

103 **One study followed sixty-three panic disorder patients:** T. A. Brown and D. H. Barlow, "Long-term Outcome in Cognitive-Behavioral Treatment of Panic Disorder: Clinical Predictors and Alternative Strategies for Assessment," *Journal of Consulting and Clinical Psychology* 63, no. 5 (1995): 754–65.

104 **exposure therapy appointments in the morning:** Alicia E. Meuret et al., "Timing Matters: Endogenous Cortisol Mediates Benefits from Early-Day Psychotherapy," *Psychoneuroendocrinology* 74 (2016): 197–202.

104 **had a greater reduction in anxiety:** B. Kleim et al., "Sleep Enhances Exposure Therapy," *Psychological Medicine* 44 (2014): 1511–19.

104 **In a 2016 study of patients:** Henny A. Westra et al., "Integrating Motivational Interviewing with Cognitive-Behavioral Therapy for Severe Generalized Anxiety Disorder: An Allegiance-Controlled Randomized Clinical Trial," *Journal of Consulting and Clinical Psychology* 84, no. 9 (2016): 768–82.

105 **the Unified Protocol:** David H. Barlow and Katherine Ann Kennedy, "New Approaches to Diagnosis and Treatment in Anxiety and Related Emotional Disorders: A Focus on Temperament," *Canadian Psychology* 57, no. 1 (2016): 8–20.

105 **asking patients to vividly imagine:** Tomislav D. Zbozinek et al., "The Effect of Positive Mood Induction on Reducing Reinstatement Fear: Relevance for Long Term Outcomes of Exposure Therapy," *Behaviour Research and Therapy* 71 (2015): 65–75.

105 **success in modifying exposure therapy:** Michelle G. Craske et al., "Maximizing Exposure Therapy: An Inhibitory Learning Approach," *Behaviour Research and Therapy* 58 (2014): 10–23.

105 **in ACT you're taught to accept:** Steven C. Hayes, *Get Out of Your Mind & Into Your Life* (Oakland, CA: New Harbinger, 2005).

107 **twelve sessions of ACT or CBT:** Joanna J. Arch et al., "Randomized Clinical Trial of Cognitive Behavioral Therapy Versus Acceptance and Commitment Therapy for Mixed Anxiety Disorders," *Journal of Consulting and Clinical Psychology* 80, no. 5 (2012): 750–65.

107 **Another 2012 paper:** Kate B. Wolitzky-Taylor et al., "Moderators and Non-Specific Predictors of Treatment Outcome for Anxiety Disorders: A Comparison of Cognitive Behavioral Therapy to Acceptance and Commitment Therapy," *Journal of Consulting and Clinical Psychology* 80, no. 5 (2012): 786–99.

108 **In a meta-analysis of thirty-nine studies:** In patients with anxiety disorders, the treatment had a large effect size of .97. See Stefan G. Hofmann, "The Effect of Mindfulness-Based Therapy on Anxiety and Depression: A Meta-Analytic Review," *Journal of Consulting and Clinical Psychology* 78, no. 2 (2010): 169–83.

108 **There's even a book:** James Jacobson, *How to Meditate with Your Dog* (Kihei, HI: Maui Media, 2010).

110 **There's emerging research that acupuncture:** See, for example, Nick Errington-Evans, "Randomised Controlled Trial on the Use of Acupuncture in Adults with Chronic, Non-Responding Anxiety Symptoms," *Acupuncture in Medicine* 33, no. 2 (2015): 98–102; Hyojeong Bae et al., "Efficacy of Acupuncture in Reducing Preoperative Anxiety: A Meta-Analysis," *Evidence-Based Complementary and Alternative Medicine* (2014); and Karen Pilkington et al., "Acupuncture for Anxiety and Anxiety Disorders: A Systematic Literature Review," *Acupuncture in Medicine* 25 (2007): 1–10.

111 **In one admittedly tiny study:** Frederick J. Heide and T. D. Borkovec, "Relaxation-Induced Anxiety: Mechanisms and Theoretical Implications," *Behaviour Research and Therapy* 22, no. 1 (1984): 1–12.

111 **Another small study of college students:** G. R. Norton et al., "Characteristics of Subjects Experiencing Relaxation and Relaxation-Induced Anxiety," *Journal of Behavior Therapy and Experimental Psychiatry* 16, no. 3 (1985): 211–16.

112 **A 2016 meta-analysis:** Stefan Hofmann et al., "Effect of Hatha Yoga on Anxiety: A Meta-Analysis," *Journal of Evidence-Based Medicine* 9, no. 3 (2016): 116–24.

119 **In a small study with GAD patients:** In the control treatment, half the time the probe replaced a threatening word; half the time it replaced a neutral word. So there was no attention training. See Nader Amir et al., "Attention Modification Program in Individuals with Generalized Anxiety Disorder," *Journal of Abnormal Psychology* 118, no. 1 (2009): 28–33.

119 **A study with social phobia patients:** Nader Amir et al., "Attention Training in Individuals with Generalized Social Phobia: A Randomized Controlled Trial," *Journal of Consulting and Clinical Psychology* 77, no. 5 (2009): 961–73.

119 **some evidence shows:** T. Shechner et al., "Attention Bias Modification Treatment Augmenting Effects on Cognitive Behavioral Therapy in Children with Anxiety: Randomized Controlled Trial," *Journal of the American Academy of Child and Adolescent Psychiatry* 53, no. 1 (2014): 61–71.

119 **In a 2015 meta-analysis, ABM:** The effect size was .42. See Marian Linetzsky et al., "Quantitative Evaluation of the Clinical Efficacy of Attention Bias Modification Treatment for Anxiety Disorders," *Depression and Anxiety* 32, no. 6 (2015): 383–91.

121 **In a 2015 study, Zilverstand:** Anna Zilverstand et al., "fMRI Neurofeedback Facilitates Anxiety Regulation in Females with Spider Phobia," *Frontiers in Behavioral Neuroscience* (June 8, 2015).

121 **In another study, researchers at Yale:** D. Scheinost et al., "Orbitofrontal Cortex Neurofeedback Produces Lasting Changes in Con-

tamination Anxiety and Resting-State Connectivity," *Translational Psychiatry* 3, no. 4 (2013): e250.

5. MAY CAUSE DIZZINESS

127 **In a 1998 study of panic disorder:** Robert B. Pohl et al., "Sertraline in the Treatment of Panic Disorder: A Double-Blind Multicenter Trial," *American Journal of Psychiatry* 155, no. 9 (1998): 1189–95.

127 **In a 2004 study looking at escitalopram:** Jonathan R. T. Davidson et al., "Escitalopram in the Treatment of Generalized Anxiety Disorder: Double-Blind, Placebo Controlled, Flexible-Dose Study," *Depression and Anxiety* 19 (2004): 234–40.

128 **Studies that reveal that:** Annelieke M. Roest et al., "Reporting Bias in Clinical Trials Investigating the Efficacy of Second-Generation Antidepressants in the Treatment of Anxiety Disorders: A Report of 2 Meta-Analyses," *JAMA Psychiatry* 72, no. 5 (2015): 500–10.

128 **He is a coauthor of a review paper:** S. Borges et al., "Review of Maintenance Trials for Major Depressive Disorder: A 25-Year Perspective from the US Food and Drug Administration," *Journal of Clinical Psychiatry* 75, no. 3 (2014): 205–14.

134 **In clinical trials by Pfizer:** "Zoloft," Pfizer, October 2016, http://labeling.pfizer.com/ShowLabeling.aspx?id=517#page=1.

135 **At least a third of people:** Eduard Maron and David Nutt, "Biological Predictors of Pharmacological Therapy in Anxiety Disorders," *Dialogues in Clinical Neuroscience* 17, no. 3 (2015): 305–17.

135 **In one study, fourteen people:** Jack B. Nitschke et al., "Anticipatory Activation in the Amygdala and Anterior Cingulate in Generalized Anxiety Disorder and Prediction of Treatment Response," *American Journal of Psychiatry* 166, no. 3 (2009): 302–10.

135 **In another study, researchers in Oxford:** Andrea Reinecke et al., "Predicting Rapid Response to Cognitive-Behavioural Treatment for Panic Disorder: The Role of Hippocampus, Insula, and Dorsolateral Prefrontal Cortex," *Behaviour Research and Therapy* 62 (2014): 120–28. For a nice summary of the state of biomarker research for anxiety disorders, see Maron and Nutt, "Biological Predictors of Pharmacological Therapy."

140 **Klonopin can cause:** "Klonopin Tablets," Genentech, 2013, www
.gene.com/download/pdf/klnopin_prescribing.pdf.

140 **Entire workbook programs:** Michael W. Otto et al., *Stopping Anxiety Medication: Panic Control Therapy for Benzodiazepine Discontinuation* (Psychological Corp., 2000).

141 **The number of American adults:** Marcus A. Bachhuber et al., "Increasing Benzodiazepine Prescriptions and Overdose Mortality in the United States, 1996–2013," *American Journal of Public Health* 106, no. 4 (2016): 686–88.

141 **And most people on benzos:** M. J. Garvey and G. D. Tollefson, "Prevalence of Misuse of Prescribed Benzodiazepines in Patients with Primary Anxiety Disorder or Major Depression," *American Journal of Psychiatry* 143, no. 12 (1986): 1601–3.

141 **One study published in the journal *BMJ*:** Sophie Billioti de Gage et al., "Benzodiazepine Use and Risk of Alzheimer's Disease: Case-Control Study," *BMJ* 349 (2014).

141 **I'm reassured by a more recent study:** Shelly L. Gray et al., "Benzodiazepine Use and Risk of Incident Dementia or Cognitive Decline: Prospective Population Based Study," *BMJ* 352 (2016).

142 **A range of pharmacological treatments:** Andrea Tone, *The Age of Anxiety: A History of America's Turbulent Affair with Tranquilizers* (New York: Basic Books, 2009), 21–24.

143 **Miltown was developed by Frank Berger:** Ibid., 35.

143 **In 1949, Berger took a job:** Ibid., 43.

144 **After a few studies in humans:** Ibid., 48–52.

144 **a full third of all prescriptions:** Ibid., xvi.

144 **a Hollywood sensation:** Ibid., 55–63.

144 **The team doctors:** Ibid., 114.

145 **One ad published:** Ibid., 75–76.

145 **At Hoffmann–LaRoche:** Ibid., 120–30.

146 **it became the bestselling:** Ibid., 137.

147 **Klein and Fink published a paper:** Donald F. Klein and Max Fink, "Psychiatric Reaction Patterns to Imipramine," *American Journal of Psychiatry* 119, no. 5 (1962): 432–38.

148 **"The chief characteristic of these disorders":** *Diagnostic and Statistical Manual of Mental Disorders* (American Psychiatric Association Mental Hospital Service, 1952), 31–34.

148 *DSM*-**II, published in 1968:** *Diagnostic and Statistical Manual of Mental Disorders*, 2nd ed. (American Psychiatric Association, 1968).

149 **he wanted the new edition:** Hannah S. Decker, *The Making of DSM-III: A Diagnostic Manual's Conquest of American Psychiatry* (Oxford: Oxford University Press, 2013).

149 **Psychoanalysts pushed back:** Ibid., 278.

149 **One study compared two groups:** Tone, *Age of Anxiety*, 90.

150 **Despite the runaway success:** Ibid., 153.

150 **A 1968 study, for example:** Ibid., 179.

150 **A Valium ad published in 1970:** Reprinted in ibid., 157.

150 **former first lady Betty Ford:** Donnie Radcliffe, "Betty Ford Dies at 93: Former First Lady Founded Iconic Clinic," *Washington Post*, July 8, 2011.

151 **Senator Edward Kennedy convened:** Tone, *Age of Anxiety*, 204–5.

152 **began recommending the SSRIs:** American Psychiatric Association, "Practice Guideline for the Treatment of Patients with Panic Disorder," *American Journal of Psychiatry* 155 (1998).

152 **GlaxoSmithKline won FDA approval:** Tone, *Age of Anxiety*, 217–18.

152 **One TV spot featured a businessman:** Paxil social anxiety ad, https://www.youtube.com/watch?v=rR8rBEFulw4.

152 **In 2009, GlaxoSmithKline said:** Greg Miller, "Is Pharma Running Out of Brainy Ideas?" *Science* 329 (2010): 502–4. A good summary of the recent retreat by pharmaceutical companies can be found at Steven E. Hyman, "Revolution Stalled," *Science Translational Medicine* 4, no. 155 (2012): 155cm11.

153 **Pexacerfont:** Vladimir Coric et al., "Multicenter, Randomized, Double-Blind, Active Comparator and Placebo-Controlled Trial of a Corticotropin-Releasing Factor Receptor-1 Antagonist in Generalized Anxiety Disorder," *Depression and Anxiety* 27 (2010): 417–25.

153 **Verucerfont:** "Neurocrine Announces Top-Line Results of Corticotropin Releasing Factor Antagonist GSK561679 for Treatment

of Major Depressive Disorder," press release, Nuerocrine Biosciences, September 14, 2010, http://phx.corporate-ir.net/phoenix.zhtml?c=68817&p=irol-newsArticle&highlight=&ID=1471129.

153 **Some scientists think that:** George F. Koob and Eric P. Zorilla, "Update on Corticotropin-Releasing Factor Pharmacotherapy for Psychiatric Disorders: A Revisionist View," *Neuropsychopharmacology Reviews* 37 (2012): 308–9.

153 **launched a program dubbed "Fast-Fail":** "FAST: Fast-Fail Trials," fact sheet, National Institute of Mental Health, http://www.nimh.nih.gov/research-priorities/research-initiatives/fast-fast-fail-trials.shtml.

154 **In a pivotal study, Davis:** William A. Falls et al., "Extinction of Fear-Potentiated Startle: Blockade by Infusion of an NMDA Antagonist into the Amygdala," *Journal of Neuroscience* 12, no. 3 (1992): 854–63.

154 **In 2002, Davis, Ressler, and colleagues:** "Facilitation of Conditioned Fear Extinction by Systemic Administration or Intra-Amygdala Infusions of D-Cycloserine as Assessed with Fear-Potentiated Startle in Rats," *Journal of Neuroscience* 22, no. 6 (2002): 2343–51.

155 **Davis and Ressler then teamed up:** Kerry J. Ressler et al., "Cognitive Enhancers as Adjuncts to Psychotherapy: Use of D-Cycloserine in Phobic Individuals to Facilitate Extinction of Fear," *Archives of General Psychiatry* 61, no. 11 (2004): 1136–44.

156 **In one trial, DCS failed:** Eric A. Storch et al., "D-cycloserine Does Not Enhance Exposure-Response Prevention Therapy in Obsessive-Compulsive Disorder," *International Clinical Psychopharmacology* 22, no. 4 (2007): 230–37.

156 **DCS sped up improvement:** Stefan G. Hofmann et al., "D-cycloserine as an Augmentation Strategy with Cognitive-Behavioral Therapy for Social Anxiety Disorder," *American Journal of Psychiatry* 170, no. 7 (2013): 751–58.

156 **One study of veterans:** Brett T. Litz et al., "A Randomized Placebo-Controlled Trial of D-cycloserine and Exposure Therapy for Post-traumatic Stress Disorder," *Journal of Psychiatric Research* 46 (2012): 1184–90.

156 **Hofmann, who had done the trials:** Stefan G. Hofmann, interview by author; and S. G. Hofmann, "D-cycloserine for Treating Anxiety Disorders: Making Good Exposures Better and Bad Exposures Worse," *Depression and Anxiety* 31 (2014): 175–77.

157 **people have taken MDMA:** For an in-depth survey of compounds being studied in anxiety disorders, see Boadie W. Dunlop et al., "Pharmacological Mechanisms of Modulating Fear and Extinction," in *Primer on Anxiety Disorders: Translational Perspectives on Diagnosis and Treatment*, ed. Kerry J. Ressler et al. (New York: Oxford University Press, 2015), 367–431.

6. COLD CALLS, AIRPLANES, AND INDECISION

159 **A 2005 study by Australian researchers:** Geoff Waghorn et al., "Disability, Employment and Work Performance Among People with ICD-10 Anxiety Disorders," *Australian and New Zealand Journal of Psychiatry* 39 (2005): 55–66.

160 **While both anxiety disorders and depression:** Inger Plaisier et al., "Depressive and Anxiety Disorders On-the-Job: The Importance of Job Characteristics for Good Work Functioning in Persons with Depressive and Anxiety Disorders," *Psychiatry Research* 200 (2012): 382–88.

160 **Of the more than ten million Americans:** *Annual Statistical Report on the Social Security Disability Insurance Program*, 2015, Social Security Administration, 2015, table 6, http://www.socialsecurity.gov /policy/docs/statcomps/di_asr/2015/sect01b.html#table6.

161 **Indeed, people with panic disorder:** Martin M. Antony et al., "Dimensions of Perfectionism Across the Anxiety Disorders," *Behaviour Research and Therapy* 36 (1998): 1143–54.

161 **Research shows, however, that anxiety:** Joachim Stöber and Jutta Joormann, "Worry, Procrastination, and Perfectionism: Differentiating Amount of Worry, Pathological Worry, Anxiety and Depression," *Cognitive Therapy and Research* 25, no. 1 (2001): 49–60.

162 **A review of more than two hundred:** Piers Steel, "The Nature of Procrastination: A Meta-Analytic and Theoretical Review of Quintessential Self-Regulatory Failure," *Psychological Bulletin* 133, no. 1 (2007): 65–94.

167 **More than a century ago, in 1908:** In Yerkes and Dodson's famous experiment, mice presented with two boxes, one black and one white, were taught to go only into the white box. The researchers did this by giving the mice shocks each time they began to enter the black box. When the task was difficult, the mice learned best when the shocks given were medium strength. When the shocks were weaker or stronger, the mice learned more slowly and made more errors. Only when the task was really easy did the mice continue to perform better as the shocks increased in strength. The researchers made the task harder by decreasing the amount of light shining on the boxes, making it tougher for the mice to tell the difference between the colors. See Robert M. Yerkes and John D. Dodson, "The Relation of Strength of Stimulus to Rapidity of Habit-Formation," *Journal of Comparative Neurology and Psychology* 18, no. 5 (1908): 459–82.

168 **a range of studies in people:** S. J. Lupien et al., "The Effects of Stress and Stress Hormones on Human Cognition: Implications for the Field of Brain and Cognition," *Brain and Cognition* 65, no. 3 (2007): 209–37.

168 **A study of beginning nursing students:** L. McEwan and D. Goldenberg, "Achievement Motivation, Anxiety and Academic Success in the First Year Master of Nursing Students," *Nurse Education Today* 19, no. 5 (1999): 419–30.

168 **Canadian researchers, for example:** Alexander M. Penney et al., "Intelligence and Emotional Disorders: Is the Worrying and Ruminating Mind a More Intelligent Mind?" *Personality and Individual Differences* 74 (2015): 90–93.

168 **A small 2012 study:** Jeremy D. Coplan et al., "The Relationship Between Intelligence and Anxiety: An Association with Subcortical White Matter Metabolism," *Frontiers in Evolutionary Neuroscience* 3, no. 8 (2012): 1–7.

168 **Ein-Dor and his colleague Orgad Tal:** Tsachi Ein-Dor and Orgad Tal, "Scared Saviors: Evidence That People High in Attachment Anxiety Are More Effective in Alerting Others to Threat," *European Journal of Social Psychology* 42, no. 6 (2012): 667–71.

174 **For decades, psychologists have theorized:** Michael W. Eysenck et al., "Anxiety and Cognitive Performance: Attentional Control

Theory," *Emotion* 7, no. 2 (2007): 336–53. Also see also Oliver J. Robinson et al., "The Impact of Anxiety upon Cognition: Perspectives from Human Threat of Shock Studies," *Frontiers in Human Neuroscience* 7 (2013).

174 **The idea is that:** Michael W. Eysenck, "Anxiety, Learning, and Memory: A Reconceptualization," *Journal of Research in Personality* 13, no. 4 (1979): 363–85.

175 **In a 2016 study, researchers at NIMH:** Katherin E. Vytal et al., "Induced-Anxiety Differentially Disrupts Working Memory in Generalized Anxiety Disorder," *BMC Psychiatry* 16 (2016): 1–9.

175 **Another study by the same NIMH:** Nicholas L. Balderston et al., "Anxiety Patients Show Reduced Working Memory Related DLPFC Activation During Safety and Threat," *Depression and Anxiety* (2016): 1–12.

176 **It sounds absurd, but a series of studies:** Alison Wood Brooks, "Get Excited: Reappraising Pre-Performance Anxiety as Excitement," *Journal of Experimental Psychology: General* 143, no. 3 (2014): 1144–58.

181 **Only one in four people:** "Workplace Stress and Anxiety Disorders Survey," Anxiety and Depression Association of America, http://www.adaa.org/workplace-stress-anxiety-disorders-survey.

181 **Still, one study published in 1999:** D. A. Koser et al., "Comparison of a Physical and Mental Disability in Employee Selection: An Experimental Examination of Direct and Moderated Effects," *North American Journal of Psychology* 1 (1999): 213–22, referenced in Kay Wheat et al., "Mental Illness in the Workplace: Conceal or Reveal?" *Journal of the Royal Society of Medicine* 103, no. 3 (2010): 83–86.

181 **A 1996 survey:** Jim Read and Sue Baker, "Not Just Sticks and Stones: A Survey of the Stigma, Taboos and Discrimination Experienced by People with Mental Health Problems," *Mind* (1996).

182 **Anxious people often have a tough time:** C. Giorgetta et al., "Reduced Risk-Taking Behavior as a Trait Feature of Anxiety," *Emotion* 12, no. 6 (2012): 1373–83. And for an overview, see Catherine A. Hartley and Elizabeth A. Phelps, "Anxiety and Decision-Making," *Biological Psychiatry* 72, no. 2 (2012).

183 **In one gambling experiment:** Andrei C. Miu et al., "Anxiety Impairs Decision-Making: Psychophysiological Evidence from an Iowa Gambling Task," *Biological Psychology* 77 (2008): 353–58.

183 **When scientists at the University of Pittsburgh:** Junchol Park et al., "Anxiety Evokes Hypofrontality and Disrupts Rule-Relevant Encoding by Dorsomedial Prefrontal Cortex Neurons," *Journal of Neuroscience* 36, no. 11 (2016): 3322–35.

7. THE ISOLATION CHAMBER

189 **I've found only one study:** Y. Tibi-Elhanany and S. G. Shamay-Tsoory, "Social Cognition in Social Anxiety: First Evidence for Increased Empathic Abilities," *Israel Journal of Psychiatry* 48, no. 2 (2011): 98–106.

189 **However, if we look at it more broadly:** For a good primer on posttraumatic growth, see Posttraumatic Growth Research Group, Department of Psychology, University of North Carolina at Charlotte, https://ptgi.uncc.edu.

191 **But one interesting 2013 study:** Jacob A. Priest, "Anxiety Disorders and the Quality of Relationships with Friends, Relatives, and Romantic Partners," *Journal of Clinical Psychology* 69, no. 1 (2013): 78–88.

191 **In another study, socially anxious women:** S. Cuming and R. M. Rapee, "Social Anxiety and Self-Protective Communication Style in Close Relationships," *Behaviour Research and Therapy* 48, no. 2 (2010): 87–96.

191 **For anxious kids, having supportive:** Julie Newman Kingery et al., "Peer Experiences of Anxious and Socially Withdrawn Youth: An Integrative Review of the Developmental and Clinical Literature," *Clinical Child and Family Psychological Review* 13 (2010): 91–128.

191 **being part of a group:** A. M. La Greca and H. M. Harrison, "Adolescent Peer Relations, Friendships, and Romantic Relationships: Do They Predict Social Anxiety and Depression?" *Journal of Clinical and Child Adolescent Psychology* 34, no. 1 (2005): 49–61.

191 **In a 2016 study, anxious teens:** N. C. Jacobson and M. G. Newman, "Perceptions of Close and Group Relationships Mediate the

Relationship Between Anxiety and Depression over a Decade Later," *Depression and Anxiety* 33, no. 1 (2016): 66–74.

191 **Good friends also enhance treatment:** J. R. Baker and J. L. Hudson, "Friendship Quality Predicts Treatment Outcome in Children with Anxiety Disorders," *Behaviour Research and Therapy* 51, no. 1 (2013): 31–36.

192 **Anxious kids generally:** Julie Newman Kingery et al., "Peer Experiences."

192 **Research has found at least:** Timothy L. Verduin and Philip C. Kendall, "Peer Perceptions and Liking of Children with Anxiety Disorders," *Journal of Abnormal Child Psychology* 36, no. 4 (2008): 459–69.

192 **A study from 1999:** D. C. Beidel et al., "Psychopathology of Childhood Social Phobia," *Journal of American Academy of Child and Adolescent Psychiatry* 38, no. 6 (1999): 643–50.

192 **Anxious kids are more likely to be bullied:** A. M. Crawford and K. Manassis, "Anxiety, Social Skills, Friendship Quality, and Peer Victimization: An Integrated Model," *Journal of Anxiety Disorders* 25, no. 7 (2011): 924–31.

192 **In one study, a staggering 92 percent:** Randi E. McCabe et al., "Preliminary Examination of the Relationship Between Anxiety Disorders in Adults and Self-Reported History of Teasing or Bullying Experiences," *Cognitive Behaviour Therapy* 32, no. 4 (2003): 187–93.

192 **Boys with social anxiety:** Kingery, "Peer Experiences."

192 **And in another example of a negative feedback:** R. R. Landoll et al., "Cyber Victimization by Peers: Prospective Associations with Adolescent Social Anxiety and Depressive Symptoms," *Journal of Adolescence* 42 (2015): 77–86.

192 **Adolescents who are frequently picked on:** Lexine A. Stapinski et al., "Peer Victimization During Adolescence and Risk for Anxiety Disorders in Adulthood: A Prospective Cohort Study," *Depression and Anxiety* 31, no. 7 (2014): 575–82.

194 **Emotional states, neuroscientists have found:** Elaine Hatfield et al., "Emotional Contagion," *Current Directions in Psychological Science* 2, no. 3 (1993): 96–100.

194 **In a 2014 study, researchers in Germany:** Veronika Engert et al., "Cortisol Increase in Empathic Stress Is Modulated by Emotional Closeness and Observation Modality," *Psychoneuroendocrinology* 45 (2014): 192–201.

194 **This might be one reason why adults:** Priest, "Anxiety Disorders and the Quality of Relationships."

199 **partners with anxiety disorders judged:** Piotr Pankiewicz et al., "Anxiety Disorders in Intimate Partners and the Quality of Their Relationship," *Journal of Affective Disorders* 140 (2012): 176–80.

200 **men whose wives had panic disorder:** Jane D. McLeod, "Anxiety Disorders and Marital Quality," *Journal of Abnormal Psychology* 103, no. 4 (1994): 767–76.

200 **A 1985 study:** W. Monteiro et al., "Marital Adjustment and Treatment Outcome in Agoraphobia," *British Journal of Psychiatry* 146 (1985): 383–90.

200 **Women with high levels of social anxiety:** E. Porter and D. L. Chambless, "Shying Away from a Good Thing: Social Anxiety in Romantic Relationships," *Journal of Clinical Psychology* 70, no. 6 (2014): 546–61.

214 **followed thirty-three heterosexual couples:** Talia I. Zaider et al., "Anxiety Disorders and Intimate Relationships: A Study of Daily Processes in Couples," *Journal of Abnormal Psychology* 119, no. 1 (2010): 163–73.

8. WORRIES ABOUT MY DAUGHTER

220 **About 10 percent of pregnant women:** William O. Cooper et al., "Increasing Use of Antidepressants in Pregnancy," *American Journal of Obstetrics & Gynecology* 196, no. 6 (2007).

220 **In the mid-2000s, studies had linked:** See, for example, G. M. Thormahlen, "Paroxetine Use During Pregnancy: Is It Safe?," *Annals of Pharmacotherapy* 40, no. 10 (2006): 1834–37; and B. Bar-Oz et al., "Paroxetine and Congenital Malformations: Meta-Analysis and Consideration of Potential Confounding Factors," *Clinical Therapeutics* 29, no. 5 (2007): 918–26.

221 **linked to a higher risk—about double:** Jennifer Reefhuis et al., "Specific SSRIs and Birth Defects: Bayesian Analysis to Interpret New Data in the Context of Previous Reports," *BMJ* 351 (2015).

221 **more likely to be born prematurely:** Rita Suri et al., "Effects of Antenatal Depression and Antidepressant Treatment on Gestational Age at Birth and Risk of Preterm Birth," *American Journal of Psychiatry* 164, no. 8 (2007): 1206–13; and T. F. Oberlander et al., "Neonatal Outcomes After Prenatal Exposure to Selective Serotonin Reuptake Inhibitor Antidepressants and Maternal Depression Using Population-Based Linked Health Data," *Archives of General Psychiatry* 63, no. 8 (2006): 898–906.

221 **serious lung condition:** Sophie Grigoriadis et al., "Prenatal Exposure to Antidepressants and Persistent Pulmonary Hypertension of the Newborn: Systematic Review and Meta-Analysis," *BMJ* 348 (2014).

221 **no more likely to have heart defects:** Irene Petersen et al., "Selective Serotonin Reuptake Inhibitors and Congenital Heart Anomalies: Comparative Cohort Studies of Women Treated Before and During Pregnancy and Their Children," *Journal of Clinical Psychiatry* 77, no. 1 (2016): e36–e42.

226 **is found in breast milk:** Tiffany Field, "Breastfeeding and Antidepressants," *Infant Behavior and Development* 31, no. 3 (2008): 481–87; and Jan Oystein Berle and Olav Spigset, "Antidepressant Use During Breastfeeding," *Current Women's Health Review* 7 (2011): 28–34.

226 **link Prozac to slow weight gain:** C. D. Chambers et al., "Weight Gain in Infants Breastfed by Mothers Who Take Fluoxetine," *Pediatrics* 104, no. 5 (1999).

226 **increased risk of autism and ADHD:** C. C. Clements et al., "Prenatal Antidepressant Exposure Is Associated with Risk for Attention-Deficit Hyperactivity Disorder but Not Autism Spectrum Disorder in a Large Health System," *Molecular Psychiatry* 20, no. 6 (2015): 727–34.

226 **twice as likely to develop autism:** T. Boukhris et al., "Antidepressant Use During Pregnancy and the Risk of Autism Spectrum Disorder in Children," *JAMA Pediatrics* 170, no. 2 (2016): 117–24.

226 **no link between antidepressants and autism:** Merete Juul Sørensen et al., "Antidepressant Exposure in Pregnancy and Risk of Autism Spectrum Disorders," *Clinical Epidemiology* 5 (2013): 449–59.

226 **more behavioral issues:** Katrina C. Johnson et al., "Preschool Outcomes Following Prenatal Serotonin Reuptake Inhibitor Exposure: Differences in Language and Behavior, but Not Cognitive Function," *Journal of Clinical Psychiatry* 77, no. 2 (2016): e176–e182.

226 **no long-term effects:** See for example, Rita Suri et al., "Acute and Long-Term Behavioral Outcome of Infants and Children Exposed in Utero to Either Maternal Depression or Antidepressants: A Review of the Literature," *Journal of Clinical Psychiatry* 75, no. 10 (2014): e1142–e1152.

226 **no difference between them:** Irena Nulman et al., "Neurodevelopment of Children Prenatally Exposed to Selective Reuptake Inhibitor Antidepressants: Toronto Sibling Study," *Journal of Clinical Psychiatry* 76, no. 7 (2015): e842–e847.

227 **to become depressed by age fifteen:** Heli Malm et al., "Gestational Exposure to Selective Serotonin Reuptake Inhibitors and Offspring Psychiatric Disorders: A National Register-Based Study," *Journal of the American Academy of Child and Adolescent Psychiatry* 55, no. 5 (2016): 359–66.

228 **Being exposed to a parent's depression:** Myrna M. Weissman et al., "Offspring of Depressed Parents: 20 Years Later," *American Journal of Psychiatry* 163 (2006): 1001–08.

229 **higher rates of anxiety, aggressive behavior:** Bea R. Van den Bergh and Alfons Marcoen, "High Antenatal Maternal Anxiety Is Related to ADHD Symptoms, Externalizing Problems, and Anxiety in 8- and 9-Year-Olds," *Child Development* 75, no. 4 (2004): 1085–97.

229 **levels of the stress hormone cortisol:** Bea R. H. Van den Bergh et al., "Antenatal Maternal Anxiety Is Related to HPA-Axis Dysregulation and Self-Reported Depressive Symptoms in Adolescence: A Prospective Study on the Fetal Origins of Depressed Mood," *Neuropsychopharmacology* 33, no. 3 (2008): 536–45.

229 **tougher time on tasks:** Maarten Mennes et al., "Long-Term Cognitive Sequelae of Antenatal Maternal Anxiety: Involvement of the

Orbitofrontal Cortex," *Neuroscience and Biobehavioral Review* 30 (2006): 1078–86; and Maarten Mennes et al., "Developmental Brain Alternations in 17 Year Old Boys Are Related to Antenatal Maternal Anxiety," *Clinical Neurophysiology* 120 (2009): 1116–22.

229 **reduce the volume in parts of the brain:** Claudia Buss et al., "High Pregnancy Anxiety During Mid-Gestation Is Associated with Decreased Gray Matter Density in 6–9 Year-Old Children," *Psychoneuroendocrinology* 35, no. 1 (2010): 141–53.

230 **babies that cry excessively:** Johanna Petzoldt et al., "Maternal Anxiety Disorders Predict Excessive Infant Crying: A Prospective Longitudinal Study," *Archives of Disease in Childhood* 99, no. 9 (2014): 800–806.

230 **feeding problems in their babies:** J. Petzoldt et al., "Maternal Anxiety Versus Depressive Disorders: Specific Relations to Infants' Crying, Feeding and Sleeping Problems," *Child: Care, Health and Development* 42, no. 2 (2015): 231–45.

230 **transmitted to them in utero:** Bea R. H. Van den Bergh et al., "Antenatal Maternal Anxiety and Stress and the Neurobehavioural Development of the Fetus and Child: Links and Possible Mechanisms. A Review," *Neuroscience and Biobehavioral Reviews* 29 (2005): 237–58.

230 **can cross the placenta:** Michael T. Kinsella and Catherine Monk, "Impact of Maternal Stress, Depression and Anxiety on Fetal Neurobehavioral Development," *Clinical Obstetrics and Gynecology* 52, no. 3 (2009): 425–40.

230 **stress during pregnancy:** Catherine Monk et al., "Distress During Pregnancy: Epigenetic Regulation of Placenta Glucocorticoid-Related Genes and Fetal Neurobehavior," *American Journal of Psychiatry* 173, no. 7 (2016): 705–13.

231 **just before getting pregnant:** L. S. Cohen et al., "Relapse of Major Depression During Pregnancy in Women Who Maintain or Discontinue Antidepressant Treatment," *Journal of the American Medical Association* 295, no. 5 (2006): 499–507.

233 **almost three times as likely:** Katja Beesdo et al., "Incidence of Social Anxiety Disorder and the Consistent Risk for Secondary Depression in the First Three Decades of Life," *Archives of General Psychiatry* 64, no. 8 (2007): 903–12.

233 **drank alcohol more frequently:** Philip C. Kendall et al., "Child Anxiety Treatment: Outcomes in Adolescence and Impact on Substance Use and Depression at 7.4 Year Follow-Up," *Journal of Consulting and Clinical Psychology* 72, no. 2 (2004): 276–87.

233 **developed an anxiety disorder:** Golda S. Ginsburg et al., "Preventing Onset of Anxiety Disorders in Offspring of Anxious Parents: A Randomized Controlled Trial of a Family-Based Intervention," *American Journal of Psychiatry* 172, no. 12 (2015): 1207–14.

235 **Thirty-nine percent of the teenage girls:** Ronald M. Rapee, "The Preventative Effects of a Brief, Early Intervention for Preschool-Aged Children at Risk for Internalizing: Follow-Up into Middle Adolescence," *Journal of Child Psychology and Psychiatry* 54, no. 7 (2013): 780–88.

239 **met criteria for social anxiety disorder:** Andrea Chronis-Tuscano et al., "Preliminary Evaluation of a Multimodal Early Intervention Program for Behaviorally Inhibited Preschoolers," *Journal of Consulting and Clinical Psychology* 83, no. 3 (2015): 534–40.

9. STAYING GROUNDED

246 **number of college students diagnosed with:** American College Health Association National College Health Assessment, *Spring 2016 Reference Group Executive Summary* (American College Health Association, 2016); and American College Health Association National College Health Assessment, *Fall 2008 Reference Group Executive Summary* (American College Health Association, 2008).

248 **a link to anxiety and depression:** See, for example, H. C. Woods and H. Scott, "#Sleepyteens: Social Media Use in Adolescence Is Associated with Poor Sleep Quality, Anxiety, Depression and Low Self-Esteem," *Journal of Adolescence* 51 (2016): 41–49.

248 **feelings of loneliness and inadequacy:** Moira Burke et al., "Social Network Activity and Social Well-Being," *CHI '10 Proceedings of the SIGCHI Conference on Human Factors in Computing Systems* (2010): 1909–12.

248 **tuition at Michigan:** "Cost of Attendance," Office of Financial Aid, University of Michigan, https://finaid.umich.edu/cost-of-attendance/.

249 **about $29,000 in debt:** *Student Debt and the Class of 2014,* Institute for College Access and Success, October 2015, http://ticas.org/sites /default/files/pub_files/classof2014.pdf.

251 **had had some previous counseling:** *College Student Mental Health Survey,* Phase III, Counseling and Psychological Services, https:// caps.umich.edu/files/caps/CSMHSfinal.pdf.

252 **don't provide psychiatrist services:** *Annual Survey 2015,* Association for University and College Counseling Center Directors. http:// www.aucccd.org/assets/documents/aucccd%202015%20mono graph%20-%20public%20version.pdf.

252 **a sign of strength:** "A Survey About Mental Health and Suicide in the United States," by Harris Poll on behalf of the Anxiety and Depression Association of America, the American Foundation for Suicide Prevention and the National Action Alliance for Suicide Prevention, 2015, https://www.adaa.org/sites/default/files/College -Aged_Adults_Survey_Summary-1.14.16.pdf.

254 **Conversion disorder is characterized:** *DSM*-5, 318–21.

254 **somatic symptom disorder:** Ibid., 311–15.

255 **mystery symptoms made up two-thirds:** Natalie Steinbrecher et al., "The Prevalence of Medically Unexplained Symptoms in Primary Care," *Psychosomatics* 52, no. 3 (2011): 263–71.

255 **evidence that it is beneficial:** John R. Keefe et al., "A Meta-Analytic Review of Psychodynamic Therapies for Anxiety Disorders," *Clinical Psychology Review* 34, no. 4 (2014): 309–23.

256 **associated with anxiety in teenagers:** M. Sarchiapone et al., "Hours of Sleep in Adolescents and Its Association with Anxiety, Emotional Concerns, and Suicidal Ideation," *Sleep Medicine* 15, no. 2 (2014): 248–54.

256 **is linked to anxiety in kids:** F. E. Fletcher et al., "The Association Between Anxiety Symptoms and Sleep in School-Aged Children: A Combined Insight from the Children's Sleep Habits Questionnaire and Actigraphy," *Behavioral Sleep Medicine* (2016): 1–16.

256 **greater risk of having more chronic illnesses:** Josine G. van Mill et al., "Sleep Duration, but Not Insomnia, Predicts the 2-Year Course of Depressive and Anxiety Disorders," *Journal of Clinical Psychiatry* 75, no. 2 (2014): 119–26.

256 **difficulty sleeping is a precursor:** M. L. Jackson et al., "Sleep Difficulties and the Development of Depression and Anxiety: A Longitudinal Study of Young Australian Women," *Archives of Women's Mental Health* 17, no. 3 (2014): 189–98.

256 **increase the risk of developing PTSD:** Rebecca C. Cox and Bunmi O. Olatunji, "A Systematic Review of Sleep Disturbance in Anxiety and Related Disorders," *Journal of Anxiety Disorders* 37 (2016): 104–29.

257 **good sleep is critical for consolidating memories:** A. K. Zalta et al., "Sleep Quality Predicts Treatment Outcome in CBT for Social Anxiety Disorder," *Depression and Anxiety* 30, no. 11 (2013): 1114–20.

257 **their amygdala activity in response to negative:** Cox and Oltunji, "A Systematic Review of Sleep Disturbance in Anxiety and Related Disorders."

258 **exercise is modestly effective:** K. Jayakody et al., "Exercise for Anxiety Disorders: Systematic Review," *British Journal of Sports Medicine* 48, no. 3 (2014): 187–96.

258 **boost brain-derived neurotrophic factor:** Lindsey B. DeBoer et al., "Exploring Exercise as an Avenue for the Treatment of Anxiety Disorders," *Expert Review of Neurotherapuetics* 12, no. 8 (2012): 1011–22.

258 **lowers activity in the HPA axis:** Elizabeth Anderson and Geetha Shivakumar, "Effects of Exercise and Physical Activity on Anxiety," *Frontiers in Psychiatry* 4 (2013).

258 **time in nature can reduce stress:** David G. Pearson and Tony Craig, "The Great Outdoors? Exploring the Mental Health Benefits of Natural Environments," *Frontiers in Psychology* 5 (2014).

258 **time in the park had decreased anxiety:** Gregory N. Bratman et al., "The Benefits of Nature Experience: Improved Affect and Cognition," *Landscape and Urban Planning* 138 (2015): 41–50.

258 **21 percent higher in urban areas:** J. Peen et al., "The Current Status of Urban-Rural Differences in Psychiatric Disorders," *Acta Psychiatrica Scandinavica* 121 (2010): 84–93.

ACKNOWLEDGMENTS

On Edge was a team endeavor. I could never have written it without the encouragement, support, and guidance of so many friends, family members, and colleagues. My agent, Gary Morris at the David Black Agency, believed in the book when it was only a few hurried paragraphs sent to him in an email. Through the years it took me to report and write it, Gary has been a fierce advocate, a stalwart sounding board, and a true mensch.

I had the good fortune to land at Crown Publishing, where the brilliant Molly Stern helms an outfit filled with the best in the business. My editor, the incredibly gifted and sharp-eyed Rachel Klayman, smoothed out my language, untangled my logic, and always pushed me to make this book better. Sarah Breivogel and Alaina Waagner got the word out about *On Edge* with creativity, tenacity, and passion. Claire Potter brought tremendous hard work and enthusiasm to the project. Jon Darga made things run smoothly and good-naturedly answered my many questions. Thanks also to Lance Fitzgerald, Robert Siek, Courtney Snyder, and everyone else on the *On Edge* team.

At the *Wall Street Journal*, editors Mike Miller and Emily Nelson have allowed me to pursue the most fun, most rewarding hybrid beat of psychology, health, and travel and gave me crucial time off to work on this book. Adam Thompson's deft editing makes me look good. Thanks to Elizabeth Bernstein, Elizabeth Holmes, and Sumathi Reddy for commenting on drafts of the manuscript. They, along with Rachel Bachman, Ellen

Byron, Ray Smith, and the entire Personal Journal crew, made it a joy to go to work every day. Former editors John Blanton and Hilary Stout were early supporters of *On Edge* and taught me so much about writing and editing and always did so with incredible generosity, humor, and grace. Thanks also to Dick Tofel, who first hired me at the *Journal*, and Jim Pensiero, who sent me on my way to becoming a reporter. Rebecca Blumenstein, Cynthia Crossen, Kathy Deveny, Laurie Hays, Dan Hertzberg, Dennis Kneale, and Paul Steiger were important early mentors. Wendy Bounds, Sam Walker, and Jeff Zaslow helped me when I was first contemplating the proposal for this book.

Anxiety researchers and clinicians are among the most generous and patient people around. Danny Pine has steered me to the best research, introduced me to important contacts, and saved me from making several mistakes. I am lucky to count him as a mentor and friend. Jordan Smoller is not only a remarkable scientist, but a wonderful writer as well: He read an early draft of the manuscript and provided important feedback.

Thank you also to Anne Marie Albano, Christine Asidao, Yair Bar-Haim, David Barlow, Katja Beesdo-Baum, Andrea Chronis-Tuscano, Michelle Craske, Christina Danko, Michael Davis, Nathan Fox, Jay Gingrich, Christian Grillon, Michelle Hampson, Steven Hayes, Stefan Hofmann, Jerry Kagan, Ned Kalin, Ron Kessler, Don Klein, Joe LeDoux, Heli Malm, Carmen McLean, Francis McMahon, Barbara Morrongiello, Danielle Novick, Ron Rapee, Kerry Ressler, Jeff Rossman, Ken Rubin, Todd Sevig, Robert Temple, Bea Van den Bergh, Greg Van Rybroek, Ulli Wittchen, and Anna Zilverstand.

I'm also very grateful to the late Alies Muskin and her staff at the Anxiety and Depression Association of America.

I'm in awe of the passion, commitment, and openness of the college mental health advocates I've met. Thank you for sharing your stories with me, supporting each other, and fighting for mental health every day. Thanks to Sara Abelson, Alison Malmon, Pam McKeta, and everyone at Active Minds. Also to Victor Schwartz and the crew at the Jed Foundation. A big shout-out to Anna Chen, Anna Learis, Grant Rivas, Shelby Steverson, and Cheyenne Stone at Michigan. Go Blue!

Receiving a Rosalynn Carter Fellowship for Mental Health Journalism allowed me to really launch this project. Our initial meeting in Atlanta was the first time I spoke about my anxiety in a professional public setting. Thank you to Mrs. Carter, Rebecca Palpant Shimkets, and the Carter Center staff, mentors, and fellows for the work you do supporting journalism and combating stigma.

So many friends have encouraged and supported me along the way. Roe D'Angelo and Ianthe Dugan read my drafts, steadied my nerves, and were the very best cheerleaders. A huge thank you also to Amy Bennett, Sabina Broadhead, Mike Cronin, Elisabeth Eaves, Chelsea Emery, Francis Freisinger, Susie Hassan, Gabrielle Kahn, Ron Lieber, Anna Loengard, Jeff Opdyke, Annie Murphy Paul, Josh Prager, Richard Robb, David Roche, Joel Smernoff, David Stone, Johannes and Karin Weidenmueller, Rubina Yeh, Leslie Wright, and Alan Zarembo. The members of the Invisible Institute are a continual source of wisdom and inspiration.

I wrote most of this book at the Ditmas Workspace in Ditmas Park, Brooklyn, where Ben Smith and Liena Zagare created a wonderful home for neighborhood writers and the indefatigable Gina, Tom, and Erica Anderson now nurture a growing creative community. Thanks to my fellow quiet room denizens Gabe Heller, David Rogers, and Adam Sternbergh for the camaraderie and conversation. We're lucky to have the Milk & Honey café a short walk away where Max and the baristas have kept me fueled with decaf.

Thank you to the therapists and doctors—especially Dr. G and Dr. L— who have helped keep me healthy.

Most of all, I thank my family. My parents, Anita and Gary Petersen, have put me back together more times than I can recall. My immensely talented sister, Dana Petersen Murphy, talked to me about her own anxiety, and she and her husband, Sean Murphy, fed and housed me during my Wisconsin reporting trips. My aunt Susan Koeferl provided crucial details about my grandmother's illness and was so open about a very painful period in her life. My cousin Renee Jahnke secured our grandmother's records from Mendota. Beverly and Bob Gallagher are the most generous, loving in-laws. Ditto to my fabulous sisters-in-law and their husbands: Jennifer and Sean Briody and Rose and Patrick Gallagher. The Bisel clan in Salem and elsewhere has been this book's unofficial marketing team. Denise Paul has taken such good care of Fiona since she was a baby and gives me the peace of mind I need to work.

If this book had an MVP, it would be my husband, Sean Gallagher. He talked me through setbacks, kept the music playing, made me pizza, and tore up his own schedule so I had the time to report and write. And he gave me Fiona. My heart, my joy. I missed out on a lot of adventures during the years I've been working on this book. But, yes, Mama can go play now.

INDEX

Page numbers beginning with 261 refer to endnotes.

abuse, physical or sexual, 44, 84
acceptance and commitment therapy (ACT), 105–7, 118, 119
    CBT vs., 107
Active Minds, 19, 181, 248
acupuncture, 110
ADHD, 44
    and antidepressants in utero, 226
    as genetic, 59
adrenal glands, 26
adrenaline, 109
adrenocorticotropic hormone (ACTH), 26, 153
aerobic exercise, 257–59
agoraphobia, 99
Albano, Anne Marie, 105
alcohol abuse, 44, 83, 84, 153
Alzheimer's disease, 35, 141
American Journal of Psychiatry, 145, 147
American Medical Association, 145
American Psychiatric Association, 151, 255

Americans with Disabilities Act, 19–20, 181
amygdala, 26–27, 32, 33, 35, 53–54, 55, 76, 84, 110, 136, 154, 260
    CBT and, 96
    in infants, 86
    sleep and, 257
Andreas of Charystos, 22
antidepressants:
    overstated effects of, 127–28
    see also specific antidepressants
Antioch College, 85–86
anxiety:
    and appearance of normality, 15–16
    attention and, 54
    bullying and, 192
    childhood events and, 37–38, 78–84, 218
    and children, 37–38, 78–84, 218, 233
    cognition and, 174–75
    on continuum, 9
    as cultural, 9
    decisions and, 182
    definition of, 8
    early treatments for, 22–25

anxiety (*continued*)
  empathy and, 189–90
  excitement vs., 176–77
  fear vs., 34
  foundation of, 25–30
  as future-oriented, 107
  as helpful, 167–69, 189
  and interpretation of ambiguity, 31
  isolation of, 188–89
  mind-body connection in, 260
  as moral failing, 22
  mothers', effect on children, 228–31
  during pregnancy, 228–29
  search for drugs for, 153
  self-absorption of, 188
  sleep and, 256, 257
  social media and, 248
  as symptom of dementia, 142
  treatment for, 25
Anxiety and Depression Association of America, 99–100, 181
anxiety disorders:
  and adult relationships, 191
  attention shifting and, 90–91
  author's diagnosis and, 4
  and brain scans of children, 53
  and childhood illnesses, 44–46
  and controlling parents, 47–49
  cost of, 6
  as disorders of brain development, 25–35
  drinking and, 20
  in *DSM*, 19
  early detection of, 233–34
  eleven types of, 5
  as fatal, 7
  friendships and, 191–94
  as gateway illness, 7
  as genetic, 59–60, 76–78, 235
  infants at risk of, 78–79, 85
  inhibitory control and, 90–91
  median onset age of, 7
  in men, 16, 78–84
  planning unaffected by, 175
  prevention of, 233–41
  procrastination and, 160–61
  rates of, 6–7
  rising rates among young people of, 246–52
  romantic relationships and, 194–203
  symptoms of, 5
  trauma and, 44–45
  treatments for, *see specific treatments*
  unemployment and, 159–60
  and witnessing parents' illness, 46–47
  in women, 6, 7, 23–24, 78–84
Anxiety Disorders Association of America, 19
Anxiety Disorders Program, University of Michigan, 93–94
anxiety neurosis, 25, 148
anxiety reaction, 148
anxiety sensitivity, 107
applied relaxation (AR), 107–8
Archives of General Psychiatry, 151
Asherman's syndrome, 222–23
Asidao, Christine, 249
asthma, 45, 46, 101–2, 103, 203, 204, 212, 259
AstraZeneca, 152–53
asylums, 96
Ativan, 141
attachment, 83
attention, anxiety and, 54
attention bias modification (ABM), 118–20
  CBT and, 119
attention shifting, 90–91
Auden, W. H., 6
Augustine, Saint, 23
autism, 77

and antidepressants in utero, 226
    and depression during pregnancy,
        228, 230–31
    as genetic, 59, 60
autonomic nervous system, 26, 86
avoidance behaviors, 17–18

baking, 256
Ball, Lucille, 144
balloon breathing, 236–37
barbital, 142
barbiturates, 142–43
Bar-Haim, Yair, 118, 119–20
Barlow, David H., 105
Beard, George Miller, 23
Beck, Aaron T., 98–99
bed nucleus of the stria terminalis
    (BNST), 32–35
Beesdo-Baum, Katja, 38
behavioral inhibition (BI), 85, 87–91
behaviorism, 97–98
benzodiazepines, 137–42, 150–51
Berger, Frank, 143–44
Berle, Milton, enthusiasm for
    Miltown of, 144
Bini, Lucio, 66
biofeedback, 108–9
bipolar disorder, 52–53, 77, 152
    as genetic, 59
BMJ, 141
breastfeeding, 225–26
Breuer, Josef, 98
Brilliant Madness, A (film), 267
bromides, 142
bronchitis, 46
Bucy, Paul, 26–27
bullying, 192

California, University of:
    at Irvine, 229
    at Los Angeles, 46

at San Diego, 31–32
Cambodia, 9
cardio, 257–58
Carter Products, 143–44, 145
catharsis, 9
CBT, see cognitive behavioral
    therapy
Celexa, 127, 221
Center for Anxiety and Related
    Disorders, Boston University,
    105
central nucleus of the amygdala, 28
Cerletti, Ugo, 66
child-directed interaction (CDI),
    237
children:
    and anxiety, 37–38, 78–84, 218,
        233
    anxiety prevention and, 234–41
    behavioral inhibition (BI) in, 85,
        87–91
    fears in, 79–80
    gender differences in, 78–79
    illnesses of, 44–46
    injuries of, 81
    panic attacks of, 38
    in pole exercise, 81–82
    stress of, 44
    trauma of, 44
chloral hydrate, 142
Cho, Seung-Hui, 250
Chronis-Tuscano, Andrea, 237
clowns, fear of, 38–39
cognition:
    anxiety and, 174–75
    exercise and, 258
cognitive behavioral therapy (CBT),
    77, 94–96, 110, 112, 118
    ABM and, 119
    ACT vs., 107
    author's experience with, 94–96,
        103, 254–55
    and brain structure, 136

cognitive behavioral therapy (CBT)
   (*continued*)
   exposure therapy and, 258
   and going off SSRIs, 157
   origins of, 97
   pregnancy and, 231
   sleep and, 256–57
   tweaking of, 103–5
cognitive defusion, 106
cognitive reappraisal, 95
cognitive therapy, 98–99
Columbia University, 227, 230
Community Mental Health Act, 268
conditioned reflex, 97
Connecticut, University of, Health Center, 233–34
contamination anxiety, 121–22
conversion disorder, 254
Cool Little Kids, 234–35, 237, 238
corticotropin-releasing factor (CRF), 153–54
corticotropin-releasing hormone (CRH), 26
cortisol, 77, 230
Counseling and Psychological Services (CAPS), University of Michigan, 249–52
Craske, Michelle, 78, 84, 105
Crisalida (Dalí), 145
cystic hygroma, 219–20, 222

Da Costa, Jacob, 24
Dalí, Salvador, 145
Danko, Christina, 237–38
Darwin, Charles, hypochondriasis of, 96
Davis, Michael, 32–34, 154–56
D-cycloserine (DCS), 154–56
decisions, difficulty in making, 182
dementia, 141, 142
depression, 7, 152, 250, 254

absenteeism and, 160
ACT and, 107
anxiety and, 52–53, 60
and childhood illnesses, 46
genes and, 77
as genetic, 59
phobias and, 41
during pregnancy, 228, 230–31
procrastination and, 162
relationships and, 199
sleep and, 256
social media and, 248
and SSRIs in utero, 227, 228
trauma and, 44
depressive reaction, 148
Diagnostic and Statistical Manual of Mental Disorders (*DSM*), 5, 8, 19, 25, 40, 118, 148, 254
Diagnostic and Statistical Manual of Mental Disorders III (*DSM*-III), 148–50, 151
disability benefits, 160
discrimination, against people with anxiety disorders, 181
divorce, and association with psychiatric disorders, 44
Dodson, John, 167–68, 280
dorsolateral prefrontal cortex, 136, 175
dorsomedial prefrontal cortex, 183
dot probe task, 31
drug abuse, 44, 83–84, 153

ecstasy, *see MDMA*
EEG, 120
Effexor, 127, 135
Ein-Dor, Tsachi, 168–69
electroconvulsive therapy (ECT), 65–66, 72–73
electrotherapy, 96
emotion regulation therapy (ERT), 108

empathy, 79, 189–90
emphysema, 46
epilepsy, 66
epinephrine, 83
Esalen Institute, 107
estradiol, 84
estrogen, 84
excitement, 176–77
exercise, 84, 256, 257–58
exposure therapy, 37, 94, 105, 106,
    237, 258
extinction, 28, 30, 55, 84
    hydrocortisone and, 156
    sleep and, 257
eye movement desensitization and
    reprocessing (EMDR), 108
Eysenck, Hans, 97–98

Facebook, *see social media*
Fast-Fail, 153
fear conditioning, 27, 28, 30, 32, 55,
    84, 94
fearful spells, 37, 38
fear hierarchy, 94
"Fearing" (song), 30
fears:
    of children, 79–80
    of women, 84
fetal brain, 230
fetal coupling, 230
fetal programming hypothesis,
    230
fight-or-flight response, 26, 28, 35,
    83, 153
Fink, Max, 146
FKBP5, 77
Food and Drug Administration
    (FDA), U.S., 120, 128, 144, 151,
    152, 153
Forbes, Bo, 115–16, 117
Ford, Betty, 151
formication, 133–34

Fox, Nathan, 87–91
France, rate of anxiety disorders in, 9
Freeman, Marlene P., 226
Freud, Sigmund, 24–25, 98

Garland, Judy, death from
    barbiturates of, 143
Genentech, 140
generalized anxiety disorder (GAD),
    5, 32, 38, 40, 63, 110, 112, 118–
    19, 120, 127, 153, 250, 258
    IQs and, 168
    relationships and, 199
    working memory and, 175
genes, 59–60, 76–78
    anxiety disorders and, 59–60,
    76–78, 235
    and environment, 77
Gilman, Charlotte Perkins, 96–
    97
Gingrich, Jay A., 227, 228
GlaxoSmithKline, 151
glutamate, 154
Gordon, Barbara, 150–51
Gray Ladies, 64
Gribbin, John, 42
Grillon, Christian, 8, 33–35
Grupe, Dan, 35
Guayasamín, Oswaldo, 185

Hampson, Michelle, 121–22
Hardy, Arthur, 99
Harvard Medical School, 44
Hayes, Steven, 105, 106–7
heart attacks, 46
heart disease, anxiety as risk factor
    for, 6
high blood pressure, 47
hippocampus, 28, 44, 136
Hippocrates, 23
Hoffmann–La Roche, 145

Hofmann, Stefan G., 112, 154–55, 156
Homer, 22
hormones:
  sex, 84
  stress, 77, 83
hospice, 177–79
House of Mirth, The (Wharton), 142
Houston, Whitney, use of benzodiazepines, 140
HPA axis, 26, 153
  and early maltreatment, 44
  exercise and, 258
human potential movement, 107
humors, theory of illness, 22–23
hydrocortisone, 156
hydros, as treatment for nervous problems, 96
hyperventilating, 94
hypnosis, 98
hypochondria, 6, 20–21, 202, 254–55, 259
hypochondriasis, 6, 96
hypothalamus, 26
hysteria, 254
hysterical neurosis, 148

Iliad (Homer), 22
Illinois, University of, shooting at, 250
illness anxiety disorder, 6
I'm Dancing As Fast As I Can (Gordon), 151
imipramine, 146–49
immune system, 6
infants:
  amygdala in, 86
  at risk for anxiety disorder, 78–79, 85
  high-reactive vs. low-reactive, 85–87
inhibitory control, 90–91

insomnia, 142, 256
Instagram, *see social media*
insula, 121, 136
insulin coma therapy, 62
integrated medicine, 110–11
internet, 19
interoceptive exposure, 258
intolerance of uncertainty, 31–32
Iowa gambling task, 182
IQ, 168
Ivie, Liz, 54

Japan, rate of anxiety disorders in, 9
Jed Foundation, 181
Johns Hopkins University School of Medicine, 233–34
Jupiter Effect, The (Gribbin and Plagemann), 43

Kagan, Jerome, 85–87
Kalin, Ned, 16
Kennedy, Edward "Ted," 151, 164
Kennedy, John F., 268
Kessler, Ron, 9, 246
ketamine, 156–57
Kidman, Nicole, 242–43
Kierkegaard, Søren, 8
Klein, Donald, 146–47
Klonopin, 137–42, 151, 180, 189, 218, 221, 244, 257, 258, 259
Klüver, Heinrich, 26–27
Klüver-Bucy syndrome, 27
Kundalini yoga, 112–17

lateral nucleus, 28
Latin America, symptoms of anxiety in, 9
learning, fear conditioning and, 33
Ledger, Heath, use of benzodiazepines, 140

LeDoux, Joseph E., 26, 27–30, 32, 154

Lexapro, 127, 136–37, 157, 221, 244

Librium, 146, 150

lung problems, association with anxiety disorders of, 46

McLean, Carmen, 80–81, 83

McMahon, Francis, 60

Macquarie University, 234–35

Malm, Heli, 227

marijuana, 10, 11, 84

Maryland, University of, 236–39

massage, 96, 109–10

MDMA (ecstasy), 157

medial prefrontal cortex, 28, 257

medication:
    FDA approval of, 152–53
    see also specific medications

meditation, 107, 108, 112, 258

melancholy, 23

Mellaril, 65

memory, *see working memory*

men:
    anxiety disorder in, 16, 78–84
    relationship problems of, 199–200

Mendota State Hospital, 58–59, 62–63, 64–67, 69–74

Mental Health Monologues, 253, 254

mephenesin, 143–44

Michigan, University of, 44, 102, 246–52

Miltown, 143, 144–45, 146

Mind, 181

mindfulness, 106, 108, 110

mindfulness-based cognitive therapy (MBCT), 108

mindfulness-based stress reduction (MBSR), 107

miscarriages, 45

Mitchell, Silas Weir, 96

Monroe, Marilyn, use of barbiturates by, 143

Morrongiello, Barbara, 81–82

mothers, 13, 17, 18, 21, 38–39, 41, 43, 45, 49–50
    anxiety of, 74–75, 228–31
    as more in sync with sons than daughters, 78

muscle relaxation, 111

napping, as adjunct to CBT, 104

Nash, John, 267

National Alliance on Mental Illness, 19

National Institute of Mental Health (NIMH), 8, 34, 53, 54–57, 153, 175

National Institutes of Health (NIH), 53, 54, 112

nature, destressing effect of, 258

negative affect, 78–79

neglect, as predictor of psychiatric disorders, 44

nervous clinics, 96

Nesse, Randolph M., 40

neurasthenia, 23, 97

neurasthenic neurosis, 148

neurofeedback, 121–22

neurons, 183, 227–28

neurotic disorders, 97–98, 149

New York Shyness and Social Anxiety Meetup Group, 122–25

New York Times, 166, 167

Nitschke, Jack, 35

N-methyl-D-aspartate (NMDA), 154–55, 157

norepinephrine, 83, 127

Northern Illinois University, shooting at, 250

Novick, Danielle, 236, 240

obsessive-compulsive disorder
  (OCD), 63, 155–56
  biomarkers of, 135
  ketamine and, 157
  and perfectionism, 161
obsessive-compulsive reaction, 148
orgasm, as Victorian-era treatment
  for hysteria, 24
OxyContin, 141
oxytocin, 83

Paddington (film), 241–43
panic attacks, 5
  in children, 38
  definition of, 12
panic disorder, 5, 24, 120, 153, 254
  asthma and, 46
  DCS in, 155–56
  in DSM-III, 148–49
  and first discussion with doctor,
    100
  and perfectionism, 161
  relationships and, 199
parent-child interaction therapy, 237
parents:
  controlling, 47–49
  death of, 44
  illnesses of, 46–47
  rejecting, 47
Pavlov, Ivan, 97
Paxil, 127, 134–35, 136, 151, 207,
  220–21
  breastfeeding and, 225–26
Percocet, 141
perfectionism, 160–61
Personal Zen app, 119
Petersen, Gladys Schneidervin,
  58–59, 60–61, 62–67, 235
  medical records of, 73
Pexacerfont, 153
phobia aides, 99
phobia reaction, 148

phobias, 22, 38
  age at onset of, 40
  as crippling, 40–41
  evolutionary reasons for, 40
  first treatment center for, 99
  hydrocortisone and, 156
  relaxation techniques for, 98
Phobia Society, 99–100
phobic disorders, 149
physical abuse, 44
Pine, Daniel, 52–54, 56
Pittsburgh, University of, 183
Plagemann, Stephen, 43
post-traumatic growth, 190
post-traumatic stress disorder
  (PTSD), 24, 32, 73, 98, 149,
  153, 250
  ABM and, 119
  biomarkers of, 135
  DCS in, 155–56
  genes and, 77
  ketamine and, 157
  MDMA and, 157
  sexual trauma and, 84
  sleep and, 256
  TMS and, 120
poverty, and association with
  psychiatric disorders, 44
prefrontal cortex, 30, 31, 35,
  53–54, 55
  CBT and, 96, 136
  dorsolateral, 120, 136, 175
  dorsomedial, 183
  medial, 28, 257
  serotonin in, 227–28
pregnancy:
  anxiety in, 228–29
  depression in, 228
  SSRIs in, 220–22, 226–28
procrastination, 160–63
progressive relaxation, 111
Prozac, 4, 19, 76, 126–27, 136,
  152, 225

in first weeks of life, 227–28
in pregnancy, 220–21
psychodynamic therapy, 132–33,
    255–56

Rapee, Ronald, 234–35, 237, 238,
    241–42
relaxation-induced anxiety, 111–12
respiratory diseases, 45–46
Ressler, Kerry, 154–55
rest cure, 96–97
risk aversion, 182–83
Ro 5-0690, 145–46
Roosevelt, Theodore, 97
Rossman, Jeffrey, 108–9
Rothbaum, Barbara, 155
Rubin, Ken, 236–37
Russell, Laurie, 54, 56, 57

Salcedo, Beth, 157
schizophrenia, 77, 152
    as genetic, 59, 60
    1950s diagnoses of, 63
selective serotonin reuptake
    inhibitors (SSRIs), 76, 77, 84,
    127, 128, 151
    pregnancy and, 220–22, 226–
    28
    stopping, 157–58
self-criticism, 161
self-doubt, 161
sensory cortex, 27
sensory thalamus, 27
separation anxiety, 40
September 11, 2001, terrorist attacks
    of, 170–74, 209
serotonin, 227–28
serotonin-norepinephrine reuptake
    inhibitors (SNRIs), 127, 151
serotonin transporters, 76
Sesame Street (TV show), 39–40, 87

Sevig, Todd, 249, 251
sexual abuse, 44
sexual assault, 84
shell shock, 73
Sivananda yoga, 113
Skinner, B. F., 97
SLC6A4, 76
sleep, 142, 256–57, 258
Smith, Anna Nicole, use of
    benzodiazepines of, 140
Smoller, Jordan, 77
social anxiety, 122–25, 251
social anxiety disorder (SAD), 56–
    57, 87, 152
    ABM and, 119
    biomarkers of, 135
    gender and, 82–83
social media, as contributor to
    anxiety and depression, 248–49
social phobia, 32, 38, 149
    ABM and, 118–19
    and first discussion with doctor,
    100
    and perfectionism, 161
somatic symptom disorder, 254
somatoform disorder, 41
Spain, rate of anxiety disorders
    in, 9
spatial navigation, 175
Special K, 156
specific phobia, 5
Spitzer, Robert, 148, 149
Stanford University, 258
startle reflex, 32–35
Sternbach, Leo, 145–46, 150–51
Steverson, Shelby, 247–48
stillbirths, 45
stress, 256
    in children, 44
    nature and, 258
Stressbusters app, 250
stress hormones, 77, 83
strokes, 46

Stroop task, 90
subgenual anterior cingulate cortex, 55
suffocation alarm system, 46
suicidal thoughts, 7
synapses, 76
systematic desensitization, 98

Tal, Orgad, 169
T allele, 77
Temple, Robert, 128
"tend and befriend," 83
Thorazine, 65
toddlers, 40, 79, 85, 86–87
Tone, Andrea, 143
tranquilizers, 144
transcranial magnetic stimulation (TMS), 120
trauma, 44–45
Turtle Program, University of Maryland, 236–39, 240

uncertainty, 182–83
unemployment, 159–60
Unified Protocol, 104–5
United States, anxiety disorder in, 16
Upjohn, 151

Valium, 137, 138, 151, 152
Van den Bergh, Bea, 228–29
Van Rybroek, Gregory, 70–73
ventromedial prefrontal cortex (vmPFC), 55, 84
Veronal, 142
Verucerfont, 153
Viagra, 129
Vicodin, 84
Vietnam, symptoms of anxiety in, 9

Virginia Tech shooting, 250
Virtual School, 56

Walker, David, 33
Wall of Faces, 31–32
Wall Street Journal, 128, 129, 157, 162–63, 165–67, 170–72, 177–81
"war neurosis," 98
Watson, John, 97
Wellness Zone, University of Michigan, 250
Wharton, Edith, 142
White Plains Hospital, 99–100
Williams, Tennessee, 144
Wisconsin, University of, 44
Wittchen, Hans-Ulrich, 230
Wofford, Harris, 164, 165
Wolpe, Joseph, 98, 99
Wolverine Support Network, 252–54
women:
    anxiety disorder in, 6, 7, 23–24, 78–84, 199, 200
    fears of, 84
    neurasthenia in, 23
    relationship problems of, 199, 200
    sex hormones of, 84
Wood Brooks, Alison, 176–77
working memory, 175
Wyeth, 144, 145

Xanax, 137, 138, 140–41, 151

Yale University, 121
Yellow Wallpaper, The (Gilman), 96–97
Yerkes, Robert, 167–68, 280

Yerkes-Dodson law, 167–68,
  280
yoga, 106, 107, 110, 112–17,
  186, 257
yohimbine, 156

Zane, Manuel, 99
Zen Buddhism, 106
Zilverstand, Anna, 121
Zoloft, 74, 127, 133, 134, 152, 221
  breastfeeding and, 226

ABOUT THE AUTHOR

Andrea Petersen is a contributing writer at the *Wall Street Journal,* where she reports on psychology, health, and neuroscience. She is the recipient of a Rosalynn Carter Fellowship for Mental Health Journalism. She lives in Brooklyn, New York, with her husband and daughter. Find her at byandreapetersen.com and @andreaapetersen.